The Regeneration of Public Parks

The Regeneration of Public Parks

Edited by Jan Woudstra and Ken Fieldhouse

Published jointly by
The Garden History Society
Landscape Design Trust
and
E & FN Spon, London, 2000
with support from
English Heritage

First published 2000
by E & FN Spon
11 New Fetter Lane, London EC4P 4EE

Simultaneously published in the USA and Canada
by E & FN Spon
29 West 35th Street, New York, NY 10001

E & FN Spon is an imprint of the Taylor & Francis Group

Printed and bound in Great Britain by
TJ International, Padstow, Cornwall

Publisher's Note
This book has been prepared from camera ready copy supplied by the editors

British Library Cataloguing in Publication Data
A catalogue record for this book is available from the British Library

Library of Congress Cataloging in Publication Data
The Library of Congress data for this book has been applied for and
may be obtained from the Library of Congress, Washington, D.C.

ISBN 0 419 25900 7

Contents

Acknowledgements

The Introduction was prepared with the help of David Jacques, Andrew Wimble, Hazel Conway, Alan Barber, Torbjørn Suneson, Klaus von Krosigk, David Lambert, Laurence Pattacini, James Hitchmough and Andy Clayden.

Many others have given editorial advice or helped with the process of refereeing for the book, or have aided with illustrations. The following are particularly thanked: Nigel Temple, Tom Wright, Roger White, John Sales, Camilla Beresford, Richard Stone, Dominic Cole, Peter Thoday, Chris Sumner, Chris Jones, Christopher Dingwall, Elizabeth Whittle, Virginia Hinze, David McQuitty, Hal Moggridge, Peter Goodchild, Theresa Baird, Richard Andrews, Mark Laird, and the University of Pennsylvania Press. Cristiano Ratti is thanked for assistance in the editorial process, and Jane Porter for design. Both the Garden History Society and the Landscape Design Trust facilitated in the publication of this book, which would not have been possible without the financial support of English Heritage.

This publication retains the conventions of *Garden History*, the journal of the Garden History Society, and the papers have been refereed and edited according to usual academic conventions.

Contributors

Frazer Chapman

Frazer Chapman is a horticulturist who has managed various London parks and has also taught garden design and horticulture. He is currently preparing a 'Parks Strategy' for Medway Council. His contribution to this book was based on a thesis completed for the postgraduate course on Conservation (Landscapes and Gardens) at the Architectural Association, London.

Hazel Conway

Dr Hazel Conway is Chair of the Conservation Committee of the Garden History Society. She is an architecture and landscape historian and has specialized in public parks. Her publications include *People's Parks* (Cambridge, 1991), *Public Parks* (Princes Risborough, 1996) and, with Rowan Roenisch, *Understanding Architecture* (London, 1994).

Edward Diestelkamp

Dr Edward Diestelkamp is Assistant to the Director of Historic Buildings at the National Trust. He is an architectural historian and writer on the use of iron in the 19th century.

Brent Elliott

Dr Brent Elliott is Librarian of the Lindley Library of the Royal Horticultural Society. He is author of various publications on Victorian and Edwardian gardening, including *Victorian Gardens* (London, 1986).

Ken Fieldhouse

Ken Fieldhouse is a landscape architect employed as Editor by the Landscape Design Trust, which includes *Landscape Design* and *Landlines*. He is publisher of the *Garden Design Journal* and has written in numerous publications on parks and gardens.

David Jacques

Dr David Jacques is Chairman of the Garden History Society. He is a landscape historian and theorist and has written various books, including a forthcoming one on 20th-century design theory, *The Millennial Landscape* (Chichester, 2000). He is a visiting professor at De Montfort University and tutor at the course on Conservation (Landscapes and Gardens) at the Architectural Association, London.

David Lambert

David Lambert is Conservation Officer of the Garden History Society, and a member of the Heritage Lottery Fund Buildings and Land Panel. He is co-author of *Public Prospects: Historic Urban Parks Under Threat* (London, 1993), and was an advisor to the House of Commons Environment Sub-Committee Inquiry into Town and Country Parks (1999).

Kim Legate

Kim Legate is a landscape architect at Landscape Design Associates in Peterborough. He has a strong interest in the history of planting design and recent projects include the Henry Ford Estate, Michigan USA, and Hestercombe gardens, Somerset. His contribution to this book is based on an MA thesis in Conservation Studies at the University of York.

Mary Lockwood

Mary Lockwood is Senior Case Officer at the Heritage Lottery Fund, where she has worked on the Urban Parks Programme. She has a particular interest in projects concerning the restoration of historic parks and gardens.

Hilary Taylor

Dr Hilary Taylor is a Director of Hilary Taylor Associates Ltd. She is an art and landscape historian and is working on the restoration of several major parks, including those at Battersea and Birkenhead.

Jan Woudstra

Dr Jan Woudstra is a Lecturer at the Department of Landscape at the University of Sheffield and is Honorary Editor of *Garden History*. He has had a long involvement with landscape and garden conservation and has tutored at the course on Conservation (Landscapes and Gardens) at the Architectural Association, London.

Foreword
I

Nick Raynsford MP
Minister for Housing and Planning, Department of the Environment,
Transport and the Regions

The Government is committed to making Britain's towns and cities more attractive and vibrant places where people will want to live. It wants to create more socially inclusive and economically competitive communities. Public parks and open spaces improve the quality of urban environments and will play an important part in bringing about this urban renaissance.

There are enormous benefits to be gained from well-designed and managed parks. Such parks provide a vital recreational resource, which can help improve the health and social well-being of people and enhance their enjoyment of the local environment. Parks also make a valuable contribution to biodiversity within urban areas and provide an important educational resource for many children, particularly those in inner urban areas.

I want our parks to be cleaner, safer and better maintained. I want to encourage more innovative thinking about the design, use and management of parks to make them more responsive to the changing urban fabric and needs of local people.

This book sets out the historical context of the development of parks, illustrates their diverse design details and offers sensible approaches to their renovation and future care. It is a good example of the type of thinking needed, and I welcome its contribution to the current debate about the future of our parks.

II: A new set of priorities

Lorna McRobie
Director of Gardens and Landscape, English Heritage

ENGLISH HERITAGE

English Heritage, sponsored by The Department of Culture, Media and Sport, is the government's principal adviser on the conservation and promotion of the historic environment. It also provides specialist advice to The Heritage Lottery Fund including the current Urban Parks Programme.

Over 120 public parks, gardens and squares are included within the 1300 sites on *The Register of Parks and Gardens of Special Historic Interest in England*. Though this designation itself brings no statutory powers of protection, Planning Policy Guidance Note 15 requires local authorities to make provision for the protection of these sites when preparing development plans and determining planning applications and, from 1995, to seek specialist advice from English Heritage and The Garden History Society before doing so. Outstanding sites on the Register, that is Grade I and II*, have since the Great Storms of 1987 and 1990 also been eligible for grant aid in the development of plans and programmes of work for the repair and the restoration of historic features and planting. Except for the initial storm damage, the funds available from English Heritage have been limited and only a few local councils have had the resources to consider tackling such projects.

English Heritage recognizes the important role played by urban parks, squares and open spaces in our cultural heritage, both in the character and life they bring to towns and cities, and in the opportunities they provide for regeneration and social inclusion. Many sites are also designated as Conservation Areas and English Heritage provides further support, advice or funding through such schemes as Conservation Area Partnerships or the more recent Heritage Economic Regeneration Scheme.

Important 19th-century public park structures such as bandstands, conservatories, pavilions, fountains and statuary may be individually listed. As such they have some statutory protection and Grade I and II* structures are also eligible for grant aid. Considerable funds have in the past been provided for these buildings and more have been targeted in *The Buildings at Risk Register* for further aid. Local councils with stretched resources and no statutory overall duty to maintain their parks have difficulty in securing match funding, or, as in the case of the majority Grade II structures, finding any funds at all for the care and conservation of these historic structures. A sustainable use for some is often impossible and unless they are seen as being of cultural value to the local community they become damaged by neglect or demolished as worthless. Unfortunately the group value of these buildings and structures is often ignored. The quality of detail in the park design, which is so important in defining local character and sense of place, is often eroded or lost, being replaced with bland concrete, mass-produced products or poor quality repairs.

Parks were designed for recreation but many councils have underrated the value of informal recreation in favour of leisure centres, sports pitches, courts, etc. for more formal and often fee-paying activities. These modern structures are visually difficult to accommodate in the park without loss of character and may be under separate management. Together with resources and expertise, standards of husbandry have also seriously declined. Parks are now often dull, drab places of mown trampled grass and tired evergreen shrubs, perceived by many as dangerous no-go areas. The current public interest and delight in horticulture expressed by the avid consumption of gardening media programmes, publications, garden centre sales, etc. has rarely been taken up by local councils as an opportunity to enhance the neighbourhood and to engage the community. With an increasingly ageing and multicultural society it must be asked if the emphasis by some councils on active formal recreation is really socially inclusive?

English Heritage has welcomed the Heritage Lottery Fund Urban Parks Programme as it has recognized the cultural as well as the recreational value inherent in these special places, encouraging many councils to reconsider their priorities and look for new opportunities for regeneration. We continue to support The Urban Parks Forum to stimulate the debate and to increase the knowledge and understanding required to enable sustainable long-term management of our parks.

III: Re-learning the lessons of the past

Alan Barber
Former President of the Institute of Leisure and Amenity Management

The neglect of Britain's heritage of public parks has been so obvious and so common that one could be forgiven for thinking that nobody cares. Of course, this is not true of the distinguished contributors to this publication; it is also not true of the many visitors who, every day, are attracted to even the poorest parks. Local people look to their local councils to take care of their parks. Perhaps more than anything else under their control, urban parks are reliant on local authorities for their good stewardship. Many must wonder why, having created this municipal heritage, so many councils are failing in their duty today.

In the late 20th century local authorities have become increasingly dependent on central government for direction, funding and support. If public parks are not made a statutory duty of local councils, if they receive no dedicated funding and, perhaps most importantly, if there is no government-sponsored national agency to act as their champion, they quickly slide down the political agenda.

All this makes the role of the local authority parks manager an uncomfortable one. Until the Heritage Lottery Fund (HLF) took up the cause, there was little awareness of just how much urban parks needed new investment. Now we are beginning to see a new and welcome appreciation of their design and social history among the more enlightened managers. Major awards are also helping to secure more dedicated management. Project managers, urban park rangers and even newly created park keepers are engaging local communities in the long-term care of their public parks.

The professional body for parks managers is the Institute of Leisure and Amenity Management. ILAM was formed in response to a reorganization of local authorities in the 1970s, which created large leisure directorates where once there were separate departments for every function. Far from absorbing a welcome spirit of entrepreneurship, horticulturally trained parks managers found integration difficult. Many saw their task as securing the lowest cost of maintenance rather than optimizing the social and economic value of great civic assets.

Now government is requiring local authorities to secure 'best value'; a demanding programme of performance review to compare the best with the rest. ILAM interprets this as best value to local people, and as upholding the long-term civic values which our urban heritage of public parks represents. Best value is a policy for a new century in which the search for sustainable development will demand easily accessible parks to add value to urban living and to help protect the countryside from suburban development.

Deprived of the institutional help so readily given to other cultural provision, local authority managers are now joined with others in a new enterprise, the Urban Parks Forum. This is a self-help organization dedicated to matching new investment with better maintenance and the introduction of community-involving programmes. Only a few parks may be helped by National Lottery money, but many could be helped by a new management philosophy. This sees public parks as the key to addressing such national issues as better health, life-long learning and social exclusion. Here we are at the dawn of a new century, re-learning the lessons of the past.

IV: A blind date between illness and cure

Stewart Harding
Policy Advisor for Historic Landscapes, Heritage Lottery Fund

The Urban Parks Programme (UPP) was launched by the Heritage Lottery Fund in 1996 to confront the crisis in the condition of our public parks. Twenty-five years of unremitting attack on public property, on our 'commonwealth', and the erosion of civic pride that went with it, had brought the wonderful legacy of parks close to ruin. If anything, the extent of dereliction and abandonment had been underestimated.

Fortunately, enthusiasts had been steadily acquiring expertise and experience in the restoration of designed historic landscape over the previous decade. The great storms of 1987 and 1990 tore holes in the parks and in our complacency. Public alarm prompted the release of the first significant funds for the restoration of historic parks and gardens. English Heritage and the Countryside Commission (Task Force Trees) worked together on the successful grant schemes to repair the parks ravaged by the storms.

However, it became obvious that the loss of over-mature trees was merely a symptom of deeper problems. The fact was that these great landscapes had been taken for granted and their survival ignored. Bringing them back to health would require much more than the replanting of trees. The Historic Landscape Survey and Restoration Plan was refined as the tool to collate all the skills needed to do justice to the past. The UPP was a blind date between the illness and the cure. Nothing on this scale had been attempted before. Were public parks different, in essence, from the private landscapes from which their designs evolved? How exactly do you mend the ravages of two decades of neglect?

Money certainly makes a difference. This was, and remains, primarily an issue of resources — the rest is down to persuasion, to understanding, to harnessing enthusiasm and to expertise. Initially allocated £50 million over three years, the UPP has now committed £130 million and looks set to spend a similar amount again over the next four years. More than £1.5 million has gone on the production of restoration plans for 130 parks. The rest has been allocated to about 100 implementation schemes for an incredible range of parks, gardens, cemeteries and historic town spaces. All the schemes are based on thorough historic research of archives and on topographical surveys. All have benefited from careful analysis and are propelled by a fresh understanding and commitment to high standards. In public parks, restoration of features means restoration of pleasure and of safety, of activity and relaxation, of contemplation and of fun. Alongside the restoration of bandstands and boating lakes goes the introduction and improvement of cafés and playgrounds. More than £6 million has been awarded for play equipment. Agreements have been reached with local authorities over better management; this will mean parks with more flowers, more music, more fun — conspicuous care and treats too.

Because Britain is so well endowed with parks — about 30,000, of which 5000 have historic character — the need for new parks is perhaps less acute than elsewhere. But it is a poor society that fails to make new parks and gardens as an essential ingredient in development of all kinds. Perhaps the nation has rested on its laurels for too long. As well as the historic parks to restore, there are thousands of nondescript open spaces that could be re-designed and managed positively. It would be great to see civic pride restored so that all of the parks and open spaces gave people what they want, and in every new development the provision of parks and gardens was made a central feature of their design.

Introduction: the regeneration of public parks

by Jan Woudstra

Figure 1: Savignyplatz in Berlin-Charlottenburg, originally laid out by Erwin Barth in 1926, was restored in 1987 with financial aid from the Berlin Department of Garden Conservation. The park is pictured here in 1991. (Photo: the author)

The sudden rise of landscape work in public parks forms the background to this publication, which collects a wide range of important insights from those involved with and responsible for public parks. It is not intended as a manual of how to carry out this work, but instead it tackles the historical context of parks, illustrates their rich and diverse design detail, suggests philosophical approaches to their renovation and future care, and offers a practical approach to aspects of conservation. General principles are provided, leaving the reader to interpret them in each case.

Owing to the enormous amount of information available, this book has been written largely from a British perspective. It does, however, offer a wider interest than the UK alone, for it discusses general principles and issues that might be applied elsewhere. Additionally, other countries are not ignored and are used appropriately as examples. This book cannot do justice to and provide a regional or national context to the rich experience provided generally by parks in other countries. Fortunately some of this information is available elsewhere; the City of Berlin, for example, has

Figure 2: Regeneration work in Central Park, New York, has been carried out by the Central Park Conservancy, a partnership between the city authority and the private sector. Shown left is the boating lake in 1987. (Photo: the author)

been at the forefront of park regeneration and in 1999 celebrated the 20th anniversary of its Department of Garden Conservation with Klaus von Krosigk *et al.*'s *Garden Art of Berlin.*[1] While such accounts of past work by those involved may not be available elsewhere, there are often published summaries of management plans. In New York, the starting point for regenerating Central Park was the formation of the Central Park Conservancy, a partnership between the city authority and the private sector. This encouraged the production of a management and restoration plan, which has been used as the basis for regeneration.[2] Boston was the first city in the USA to make the improvement of public parks part of their Poverty Action Programme, thus attracting State and Federal funding. The argument was that 'free to enter public parks' are proportionately more important to people of low income, and that outdoor recreational programming aimed at young people aids the development of positive lifestyles necessary to break the spiral of deprivation.[3] The most successful regeneration schemes in Europe have been in those instances where parks issues are connected with topics of political interest, which can be seen in cities such as Amsterdam, Brussels, Copenhagen, Strasbourg, Stockholm and Stuttgart. Unfortunately not all of this is easily available in print.

Since the 19th century public parks have been

considered as lungs for the city. The 1992 Rio de Janeiro conference on environment and development may be cited as a sign of renewed awareness of the contribution parks make to the quality of life through recreation and the environment.[4] The conference incorporated the recommendations of *The Brundtland Report* (1987) on sustainability,[5] which was defined as 'development that meets the needs of the present without compromising the ability of future generations to meet their own needs'. Vegetation cleans the air by absorbing pollutants, moderates the city climate and encourages airflow, thus providing physical benefits. It also has psychological advantages and a calming effect. These benefits are fully exploited in cities where parks form an important part of the civic infrastructure. Additionally parks help in attracting tourism, provide evidence of the quality of the city, enable space for large events and are spaces for recreation.

In the UK, the Garden History Society and the Victorian Society produced a joint report in 1993 highlighting the state of urban parks.[6] Meanwhile national agencies responsible for identifying landscapes of historic importance — English Heritage, Cadw: Welsh Historic Monuments, and Historic Scotland — began to focus more on them. Comedia, in association with Demos, published research on social aspects of urban parks, providing justification

Figure 3: Public parks allow space for occasional large events, such as this funfair at Clissold Park, London. (Photo: the author)

for reinvigoration.[7] The Heritage Lottery Fund soon after, in 1996, offered grant-aid for the regeneration of public parks through its Urban Parks Programme. It was now possible to move from concern and assessment to rectifying the overwhelming neglect of many years.

Parks for the people

Traditionally public parks were intended for all members of society, and they have provided a variety of uses. The earliest use foreseen was informal promenading, and this was followed by sports, such as cricket and football, and then children's play. These uses are as valid today as when the parks were laid out. Nevertheless visitor numbers have declined steadily in the second half of the 20th century, a fact that can be attributed to factors such as car-borne recreation, a lack of modern attractions, vandalism, poor security and indifferent standards of maintenance.

In their weakened state public parks may fall victim to pressures which, if unchecked, can lead to appropriation by special interests and an overall loss to the general public. There is pressure from organized sports for improved facilities, artificial surfaces, indoor sports or leisure centres. Again, as available open space for development in cities becomes scarcer, there are pressures for new housing or shopping centres, developments seemingly made more attractive if 'planning gain'

promises better facilities, restoration or a higher standard of maintenance for the remainder of the park. In the long run, though, the integrity of the park is threatened.

Biodiversity

In the wake of the Rio de Janeiro convention biodiversity has risen up the list of political priorities.[8] The UK Steering Group has defined its task as being to 'conserve and enhance biological diversity within the UK, and to contribute to the conservation of global biodiversity through all appropriate mechanisms'.[9] Parks perform an important role for wildlife in cities, though this has to be kept in perspective: parks were created to provide facilities for people and are thus designed landscapes, rather than primarily nature reserves. Nevertheless, there will often be good opportunities to enhance wildlife value through considered planting and maintenance, and the means for people to enjoy and learn from it.

Local distinctiveness

Instant makeovers of gardens, so much favoured currently by the media as short-term challenges, unfortunately do nothing to imbue the public with values of sustainability and long-term planning. If public parks are to have any future, they must be regarded as beacons of consistency, where links with past matter and value can accumulate. Each

3

Figure 4: Queen Mary's Rose Garden, Regent's Park, London. (Photo: the author)

4

Figure 5: Fountain in Vivary Park, Taunton. (Photo: the author)

Figure 6: Boats on the lake edge at Finsbury Park, London. (Photo: the author)

Figure 7: Clissold Park paddling pool: without appealing to children, public parks would quickly lose their richness and purpose; water is one way to attract them to a park. (Photo: the author)

park provides a unique experience. Its distinctiveness is related to its particular history, for example if the park evolved from a private estate or was a purpose-built open space. It will also be host to an infinitude of personal associations. Parks are landscapes of memory.

Care of the old and design of the new

Over time many well-designed parks have deteriorated due to a lack of maintenance, vandalism, poor-quality repairs, poor new design, poor location of new features, ill-informed planting and the removal of existing features, including planting and bedding. In many instances these decisions have been taken in an *ad hoc* manner without considering the way this might affect the overall design of a park. An amalgamation of such changes may adversely affect the appearance and usage of the park. Laid out with turf, water and hard surfaces within a framework of planting, the composition of these various elements determines the park's character, though it may alter subtly over time with the growth of vegetation. As all plants have a limited life expectancy, the framework of trees and shrubs should be attended to at regular intervals.

Considered management sets out to maintain a balance between the vegetation and the various elements of the site and requires skilled horticultural management, now ever more needed as a result of the restructuring of former Municipal Parks Departments, which as a result of the Bains Report (1972) became subsumed in Leisure and Amenity Services Departments.[10] This meant that parks had to compete for funds with other leisure services, and responsibility for the management of parks was often split between different departments. Since then successive reorganizations have continued to jeopardize funding and parks were often considered as a soft option where financial cuts might be made.

Where the period of long, slow decline has been extended, thoroughgoing repair will be desirable. It will be important to make an assessment of the extent of past changes, in other words to chart the historical development of the park. Once this is properly understood, qualified and experienced professionals generally can 'tweak' the existing layout by devising a programme of repair of hard elements and rejuvenation of planting. Hence, slow and sensitive upgrading, which recognizes the value of distinctiveness and the importance of memory in parks, is generally preferable in older

5

parks to redesign. It is one of the qualities of the designer to show humility, and an appreciation of existing fabric and character. In sites of historic importance there is generally a requirement for accurate restoration work and sometimes there is scope for reconstruction of former features.

Nevertheless there will be occasions, for example where a park has been mutilated beyond recognition, where rejuvenation is pointless and a redesign may be preferable. As with care and maintenance, the basis for any (new) design within public parks should be a profound understanding of the site and its connections with the surroundings, with reference to its spatial, historical, environmental and ecological qualities. Most poorly considered new design is due to a lack of understanding of the existing environment.

There are still landscape architects who consider neglected parks as opportunities 'to express the taste and preferences of our own time'. However, loss of integrity in today's parks often results from previous generations of such designers, whose work quickly became dated and incongruous with the surroundings. Today's keen designers, despite their excellent intentions, may then merely be continuing a cycle of *ad hoc* decisions and community alienation. This is not an argument against all change, merely against opinionated and hasty design. Decisions on altering a park's design need to be taken for profound reasons, weightily considered and accepted by consensus.

New facilities

Regeneration projects sometimes revolve around the generation of revenue at built features e.g. cafés and restaurants. These generally require vehicular access which, with some exceptions such as Victoria Park, London, and Birkenhead Park, Liverpool, vie against the traditional pedestrian scale of parks. First, facilities often heavily rely on car-based customers. Additionally, there are usually statutory requirements to enable access by emergency vehicles and there are continual deliveries to these buildings.

Modern sports facilities tend not to complement a park. They generally provide for a minority of users, and modern facilities, including hard surfaces, flood lighting, associated buildings and car parking, can severely detract from the appearance of the park. As with other features in parks, sports facilities have to be considered in terms of the purpose of the park as a whole so that a balanced view can be maintained.

New materials

The introduction of new features such as seats, lighting columns, gates and other park furniture can severely affect the appearance and character of a park. Certain 'heritage' ranges have been considered as safe options. However, many are crude mild steel or aluminium versions of historic designs and have none of the quality or craftsmanship reflected in the cast-iron versions. The modern versions tend to have meaner dimensions and proportions and lack detail found in earlier cast- or wrought-iron work. In these cases modern furniture is an infinitely preferred option. Fortunately it is still possible to acquire quality wrought-iron furniture from artist-blacksmiths who accurately match any historic design.

Once common, traditional materials such as walks of gravel have disappeared in most public parks, where the maintenance skills of repair of raking, rolling and occasional replenishing have been lost. Most parks now use the low-maintenance solution of tarmac, which can be swept easily and can carry vehicles. Tarmac certainly does not have the aesthetically pleasing colour and texture of its predecessor.

Without appealing to children, public parks would quickly lose their richness and purpose. Children may be attracted by various means, such as by water and animals, and the opportunity for play is a prerequisite for a successful park. While planting may inspire informal play, the conventional way is to do this by provision of play equipment. Traditional play equipment is now often considered dangerous, whereas modern custom designed equipment is safer and more exciting, educational and challenging. Modern equipment also caters for a broader age range of

Figure 8: CCTV is not necessarily the solution to security problems in parks. Bournemouth, 1997. (Photo: the author)

children, and allows parents to interact with children. Fences, too, have also become a modern adjunct to playgrounds — to keep out dogs and to control children. The major issue limiting the success of playgrounds, however, is adequate funding for maintenance, supervision and safety.

Security issues

The traditional park keeper has become a victim of budgetary cuts and a change of managerial attitudes with the result that many parks are unprotected and open to vandalism and other abuse and antisocial behaviour. A common problem in encouraging wider use of these places is the popular perception that the parks are unsafe. The introduction of closed circuit televisions (CCTV) is seen as an option, but those that merely record events may provide an illusion of security. For such a system to be effective, cameras need to have high-definition colour images to allow clear identification of individuals along with constant 24-hour monitoring with effective links to those who can provide a quick response. The only viable option, therefore, requires expensive equipment, high maintenance and monitoring costs. The cameras tend to be conspicuously sited on tall poles and are of insufficient number, both to achieve comprehensive surveillance and to act as a deterrent. Consequently their scale and location can have a damaging impact on the landscape, particularly if lighting is required. CCTV, therefore, is no substitute for supervision preferably by gardening staff or alternatively by specifically employed personnel and adoption of the park by the local community.

Parks policy

A recent inquiry by the Environment Sub-Committee of the Environment, Transport and Regional Affairs Select Committee of the House of Commons has brought parks to the forefront of political thinking in England. Its report highlights the problems and reinforces the significance of public parks generally and makes recommendations about funding and future management. A new National Agency, loosely based on the Royal Parks Agency, is suggested to arrest and reverse the decline of parks. These and other efforts in the current renaissance will undoubtedly provide regenerated public parks with a new perspective.[11]

Structure of this book

This book contains carefully selected contributions by specialists in their fields. The first part deals with general issues relating to public parks, while the second relates to specific elements within parks. Each chapter is self-contained and fully referenced. A bibliography completes the publication — it contains the main literature referred to in the text.

Notes

1. Klaus von Krosigk, Gesine Sturm *et al.*, *Garden Art of Berlin: 20 Years of Conservation of Historic Gardens and Parks in the Capital* (Berlin: Schelzky & Jeep, 1999).

2. Elizabeth Barlow Rogers, *Rebuilding Central Park: A Management and Restoration Plan* (Cambridge, MA: MIT Press, 1987).

3. Mark Primack (ed.), *The Greening of Boston* (Boston: Boston Foundation, 1987).

4. UN Conference on Environment and Development, 'Agenda 21: Programme of Action for Sustainable Development', Rio de Janeiro, Brazil, 1992. The conference resulted in Secretaries of State of the Environment *et al.*, *Sustainable Development: The UK Strategy* (London: HMSO, 1994).

5. World Commission on Environment and Development (The Brundtland Commission), *Our Common Future* (Oxford: Oxford University Press, 1987), 8.

6. Hazel Conway and David Lambert, *Public Prospects: Historic Urban Parks Under Threat* (London: Garden History Society and Victorian Society, 1993).

7. Liz Greenhalgh and Ken Worpole, *Park Life: Urban Parks and Social Renewal* (London: Comedia in association with Demos, 1995).

8. Secretaries of State of the Environment *et al.*, *Biodiversity: The UK Action Plan* (London: HMSO, 1994).

9. UK Steering Group, *Biodiversity, vol. 1: Meeting the Rio Challenge* (London: HMSO, 1995), 5.

10. Bains Committee, *The New Local Authorities: Management and Structures* (London: HMSO, 1972).

11. Environment, Transport and Regional Affairs Committee, *Town and Country Parks*, 20th Report, vol. 1 (London: HMSO, 1999).

Parks and people: the social functions

by Hazel Conway

Figure 1: Clarence Gardens, Scarborough, c.1905. (From the collection of Nigel Temple)

Every town has its public parks, gardens and recreation grounds, and for very many of us these parks form an important part of the background to our lives — particularly if one lives in a town of any size. Yet, over the past two decades parks have been under increasing threat from neglect, from vandalism, from lack of funds for maintenance and from development proposals.[1] Indeed, some question whether historic urban parks are relevant to urban living in the 21st century. It is argued that people have changed, that their leisure needs have changed and that parks designed for the leisure needs of over a century ago, when the first public parks were created, are at best irrelevant if not completely redundant for the needs of today. If one looks more closely at the reasons why these parks were created during the 19th and 20th centuries, for whom they were created and how they were used, a fuller understanding of their social role in the past and their relevance to today and to the future becomes possible.

The park movement

During the mid-19th century urban parks were created throughout Britain as a response to the appalling problems of the urban environment brought about by industrialization and rapid population growth. Britain was at the forefront of the Industrial Revolution and ours was the first country to 'invent' the municipal park. Official recognition of the need for parks dates from 1833 when the Select Committee on Public Walks presented a Report to Parliament about the open space available for recreation in the major industrial centres and the smaller towns. The Committee concluded that the poorest people living in the largest urban centres in overcrowded conditions of utmost poverty had the greatest need for parks. Only London had adequate parks, the Royal Parks, but there were no parks in the East End, or south of the river, except for Greenwich Park. The Committee identified the benefits of parks in physical, moral, spiritual and political terms. Parks would be the lungs for the city and would refresh the air; would improve people's health and provide places for exercise; would be an alternative form of recreation to the tavern; and would provide beneficial contact with nature, so elevating the spirit. Furthermore, as all members of society would use parks, social tensions would be reduced and the classes would learn from each other.[2]

The park movement began slowly in the 1830s and 1840s when parks began to be created in the major industrial centres of the north-west of England and in Glasgow, Scotland. The first of the new industrial centres to create a municipal park was Preston, where Moor Park opened in 1833. Manchester was the first of the major industrial centres to create parks: Philips Park, Queen's Park and Peel Park, Salford, designed by Joshua Major opened in 1846. Glasgow created its first park, Kelvingrove Park, in 1854. As the park movement expanded benefactors and philanthropists donated parks, but by far the greatest number was created by local authorities and these parks were a cause for great civic pride.

The early parks were created *ad hoc* on available land, often on the outskirts of expanding towns where the land was cheaper. They were created out of the estates of substantial mansions that were being pressed by the tide of urbanism, on the greens and commons that were traditionally the people's playgrounds, and out of quarries, spoil heaps and other marginal land. By the 1880s it had become increasingly recognized that accessibility was important and that large prestige parks were not necessarily the best solution. What was needed were more small parks in inner-city areas. The work of the Metropolitan Public Gardens Association set up in 1882, the Kyrle Society set up in 1875 and other organizations in transforming disused burial grounds into parks, gardens and recreation grounds represented a very great achievement, particularly in view of the religious feelings of the period.[3]

By the 1880s the message that parks were an attractive amenity had become evident to the fast-developing seaside resorts. A well-designed park would not only add to their attractions, but also, if they were equipped with large palmhouses and winter gardens, then the vagaries of the British climate on holiday-makers could, to a certain extent, be mitigated. The years 1830–85 mark the pioneering phase of park development. Thereafter, this was assured and many more parks were created from 1885 to 1914 than in the pioneering phase. By this time the battle for parks had been won, but the need for parks continued. It is interesting to see how these needs reflect those first voiced by the Committee in stressing that parks would improve people's physical health, make them happier and better citizens, and encourage them to be virtuous.[4]

Between the two World Wars the momentum of park development was maintained and the link between public health, recreation and sport was further emphasized. Across the country as a whole in the interwar period 4 million houses were built on green field sites, with a huge expansion of the suburbs and the building of satellite towns such as Speke and Knowsley near Liverpool. Between 1921 and 1937 some 1.4 million people moved to the outer London suburbs.[5] Parks and recreation grounds were integral parts of this suburban development.[6]

After the Second World War the emphasis was on slum clearance, urban renewal and the creation of New Towns. New Town design was strongly influenced by the Garden City Movement and adequate provision of parks and open space was an integral part of the planned New Towns of the 1950s and 1960s. During the 1960s and 1970s a major area of park development concerned the post-industrial landscape: the transformation of derelict industrial wastelands into parks and gardens. The Tyne Landscape Plan dates from 1965; the Stoke on Trent reclamation programme from 1970. Central Forest Park, Hanley, was part of a wide reclamation project, which included some 50 sites and the creation of Greenways. These designs were based on visions of the landscape in which the industrial memory was almost completely wiped out. In the 1970s large numbers of country parks were created on the urban fringe and in open country. As these attracted grant aid, local authorities found them economical to maintain and they were also popular with car-owners. As a result urban parks were increasingly ignored and their use for those that did not have access to cars — children, the elderly and the disadvantaged — was also ignored. During the 1980s this decline accelerated to such an extent that in 1993 the Garden History Society and the Victorian Society decided to draw attention to what was happening.[7] *Public Prospects* illustrated the extent of the decline, spelled out the reasons for it and recommended action to halt it. The first signs of rescue came three years later, in 1996, when Lord Jacob Rothschild, then Chairman of the Heritage Lottery Fund (HLF), launched the Urban Parks Programme (UPP). As a result there has been a major shift in the perception of public parks and they are now on the main political agenda. Chris Smith, Secretary of State for Culture, Media and Sport, speaking of the UPP in 1997 said, 'these are . . . the sort of grants that [provide] real benefits to millions of ordinary people . . .'. At local authority level there has been a major change in attitudes towards parks, with optimism and positive thinking replacing a pervading sense of defeatism, and it was only when the money became available under the UPP that this change occurred. The restoration of urban parks has been by far the most popular of the HLF's initiatives.

Park use

The parks created in the 19th and early 20th centuries were designed for all members of society and were very popular places. When a new park opened, people travelled by train from miles around to join in the celebrations. In 1883 Glasgow took a census of park use and recorded 100,000 people entering Glasgow Green on an ordinary Sunday in July and 48,000 people entering Kelvingrove Park. These numbers were matched on other days of rest.[8] People put on their best clothes to visit parks. In the summer many parks put on special events that attracted huge numbers to the parks (see colour section). Charles

Blondin, the hero of the tight-rope crossing of Niagara Falls in 1859/60, performed in Queen's Park, Longton,[9] while at a free gala in Peel Park, Bradford, there were balloon ascents and demonstration rapier fights. The ground around was packed with spectators.[10] During the Second World War parks in the major cities became the focus for Holidays at Home, since travel was discouraged. The use of parks for special events has continued to this day, from Luciano Pavarotti in Hyde Park to the Irish Festival in Peckham Rye, London, from the Bradford Mela in Lister Park to the Leeds West Indian Carnival in Roundhay Park, to name but a few. Parks are one of the few places where events for large numbers of people can be held.

Special events in parks, by their nature, happen rarely. What is more important is the day-to-day use of parks and their relationship with the local community. A survey of the main purpose of day visits outside the home made in 1996 showed that for 18 per cent of people it was to visit friends, another 18 per cent went out to eat or drink, while 15 per cent went out for a walk and 11 per cent went shopping. The destination of the walkers was not revealed.[11] In 1992 an Audit Commission-sponsored MORI survey on recreation found that while 46 per cent of people had used a local authority leisure centre or swimming pool within the past 12 months, nearly double that number (70 per cent) had used parks, playgrounds and open spaces, and half had used them more than ten times in the period surveyed.[12] Today, it is estimated that some 8 million people visit a park on any one day.[13]

Park facilities

Parks offered a range of facilities for both young and old and for all sections of society. Their design enabled some to enjoy quietness and privacy, while others enjoyed group activities, for park users are individuals each of whom brings their own world and needs when visiting. The open areas of grass could be used for sports, grazing, hay or meetings, but generally not for religious or political meetings, although there were exceptions to this. Glasgow Green and Victoria Park, London,

11

Figure 2: Queen Victoria (1898), Victoria Park, Newbury. (Photo: the author)

12

became well known venues for religious, social and political debate, and both William Morris and Bernard Shaw addressed meetings in the latter.[14] Many parks had lakes and offered activities such as boating, model boating, swimming, skating and fishing. What one was allowed to do depended on the local bylaws. For example, fishing and skating were permissible in Birkenhead Park, but not swimming, whereas in Victoria Park one could swim at specified hours.

If people were to use parks for any length of time it was important to offer refreshments, drinking water and toilets, and to supply these needs many parks had a range of buildings including pagodas, shelters, refreshments rooms and bandstands. As a result of the decline in investment in parks during the 1980s, by 1994 less than 10 per cent of parks had cafés, refreshments or kiosks and only about 25 per cent of parks still had toilets.[15] The recent trend has been to close toilets and to convert them into cafes and restaurants.

In addition to their practical functions parks had educational, social, political and psychological roles to play for they reflected the aspirations not only of the period in which they were created, but also of subsequent periods. These layers of meaning brought about by time, history and the memory of the generations that have used them adds to the significance of parks. This brief examination can only hint at the richness of these landscapes, how they have been used in the past and their significance today.

Moral geography/education

In the 19th and early 20th centuries public parks provided a place where the new industrial class could meet their so-called betters in a safe, respectable and structured setting. The moral geography of the public park included in its design lodges, statues, drinking fountains, bandstands and planting. These were intended to 'improve' the park users and to encourage local pride and patriotism. The park promoters may well have had these aims and designers may well have striven to incorporate them in their plans, but that is not to say that they were successful, for the park users were a most resilient sector of society and the idea of 'social control' has been increasingly questioned among historians in recent years.

Parks were places to celebrate and commemorate local, national and international events. Statues of the Queen, Prince Albert, local MPs, aristocrats, entrepreneurs and benefactors were those that featured most (figure 2). Placed on plinths and standing high above the park, they were looked up to by visitors both physically and metaphorically. Often statues were paid for by public subscription, thus strengthening the link between the park and the local community. These statues promoted local and national pride as well as having an educational role. Around the palmhouse in Sefton Park the importance of those associated with the natural world was placed on a par with the greatest figures in navigation and discovery. Six statues stood around the palmhouse: Charles Darwin; John Parkinson, 'Apothecary to James I'; André Le Nôtre, 'The most famous of all garden architects'; James Cook, 'Explorer of Australia'; Henry the Navigator, 'Father of Atlantic Exploration'; and Gerardus Mercator, 'Father of Modern Cartography'. Pride and education went hand in hand, with inscriptions explaining the significance of each figure. (These statues have been removed for safety pending the restoration of the park and palmhouse under the UPP of the HLF.)

By the end of the 19th century most parks featured a bandstand: light and airy, painted in bold colours and set against a background of green, it came to symbolize the public park, recreation, relaxation and fun. A wide range of classical music was played and this was popular both with the park visitors and with the social reformers who thought that such music had a refining influence.[16] Drinking fountains provided the ideal opportunity for promoting the values of temperance and generally no alcohol was sold in parks. One of the few exceptions to this was in Roundhay Park, Leeds, where the Mansion was let as a hotel.

The didactic role of parks has changed and one of the clearest symbols of this was the removal of the 'keep off the grass' notices after the Second World War. Today parks have both a formal and an informal role to play in education. They are part of our history, reinforcing the sense of local and national identity as well as that of memory and personal identity. The role that the natural environment can play in education has been well

recognized, but the potential role of designed landscapes such as urban parks has until recently not been explored.[17] There are signs that this is now changing. Recognition of the role that parks can play in children's education is illustrated by the recent introduction of publications and education packs enabling children to study their local park.[18]

Safety

In the past safety in parks was secured by the presence of park keepers and superintendents and by the swearing in of park police. To those who subscribe to the idea of 'Victorian values' vandalism is a modern ill. Yet behavioural research shows that people are not more inherently wicked today. What is different is the economic climate and that in the majority of parks there are no park keepers or security staff. With Compulsory Competitive Tendering (CCT) park budgets were cut and park keepers replaced by teams who come once a week to cut the grass. If the parks are not policed regularly, then people, especially women and children, become fearful of using them. By 1996 an Association of Direct Labour Organisations (ADLO) survey showed that only 39 per cent of respondents had dedicated park staff and that 90 per cent of local authorities experienced vandalism in their parks.[19] Now CCT is being replaced by Best Value and park rangers are once more being introduced into some parks.[20]

Some argue that historic urban parks must change if they are to survive in a modern society, because the parks themselves and the features within them act as a stimulus and challenge to those who are alienated from society. In this argument parks in effect promote vandalism. Indeed, according to one local authority an Edwardian wooden shelter was 'socially and functionally obsolete' because it attracted vandals! The design of buildings, towns and landscapes affects the ways in which people relate to each other. Neglected parks with burnt-out buildings, supermarket trolleys and cars abandoned in the lake, broken seats, and graffiti clearly proclaim that no one cares. There is now sufficient research to show that neglected environments foster anti-

13

Figure 3: Nottingham Arboretum aviary c.1900. Aviaries, deer and guinea pig enclosures, small zoos and sandpits were introduced for children in many parks by the end of the 19th century. (From the collection of the author)

14

social behaviour. But this is not the same as saying that a well-cared for park with an array of well-maintained buildings, statues and planting *per se* issues challenges to vandalize.

Playgrounds

The playground was an important feature of historic urban parks. In the first Manchester parks separate playgrounds were provided for girls and boys, not for any moral reason, but because the parks committee found that if both shared the same facilities then the boys monopolized the equipment and the girls never had the opportunity to use it.[21] In addition to playgrounds there were gymnasia with climbing poles, ropes to swing on and poles to swing over, which were used only by males.[22] By the end of the 19th century the facilities for children expanded with the introduction of aviaries, deer and guinea pig enclosures, small zoos and sandpits (figures 3, 4). The 20th century saw further introductions such as model villages (Vauxhall Park, *c.*1920) and model traffic areas where children could go to drive model cars (Lordship Lane Recreation Ground, Tottenham, 1938).[23]

During the Second World War bombsites became playgrounds and afterwards the sculptor

Jamie McCullough pioneered Meanwhile Gardens on derelict sites.[24] Play streets were designated and a new form of inner-city park was the adventure playground. The design of playground equipment is changing and the new playground created in Emslie Horniman Pleasance, North Kensington, and the design for the Princess Diana Memorial Playground in Kensington Gardens, both in London, re-think the form they should take. This park was the first to open after complete restoration under the UPP in August 1998. One of the major uses of parks still is going there with children or grandchildren, but playgrounds are not necessarily the most important attraction (figure 5). Water is a popular feature and feeding the ducks is still a thing that children love to do (figure 6).

The one age group that has few facilities set aside for it is that of young teenagers. Often they can be seen congregating around the swings, only to be chased off by parents with young children.

Health and sports

From the early 19th century it was thought that parks would be the lungs of the city and provide a respite from air pollution. The Clean Air Act of 1956 banned the burning of solid fuels and air pollution today takes a different form in which

Figure 4:
Victoria Park,
the Aviary. (From
the collection of
Nigel Temple)

parks still have an important role to play. Trees filter the dust from the air and lower the temperature in cities. One hectare of urban park with trees, shrubs and grass can remove 600 kg of carbon dioxide from the air and can deliver 600 kg of oxygen in 12 hours. Trees can also filter out up to 85 per cent of suspended particles.[25]

Urban parks also have a role to play in mental health and research is being undertaken on the role of nature on psychological states. Hospital patients who can look out on trees and nature recovered more quickly that those patients whose views were restricted to other buildings. The Victorians were well aware of the calming effects of nature and recent research is beginning to substantiate this.

The earliest parks offered sports such as cricket and other middle-class pursuits such as archery. In the Manchester parks special sites were set aside for skipping, but skipping in Victoria Park, London, was liable to attract a fine. In other words, opportunities for both active and passive forms of recreation were present in the parks from the beginning. As the 19th century progressed so more sports facilities became available, including cricket, tennis, football, cycling, putting and bowls. Class and gender in sports reflected

contemporary power relationships: throughout the 19th century and well into the 20th, middle-class males were the arbiters of sporting culture. Cycling, tennis, golf and hockey were sports that became available to women and the link between this and emancipation was an important one.[26] Poole Park in Poole, Dorset, still features a circular cycling track built as part of the park when it opened in the 1890s. With imagination it could now provide the focus for summer bicycle pageants for children and parades of historic bicycles.

Today the pressure is on historic parks to accommodate more sports, but this pressure is not for more pitches and tennis courts, but for leisure centres. The Park Manager of Pallister Park, Middlesborough, had become fed up with the dual standards operated by the Leisure Services. He argued that leisure centres and parks should get parity of funding and that parks were in effect leisure centres without a roof. As a result the park has had a leisure centre built in the middle of it under a £3 million City Challenge Scheme. In 1993 it was awarded 'Park of the Year' by ILAM.[27] Leisure centres mean large buildings and larger areas of parking space, which can have a most detrimental effect on historic parks.

16

Figure 5 (top): Wicksteed Park, Kettering, in 1985. One of the major uses of parks still is going there with children or grandchildren, but playgrounds are not necessarily the most important attraction. (Photo: the author)
Figure 6 (bottom): Simply feeding the ducks is a thing that children love to do, whether in the 1890s or 1990s. (Photo: Jane Porter)

The argument that leisure needs have changed needs to be challenged. The most popular physical activity for both men and women is walking (49 per cent males; 41 per cent females over 16 years of age). Between 1987 and 1996 the number of people walking increased from 37.9 to 44.5 per cent.[28] For the majority of park users sports are not high on their agenda. Only 6 per cent of park users come for organized sport, whereas sport takes up 25 per cent of the space and 50 per cent of the budget. There is a tendency for parks to promote male physical fitness at the expense of children, women, family groups, the elderly and the disabled.[29] What most people like about parks is the freedom to do what they want, to be alone or in company as they choose, away from the pressures of the city and to enjoy the space, the flowers, the greenery and the wildlife (see colour section).

Nature

The early parks reflected the mid-19th-century interest in studying all aspects of the natural world, including that of prehistory. Fossilized tree trunks and roots were displayed at Lister Park, Bradford, Victoria Park, Glasgow, and many other parks. The most dramatic of these displays of prehistory was undoubtedly the dinosaurs on islands in the lower lake at Crystal Palace Park, London. This interest in the natural world could also be seen in the plants displayed in public parks and in the palmhouses. At the Derby Arboretum in 1840 John Claudius Loudon planted more than 800 species of trees so that the individual character and beauty of each could be appreciated. Each species was labelled with its name, history, uses and country of origin.[30] The huge palmhouses added to so many parks at the end of the 19th century introduced people to a far wider range of plants and presented the flora in beautiful, warm surroundings: somewhere delightful to go on a cold or wet day. Many palmhouses are now in a decayed state, awaiting restoration and seeking new uses. An extremely successful example of the modern use of a palmhouse is the Tropical World at Roundhay Park, Leeds, which attracts more than a million visitors annually.

Parks provided intense horticultural experi-

ences. Visitors loved the floral displays, the carpet bedding, the commemorative and sculptural planting with their brilliant masses of strong colours. To the 19th century park promoters these floral displays had an elevating function: 'Flowers not only charm, they teach'. Indeed, the very order in which the parks were kept was thought to provide lessons in 'neatness . . . conduct and behaviour'.[31] The controlled ways in which nature was presented in the parks was very different from that of nature in the wild and reflected the ways in which working people were controlled in life. This point was clearly recognized by William Morris.

Bedding planting is very labour-intensive. Philips Park, Manchester, had a wonderful reputation for its tulips and Tulip Sunday was an important annual event. In the mid-1980s the planting of tulips ceased as part of a cost-cutting exercise and roses were planted in their stead. In the late 1980s the tulips were reinstated, but in 1991 vandals entered the park on the Saturday night and decapitated every tulip. After this the beds were grassed over. The park then went into a spiral of decline, but in 1997, for the first time in about a decade, the tulips were planted and Tulip Sunday was again celebrated (figure 7).

Public parks have always featured a wide variety of gardens and reflected contemporary trends and interests. The Festival Gardens in Battersea Park, London, in 1951 are one example. In Lister Park, Bradford, the successful application to the UPP includes the building of a new Mughal garden on a derelict site. Lister Park lies at the centre of a large Asian population and this will add to the attractions of the park and reinforce its links with the local community.

It was generally agreed among park superintendents that the vivid floral displays attracted park visitors. Some recent research acknowledges that park users today place a high value on scenery and natural features, but there is no research on the enjoyment of flowers, or how looking at bright flowers cheers people up. The lack of dedicated park staff, the closure of nurseries and the dispersal of specialized collections of plants means that today the opportunities for training in horticulture are greatly diminished, and what planting there is tends to be is more uniform because plants are bought in from garden centres. Yet gardening is an increasingly popular home-based leisure activity. In 1987, 46 per cent of the population participated; by 1998 this had risen to 48 per cent.[32]

Gardens form an increasingly popular tourist attraction. The most popular garden attractions were Hampton Court Palace, followed by Tropical World, Roundhay Park, Leeds. Over 10 years, from 1986 to 1996, visits to gardens increased from 105 visits in 1986 (index: 1985 = 100) to 163 in 1996. This compares with museum visits in 1986 at 98.2, rising to 113.8 in 1996. Thus, garden visits saw a 55 per cent increase in this period compared with a 15.8 per cent increase in museum visits.[33] Between 1975 and 1993 National Trust figures for visits to 16 gardens showed an increase of 131 per cent. This was more than twice the increase in visits to historic properties.[34]

Parks and the urban environment

Historic urban parks have been and still are the subject of conflicting pressures. The people's love of their local park as a constant in their lives contrasts with the attitude of some politicians and local authorities who see parks as a resource to be built on and moulded in response to changes in patterns of life.[35] In the past urban parks were seen as *rus in urbe*. Today our place in nature and our relation to it is being re-examined. One is increasingly aware of the impact on the environment of the growing use of cars, and also that decentralization and the building of towns in the countryside is not an urban solution. More than 80 per cent of the population lives in towns, and a policy is needed to enhance them and to make them places that are enjoyable to live in. Local Agenda 21 means that local authorities must consider the implications of sustainability and complete a strategy by December 2000. The annual survey of local authority budgets for 1996/97 showed plans to increase spending on environmental issues, while at the same time planning to spend £15 million less on parks and recreation.[36]

The conservation of the historic environment includes designed landscapes such as historic urban parks. They are a fundamental part of sustainability for they are an important part of local distinctiveness, important to the local community and part of our national identity. All these factors are stressed in Local Agenda 21. Too often conservation is seen as standing in the way of urban development. The evidence however contradicts this.[37] In Sheffield, the restoration of Norfolk Park is stimulating economic growth in the adjoining estates. Historic parks are part of the historic environment and have a role to play in arresting urban decay, promoting cities that are liveable in, encouraging people to move back into the city centre to live, thereby reducing pressure on the countryside. The restoration of the historic West Park was an integral part of Wolverhampton's city centre regeneration strategy. Glasgow's wide-ranging park strategy includes parks, open spaces and the urban fringe.[38]

New parks and all types of green space have a role to play. In Limehouse, London, new parks and open spaces have been created as part of the urban regeneration scheme of Docklands. Ropemaker's Fields features a new bandstand that uses cast-iron columns from nearby warehouses at St Katherine's Dock, so the new retains the memory of the old, not only in the name, but also in the fabric. In Glasgow a range of new parks and open spaces is being created as part of Glasgow 1999 City of Architecture and Design.[39] The New Opportunities Fund is to direct National Lottery money into health, education and the environment: green spaces and sustainable communities are among the new initiatives.[40] The Fund proposes to help urban and rural communities to 'understand, improve and care for their natural and living environment', by creating or improving public spaces, parks, play areas and community gardens. It will, therefore, make it possible to reach parts of the environment that the HLF cannot reach, that is those parks, gardens and open spaces that do not have sufficient heritage merit to qualify for a HLF grant. It is important that this initiative be in addition to the UPP, for there remain thousands of

Figure 7: Tulips for Tulip Sunday, Philips Park, Manchester, in 1997. (Photo: Manchester City Council)

parks in the most deprived areas of our cities that are still in great need of attention.

Conclusion

Parks are for people of all ages and all walks of life. They were designed for a different age, but all the evidence contradicts the assertion that people and their leisure needs have changed. What has changed are the standards of maintenance and the lack of a dedicated park staff. Some parks lost their character not from vandalism or neglect, but because of ignorance — nobody thought there was anything there to understand, or of value. Historic parks were designed to improve the urban environment in many ways: financially, by raising the value of the property around them; practically, by cleaning the air and being lungs for the city; physically, by providing a place for sport and exercise; and psychologically, by providing a place where people could relax and enjoy the sight of trees and grass. If one looks at the role of parks today one finds that all of these points are still as valid. The original designers knew what they were doing. They provided subtle, flexible designs that accommodated a wide range of activities and there is no reason why these parks should not have an equally important role to play well into the 21st century.

Notes

1. Hazel Conway and David Lambert, *Public Prospects: Historic Urban Parks Under Threat* (London: Garden History Society and Victorian Society, 1993).

2. *Select Committee on Public Walks*, BPP, vol. XV (1833), Cmnd. 448.

3. Hazel Conway, *People's Parks* (Cambridge: Cambridge University Press, 1991); *idem*, *Public Parks* (Princes Risborough: Shire, 1996).

4. Harriet Jordan, 'Public parks, 1885–1914', *Garden History*, 22/1 (1994), 85–113.

5. Alan Jackson, *Semi-detached London* (London: Architectural Press, 1973).

6. *Journal of Park Administration* (November 1937), 195.

7. Conway and Lambert, *Public Prospects*.

8. *Gardeners' Chronicle* (12 April 1884), 477.

9. *Farmers' New Almanack* (1890), 3–4.

10. Susan Lasdun, *The English Park: Royal, Private and Public* (London: André Deutsch, 1991), 156.

11. *Social Trends*, No. 28 (London: Office of National Statistics, 1996), 223.

12. *Environmental and Recreational Indicators*. Report for Audit Commission (London: MORI, 1992).

13. Ibid., 31.

14. Charles Poulsen, *Victoria Park* (London: Stepney Books and Journeyman, 1976).

15. *The Quality Exchange Survey of Parks and Open Spaces Managed by the London Boroughs, Metropolitan and District Councils of England and Wales* (London: Audit Commission, 1994).

16. Conway, *People's Parks*, 202.

17. *Watch this Space!* (London: London Boroughs Association [LBA], 1995), 53–62.

18. Susan Marcus and Rosie Barker, *Using Historic Parks and Gardens: A Teacher's Guide* (London: English Heritage, 1997); *Park Discovery Project: Teachers' Pack* (London: London Historic Parks and Gardens Trust, 1998).

19. *More Grounds for Concern* (London: GMB, 1997), 21, 31.

20. Ibid.

21. Conway, *People's Parks,* 195.

22. Lasdun, *The English Park*, 160.

23. Ruth Guilding, 'The Model Traffic Recreation Area at Lordship Lane', *London Gardener*, 2/2 (1996–97), 18–22.

24. Jamie McCullough, *Meanwhile Gardens* (London: Calouste Gulbenkian Foundation, 1978).

25. *Watch this Space!*, 39.

26. Conway, *People's Parks*, 195.

27. Conway and Lambert, *Public Prospects.*

28. *Social Trends*, No. 28.

29. *Urban Parks Discussion Paper* (London: Landscape Institute, 1992), 8.

30. John Claudius Loudon, *The Derby Arboretum* (London: Longman, Orme, Brown, Green & Longmans, 1840).

31. Conway, *People's Parks*, 182–3.

32. *Annual Abstract of Statistics*, No. 134 (London: HMSO, 1998).

33. *Annual Abstract of Statistics*, No. 134.

34. 'Feasibility Study for an Organisation to Assist in the Conservation of Historic Parks and Gardens' (London: Elizabeth Banks Associates, 1995), Appendix 2.

35. *People, Parks and Cities* (London: Department of the Environment, 1996), 25.

36. *More Grounds for Concern*, 15.

37. *Conservation-led Regeneration* (London: English Heritage, 1998); *Catalytic Conversion: Revive Historic Buildings to Regenerate Communities* (London: SAVE Britain's Heritage, 1998).

38. *A New Vision, A New Future* (Glasgow: Glasgow City Council, 1996).

39. *Blueprint*, no. 157 (January 1999), 22–3.

40. *New Links for the Lottery: Proposals for the New Opportunities Fund* (London: HMSO, 1998).

Memory and value

by David Jacques

Figure 1: Scenes like this, from Chiswick House grounds in the 1980s, are what memories are made of. (Photo: the author)

'Conservation' is best understood as an attitude of mind, namely a concern for value in the physical world. It is less easy to give 'value' a simple definition because the numerous interests that see value in landscape raise the question of 'value to whom?'

Public parks were created with the expectation that they would provide spiritually uplifting picturesque scenes reminiscent of the then-current understanding of nature, and of art's role within it, and fresh air for healthy physical recreation. In the wider landscape the values still given most attention by the countryside agencies are aesthetics and nature conservation, though the ancient fabric (a term that here includes hard and soft materials) of the countryside and its patterns are a recent interest.

Such perceptions are those of the designer and planner, those who view such places from a lofty professional viewpoint. However, seen through the eyes of the everyday users of such landscapes, including urban parks, the complexion of values invested in them will generally have colouring applied, and often obscuring, the professional ones. The user re-focuses the expert perceptions in a subjective fashion through the lens of oft-repeated personal experience.

Memory is the unseen but guiding force determining most park users' responses. 'The landscape is a storehouse of impressions, of knowledge, of loyalty', wrote Christopher Tunnard. 'Our view of the landscape is conditioned by familiarity.'[1] He was one of the first to see memory as a value in landscape. More recently, the ICCROM/ICOMOS *Management Guidelines for World Heritage Sites*, based on experience around the world, headed its list of cultural values with 'identity value', which was seen as 'related to the emotional ties of society to specific objects or sites'.[2] As places come to be used and associated with events they become emotionally charged in the minds of users. Visiting the place again is the trigger to remember and re-live past events and pleasures. It becomes a dimension to one's self and society's self-image.

Emotional attachments to landscapes should not be dismissed as mere sentimentality; while they are held they stimulate memory and awareness of self. Change to familiar landscape causes disorientation as treasured memory loses its grounding. Margaret Drabble, the writer, saw that: 'the landscape . . . is a living link between what we were and what we have become. This is one of the reasons why we feel such profound and apparently disproportionate anguish when a loved landscape is altered out of recognition; we lose not only a place, but [also] part of ourselves, a continuity between the shifting phases of our life'.[3]

People indeed crave continuity in their surroundings, unless it is they themselves that change them.[4] They like to think that places remain intact, 'unspoiled', to allow their enjoyment to be repeated. In public parks, instead of aesthetics, nature conservation and archaeology, one hears of dog-walkers and mothers pushing buggies complaining, often seemingly perversely, about improvements or changes to the paths, shrubs, trees and seats they habitually see and use. Academics and civil servants then try to rationalize these responses in terms of 'the familiar, cherished, scene', 'the sense of place' or 'local distinctiveness'.

David Lowenthal asserted long ago that popular tastes reveal 'a deeply held and deeply rooted system of shared beliefs'.[5] Peirce Lewis, Professor of Geography at Pennsylvania State University, has been interested in the public's tastes in landscape because 'they are part of a larger value system through which people identify themselves as members of a community'.[6] He has postulated three 'canons' of popular landscape taste:

Canon 1: Popular taste is not a trivial matter; it is a fundamental part of all cultures, and a crucial means by which nations and cultures identify themselves and separate themselves from other nations and cultures.

Canon 2: Landscape taste, like all taste, reveals itself at two quite different levels within any given culture. One level is fundamental; the other is ephemeral.

Canon 3: The cultural landscape is divided into two large spatial categories: areas where standards of taste are routinely invoked, and areas where they are not.

In this review of popular landscape taste, Peirce was assiduously non-judgemental. He just tried to understand it as an aspect of culture, not to examine standards of taste. However, designers and politicians acting on others' behalf do not have that luxury: they must invoke standards of taste in proposing and judging schemes. Unfortunately the Diana, Princess of Wales, Memorial Garden episode in 1998 demonstrated that the rôle of memory was far from being understood. Those who proposed it for Kensington Gardens had no clear conception of the difference between a garden of memory and a memorial garden. The former would have conserved a familiar place to enable visitors to recall their memories and feelings; the latter would have eradicated the cherished scene with an entirely new themed garden.

There was a time, as recently as the 1970s, when landscape evaluation was supposed to be an 'objective' affair. However, most landscape

Figure 2: Engraving by Pieter Andreas Rysbrack of the orange tree garden at Chiswick House, *c.*1730. Documents such as this are invaluable in restoration work. (Illustration: Department of the Environment)

23

planners now accept that there are many valid landscape tastes; and it may be that some people have no clear visual preferences as such, but just feel comfortable in familiar places. The rôle of the professional is thus shifting from being the 'expert', giving detached but objective evaluations, to that of interpreter of the public's perceptions. Typically, the professional is presented with a mass of viewpoints and other data, perhaps from a public consultation exercise, that needs somehow to be structured in a form that is comprehensible and useful to decision-makers.

Often, in practice, the most valued areas are the intimate and familiar ones that play a part in people's daily lives, rather than the distant parks and outstanding landscapes far from home.[7] The social contact at such places is important, but so too are the direct sensuous encounters with nature, such as being outside in open space, enjoying the changing seasons, feeling the sun, the wind and

the rain, being able to run or walk, or just sitting and enjoying the view. Simple contact with nature will suffice; ordinary plants, and any birds or animals are good to see. Successful parks combine formal flowerbeds and naturalistic areas with a mix of recreational facilities and a variety of congenial social settings. They are best able to provide both associative and material access to a better world through providing sensory and natural experiences, a world of adventure play, and a more supportive social community where common experiences are shared.

Translated into a designer's perceptions, this argues that the quality of a park derives from a composite of a complex design that provides a range of interesting spaces and promotes varied experiences, as well as a benevolent regime of management that allows the enrichment of the place's attributes. If this sounds like a conservationist's plea for maintenance and repair rather than re-design, that indeed may be the practical outcome in many cases. However, the imperative for a conservation approach in traditional parks does not derive principally from the professional's or art historian's 'top-down' viewpoint. It flows from a 'bottom-up' appreciation from the everyday user.

Change and decay

No one involved with landscapes needs reminding that landscapes change through the processes of natural growth and decay, and the style of maintenance. However, sudden extreme change at one or maybe several points in a landscape's history may be even more important to the overall character and value of a place. These changes are generally planned events, like the ruling class re-ordering fields or their drainage for better agricultural production, or reshaping by a landscape designer. Cultural landscapes are thus best characterized as deriving their form from a series of 'overlays' and their content from the style of recent management. In this, they differ from natural landscapes, which evolve relatively slowly in response to climate and geology in order to reach eventual equilibrium.[8]

With each new overlay, the elements of former ones can be destroyed or recycled. The historical tendency of landscape designers to incorporate substantial numbers of earlier landscape components is too often overlooked. It is common to find that, for example, earthworks and trees in parks and gardens have been repeatedly re-cycled. In many urban parks a former country house or villa landscape has been adapted wholesale, and even in new designs earlier landscape elements are gratefully incorporated as a matter of course.

As the previous chapter by Hazel Conway indicates, though, landscapes can drift between events in response to natural processes, economic imperatives or social conditions away from their planned state. Typically, in such circumstances, aesthetic and associative values ebb away, even if nature conservation value may be retained or enhanced. A landscape's carefully crafted form can thus be disturbed not only by a new overlay, or deliberate incremental change, but also through forms of maintenance including, of course, neglect.

The principle of sustainability is that an asset should be managed so that there is no diminution of its value over time. This applies to the cultural heritage as it does to the natural; even more so, in fact, because landscapes are non-renewable as living links to memory. The struggle to conserve the human and material value of urban parks is thus a key aspect of sustainability and quality of life in cities.

Management planning: logic and process

Anyone concerned with conserving value in a landscape must address the questions of what, precisely, is being attempted and how it can be achieved. The management plan commits such thoughts to paper and enables others to participate in the thought process. The logic of evaluating the present, defining the aims for the future, setting out the practical proposals and then inviting criticism before decisions are taken is now familiar. Implementation then starts a process that continues into the distant future with monitoring and review.

There is advice from the Heritage Lottery Fund (HLF) in the form of *Conservation Plans*.[9] As this implies in its 'Introduction', it is not the comprehensive advice that is needed for a practical management plan, and concentrates simply upon conservation policies. The HLF's 'Recommended Brief to Applicants and Historic Landscape Consultants' provides a better model of the management planning process that is specific to landscapes.[10] Broad advice can also be sought from the Countryside Commission's *Site Management Planning: A Guide*,[11] which, although not specific to urban parks, gives hints on non-conservation aspects, creating a work programme, financial planning, implementation, monitoring and review.

Evaluating the present will be based on survey and historical research.[12] The ensuing analysis will aim at an understanding of the dynamics of the landscape, and that in turn will be informed by an examination of underlying natural factors, and past and present human aspirations, in an explanation of the changes seen in historical times and in the present. Historical interest may be just one value among many identified: ecology, horticulture, aesthetics and, of course, finance may justify consideration and integration into the plan. Then it is time to assess condition and identify the problems and dangers inherent in the current state of affairs.

The next stage is the definition of a long-term vision, say 20 years in the future. The essence of defining a vision is specifying the values that a place might conceivably achieve through benign management. It may be that a range of interests will need to be reconciled or given priorities and so the vision should expand on the nature, intensity and mix of values intended.

Translating the vision into drawn, quantified and costed prescription takes place through intermediate steps referred to variously as objectives, policies, proposals or methods. A long-term continuity of purpose and the careful planning of change are the necessary preconditions to the accumulation of value. Hence, involving the managers, so that the plans become theirs, is a sensible precaution.

The rôle of monitoring and review is often underplayed. No doubt this is because they are the most difficult stages to ensure as they depend upon some future manager not only being aware of a former management plan, but also being willing to engage in time-consuming reviews. Human nature often dictates that every new person in charge wishes to start afresh, unbound by previous decisions. It is thus seldom possible for any manager to ensure compliance from 'beyond the grave', but public agencies are in the best position to do so through their enforcement of grant conditions. It is a tragedy getting worse annually, then, that there is no register of management plans.

Continuity through maintenance and repair

Practical prescription for the retention of fabric and design as the embodiment of memory may take various forms. Foremost among them is maintenance. Continuity of management creates the conditions for the development of archaeological, historical and often ecological interest. Normally, continuity is achieved through planned maintenance that slows the processes of decay while allowing incremental adjustments to combat that which is unavoidable. Landscape components are thus given an extended life, always a significant aim of conservation.

The politicians' cycle of neglect-blitz-neglect, which may give a fleeting impression that action is being taken, is anathema to sensible landscape management on historical, ecological and aesthetic grounds. Hence, many of the more interesting historic gardens are those modest places where maintenance has been sustained over long periods. This is not preservation; the inevitability of decay determines that. Arguably, one of the few examples of preservation in landscape is the retention of grassed earthworks by mowing. Another vital ingredient besides continuity is the use of craft skills. The difficulty of finding craftsmen suitable for conservation work can be serious, so one aspect of conservation is to keep alive the craftsmanship that maintains the forms.

Eventually the point is reached, though, when the fabric has decayed past the point when it makes a viable contribution to the design. In some circumstances, especially planting, it will not just have decayed; it will have substantially disappeared. Nevertheless the design intentions can be perpetuated through repairs, and, in areas for which there is inadequate knowledge of the detail, through conjectural detailing. An emphasis on conserving historic fabric thus has to give way progressively to the perpetuation of design intentions and the familiar scene by replacing lost or damaged landscape elements. Providing an orderly transition from one to the other becomes the challenge. In summary, the scope of conservation-based treatments is thus maintenance, repair and conjectural detailing.[13]

Reconstructions — the wholesale reinvention of fabric removed in the past — are invariably problematic. They may involve the removal of a later overlay, yet an overlay considered unimportant at first frequently comes in time to be

25

Figure 3: Chiswick Villa garden front.

recognized as historically interesting. Any judgement that one particular overlay represented the greatness of a site is very subjective and ignores the accumulation of interest over several periods. There is seldom adequate justification for removing overlays that contribute positively to a sense of place.

On the other hand, aesthetic as well as practical reasons frequently argue that 'accretions' of very limited merit that have outlived their usefulness, like redundant 1930s toilet blocks or 1960s playgrounds perpetually closed for repairs, should be removed. It can always be argued, though, that any component is part of the memory of the site, even though it may be disruptive of design interest and aesthetic value. On what basis, then, can one apply the pejorative term 'accretion'? Few would argue that overgrown hedges should not be cut, or that large areas of unused tarmac are worth retaining, but should plantings now regretted be dismissed as worthless intrusions, or regarded as part of the evolution of the site? This is where the manager must make the leap of judgement; but a useful test is to ask whether the accretion was the result of careful consideration, or arose through thoughtlessness, short-sightedness or neglect.

Sometimes one hears the observation that restorers are trying to 'put the clock back'. This may be true with reconstructions of past overlays, but misrepresents the rôle of repair in making good that which is of the present, though decayed. In effect, this will mean rediscovering the qualities it must have had when it was previously in peak condition. Repairs can be seen not only as a historian's desire to preserve fine art interest, but also as a process to knit together a degraded or dissembled park, to reset the clock and allow the process by which value was formerly accumulated to re-commence.

What to do about poor past restoration

Poor past restoration presents particularly intractable problems. Are they overlays or accretions? Should they stand as testimony of the attitudes to conservation in their day, or are they dispensable like other accoutrements of past presentation? Is it possible to re-restore and this time get it 'right'? At Chiswick House, Middlesex, the rather inaccurate 1950s restoration-in-spirit of the Burlington gardens immediately around his villa had a degree of historical value in its own right by the 1990s. On the other hand, the villa had been altered to recover its appearance in Burlington's time accurately, and the original form of the gardens was recoverable too, with only a small degree of conjecture, with the aid of archae-ology. In this case the 1950s attempt at restoration was deemed dispensable and a fresh attempt 'to

Figure 4: Old photographs, such as this one of Chiswick House from *Country Life c.*1898, often reveal lost details; for example, the pathway shown here was later grassed over, as the more recent photograph shown in figure 3 demonstrates. (Photos: this page, Country Life; opposite, Jan Woudstra)

get it right' was the least bad option.[14]

The Great Garden at Kenilworth Castle, Warwickshire, has so far provided the most intractable problem. Lord Leicester, Elizabeth I's favourite, formed it in the 1570s. It afterwards became a kitchen garden following the castle's slighting by Oliver Cromwell in the 1650s. In the 1960s a Ministry of Works inspector determined to restore it to its state in its heyday in Elizabethan times. The potential of garden archaeology was barely understood at the time and even if well conducted may have shown little after three centuries of double digging. The inspector thus designed a pastiche in what he thought was the spirit of Elizabethan times. As a result, the present garden has neither historical integrity nor historical interest; effectively there is nothing now worth conserving. The moral of these tales is that restoration, whether at a country house or in a public park, is only worth doing well.

Conjectural detailing

Landscapes' inherent ephemerality often causes restoration to go further than 'conservative repair'. The drawbacks of over-restoration — passing off a bogus scene as the authentic past — may not be serious if missing elements came from a uniform construction, like a wall, or a repetitive pattern, such as trees in an avenue. Difficulties emerge, though, where the original detail was non-uniform or non-repetitive, such as rockwork or shrub planting.

The problem for parks is magnified because, typically, the precise form of much of their original planting, and also edges, paths and paving, may have gone unrecorded. Meanwhile, it is quite common to find that the constructed elements of a park, such as paths, steps and buildings, require no more than modest repairs, while the accompanying shrubbery is drastically reduced to just a few yews among invading elder, or thickets of *Aucuba japonica* or *Rhododendron ponticum*. All the choicer smaller shrubs and associated bulbs and flowers may have disappeared decades ago, probably without being recorded either. Even if good information existed on the original planting, exact like-for-like replacement is often not possible for horticultural reasons. Adjacent plants may have grown and, by shading and taking the nutrients and moisture from the soil, may have altered the growing conditions.

Nevertheless, to refuse to restore the planting on the basis that not enough is known would be perverse. The most sensible answer is to carry out 'conjectural detailing' that provides a best-guess repair, but to make the nature of such a decision abundantly clear in any boards, press releases or literature (see the chapter by Kim Legate).

Interpretation

The moral obligation of recording and interpreting accompanies any position as manager of a publicly owned site. Local memories and traditions may be passed on to younger residents, and deepen their perceptions of the special nature of the place. Recording of both fabric and memory are the basis for such interpretation as well as defining a conservation approach. Usually it will be helpful to users if interpretation can be extended to time out of mind, say to the origins of the park, as this will help them make sense of the design and components.

The manager will often need the assistance of professional historians and interpreters. These people are enablers, with skills in identifying the pertinent, and often difficult and uncomfortable, questions raised by the place so that interested visitors can reconstruct events or scenes, and seek enlightenment through observation and reflection. The use of imagination can be stimulated by such means as education packs for schools, posters, children's books, guidebooks, information boards, artist's impressions, models and videos. The places themselves then become evocative templates for journeys in the imagination.

Rehabilitation and the 'new uses' rhetoric

Adaptation (or 'rehabilitation') of parks may seem attractive because it is an approach designed to accommodate changing uses. The past tendency to spread tarmacadam over all paths was generally justified by a combination of coping with visitor pressure and ensuring low maintenance. However, it can be highly debilitating to the historic character, especially at a property started as a country house or villa, and which subsequently became a public park. These days there is often a strong perceived need to adapt a public park for 'modern needs' with parking areas, active recreation facilities or just new design with concrete paving blocks and 'heritage' furniture.

The 'new uses' rhetoric was overtly concerned with the 'needs of the people'. When H. Frank Clark wanted to restore Chiswick House Grounds in 1951 the argument he had to deploy was that they were run down and needed rehabilitation for greater use.[15] Meanwhile he argued that a concern about their precise form would be 'pedantic', with the result that his scheme was not expensive — but then neither was it accurate. Rehabilitation likewise provided the basis for a consensus, brokered during the 1970s, between architectural conservators, Modernist architects and borough treasurers for justifying keeping old buildings.

Adaptation to new uses has become a strong theme in American urban parks. 'Rehabilitation' is one of the categories of the treatment of historic properties recognized in the Secretary of the Interior's *Standards for Historic Preservation Projects* (1983). During the 1990s these standards

Figure 5: Engraving by John Donowell (*c*.1753) showing 'A view of the Back Front of the House, & part of the Garden of the Earl of Burlington, at CHISWICK; with a distant view of the Orangery, Greenhouse, Inigo Jones's Gate &c.' (Illustration: private collection)

were extended to historic landscape.[16] In this context it was defined as treatment that 'retains the landscape as it has evolved historically by maintaining and repairing historic features, while allowing additions and alterations for contemporary and future uses'. The defining characteristic of rehabilitation is thus the handling of use rather than the treatment of the historic fabric, and in this respect it differs from the other categories of stabilization, preservation, restoration and reconstruction. Despite its defects in providing guidance for the conservation of fabric, though, rehabilitation has been promoted as the preferred approach in the USA.[17]

The irony is that the 'new uses' rhetoric has little force in recreational landscapes that have no 'use' in the commercial sense implied in connection with buildings. Furthermore, there is the danger of frequent adaptation obscuring the clarity

of design intentions and disturbing the patterns of long-term care that landscapes need, without completely satisfying up-to-date requirements. All too often some cheap or halfway scheme results. It will often be preferable to resist such change until the case for a new overlay is overwhelming, and then to insist upon new work of merit.

The conservation ethic in new work

The term 'conservation' implies an ethic seeking the beneficial management of value. Two philosophers have defined it in these terms: 'Conservation is about negotiating the transition from past to future in such a way as to secure the transfer of maximum significance'.[18] While this definition is helpful in most respects, it does not address the ethics of change.

Stewardship of the landscape and the values it

embodies springs from the guiding principle that the sum of the qualities found in a landscape should only be enhanced through change. New work is welcome where it will add to the enrichment of the place. This will not be based on a judgement of immediate gain, but on whether new work will be of more lasting quality than that which it replaces. There will be the additional test that change should be managed with a respect for user's memories. Furthermore, the onus is upon those who would alter in the cause of progress to answer these points; it should be the designer's responsibility, not the conservationist's, to initiate such debate.

Usually, where the value, or mix of values, in a landscape is already high, the emphasis of treatment is, rightly, on protection, maintenance and repair. Where existing value is less pronounced, it might not be difficult to argue that new work would be beneficial. Even so, the scope for new design on a clean drawing sheet is limited today. That suits the mood of the time, which is cautious of grandiose gestures for short-term political gain. Instead, careful interventions, based on a solid understanding of the landscape and the demands upon it, are the more appropriate.

Managers could think more in terms of adding a layer that accommodates past value, and that provides the framework within which new value can be generated. People trained to understand and welcome complexity, who seek the good of many interests, but recognize that the balance will be different in each locality, are at a premium. Design skills have a major contribution to make, but should be deployed as a consequence of landscape management and landscape planning, and not for their own sake.

The interplay of conservation and change

The Heritage Lottery Fund does not define the 'heritage merit' that it seeks,[19] but its 'Recommended brief to applicants and historic landscape consultants' notes that consultants should 'demonstrate how the historic character and value of the site will be preserved'.

Meanwhile the HLF is not averse to change where the case for it is solid.

However, a balanced vision embracing conservation and change does sometimes encounter friction deriving from competing professional viewpoints. The Crystal Palace case[20] brought the rhetoric relating to the supposed opposition between 'progress' and 'protection' to the fore once more. Modernists have always found it convenient to view 'history' as a problematic counterpart against which Modernism could be contrasted to seem progressive. Modernism was presented as the future, one that had to overcome the anti-progressive forces of the old order. Conservationists are caricatured as championing the 'traditional', itself defined from the perspective of the modern.[21] In creating designations, enforcing stasis, conservationists merely seem to confirm that the dead hand of history had no meaningful place in the changing everyday world.[22]

A criticism still frequently levelled against conservationists is that they concentrate on the negative aspects of change. Clearly it cannot always be detrimental, though, because the present mix of value in the landscape is the result of past change and the subsequent accumulation of interest that it allowed. These days it is generally recognized that having policies to preserve or enhance conservation value does not mean that all further change should be stopped. Yet there is a fundamental problem in achieving a reliable perspective on change. The benefits of past actions are understood, and can be loved. Meanwhile, the immediate disbenefits of change can be relatively vividly appreciated, while the benefits of future actions are unknown, and are as yet unloved.

Despite this, possible heritage benefits from restoration or new works can be envisaged thus:

1. The safeguarding of historic fabric through an improved maintenance regime.

2. The burial of historic fabric in the event of a new overlay so that it can be recovered at some future date.

3. The mechanical strengthening of

historic fabric through repairs.

4. The recovery of historic landscape components or areas through replacement of fabric and conjectural detailing.

5. The clarification of an historic design by the removal of overgrowth, dirt, debris and accretion.

6. The interpretation of a site and its components to the everyday user.

7. The collection and archiving of information that will support future restoration or interpretation.

An integrated vision of conservation and change is not just a present imperative; it has always been the reality. Unfortunately, historic fabric is too often presented simplistically as the then new, ignoring its continuing contribution to the present. A better understanding, more complex but more realistic, recognizes that at no point were the ancient and the new mutually exclusive, but they connected and interpenetrated each other. The past has always been a source of inspiration and the yardstick for change.

Conservation is thus about the present, not the past, about the wise use of resources, and about how a culture uses and takes what it inherits into the future. A creative interplay between conservation and change is the surest way of achieving enhanced value in our complex and uncertain future.

Notes

1. Christopher Tunnard, *A World With A View: An Inquiry into the Nature of Scenic Values* (New Haven and London: Yale University Press, 1978), 1, 2.

2. Bernard M. Fielden and Jukka Jokilehto, *Management Guidelines for World Heritage Sites* (Rome: ICCROM, 1993), 18. ICCROM is the International Centre for the Study of the Preservation and the Restoration of Cultural Property in Rome; ICOMOS is the International Council for Monuments and Sites in London.

3. Margaret Drabble, *A Writer's Britain:*

Landscape in Literature (London: Thames & Hudson, 1979), 270.

4. J. J. Costonis, *Icons and Aliens: Law, Aesthetics, and Environmental Change* (Urbana: University of Urbana-Champaign Press, 1989), written by a legal theorist, puts forward a 'cultural stability-identity' hypothesis by which communities apply aesthetic controls to protect their identities through stabilizing their environments.

5. David Lowenthal, 'The American scene', *Geographical Review*, 58 (1968), 61.

6. Peirce Lewis, 'American landscape tastes', in *Modern Landscape Architecture: A Critical Review*, ed. Marc Trieb (Cambridge, MA: MIT Press, 1993), 2–17.

7. Jacqueline Burgess *et al.*, 'People, parks and the urban green: a study of popular meanings and values for open spaces in the city', *Urban Studies*, 25 (1988), 455–73.

8. Landscape ecology, in claiming that landscapes evolve largely in response to natural factors, tends to place humans in an unrealistically passive rôle. The cultural landscapes approach differs in emphasizing human values, and the active rôle played by humans in shaping landscape.

9. *Conservation Plans for Historic Places* (London: Heritage Lottery Fund, 1998).

10. *Application Pack* (London: Heritage Lottery Fund, 1998).

11. Richard Clarke and David Mount, *Site Management Planning: A Guide*. Publication no. 527 (Cheltenham: Countryside Commission, 1998).

12. David Lambert, Peter Goodchild and Judith Roberts, *Researching a Garden's History: A Guide to Documentary and Published Sources* (Reigate: Landscape Design Trust, and York: University of York Institute of Advanced Architectural Studies, 1995).

13. David Jacques, 'The treatment of historic parks and gardens', *Journal of Architectural Conservation*, 1/2 (1995), 21–35.

31

Figure 6: The Rosary at Chiswick House was reinstated as part of the most recent restoration programme. (Photo: Jan Woudstra)

14. David Jacques, 'Restoration and Management Plan', unpublished report for English Heritage (1986); *idem*, 'What to do about earlier inaccurate restoration?: a case study of Chiswick House grounds', *APT Bulletin: The Journal of Preservation Technology*, 24/3–4 (1992/93), 4–13.

15. Clark remained a garden history luminary following his *The English Landscape Garden* (London: Pleiades, 1948), and was the first President of the Garden History Society on its foundation in 1965. For his work at Chiswick, see Jacques, 'What to do about earlier inaccurate restoration?'

16. Charles A. Birnbaum, *Guidelines for the Treatment of Historic Landscapes* (Washington, DC: US National Park Service, 1997).

17. Charles A. Birnbaum, 'A reality check for our nation's parks', *CRM Bulletin*, 16/4 (1993), 1–4. Virtually all historic landscape projects involve some degree of design adjustment for modern usage, and there is a danger that landscape designers proclaim them as rehabilitation, glossing over the tricky questions on the approach to the treatment of historic fabric and the justification for what are often, in effect, new overlays in the landscape.

18. Alan Holland and Kate Rawles, 'Values in conservation', ECOS, 14/1 (1993), 14–19. The authors were from the University of Lancaster on a contract from the Countryside Council for Wales to examine the ethics of conservation.

19. 'Special guidance', in *Application Pack*, 6.

20. A bold scheme by Kathryn Gustafson for the upper terraces was not eligible for a HLF grant, much to the chagrin of the local authority officials who chose to present the issue as entrenched conservatism frustrating a progressive modern solution.

21. Kathleen Watt, 'On the need to re-theorise tradition', unpublished paper, Hull School of Architecture, 1996.

22. This view was expressed as long ago as Christopher Tunnard, *Gardens and the Modern Landscape* (London: Architectural Press, 1938), 161.

Study methods

by Mary Lockwood

Figure 1: Old postcards are a very valuable source of information about a park's history. Simmons' Park, Okehampton. (From the collection of Nigel Temple)

The Friends of Birkenhead Park in the Wirral have a motto: 'that which is good should be preserved'. It is a view shared by the many people who believe that historic public parks are a valuable and relevant part of urban life, and should be restored and managed accordingly. It is to be hoped that we are living in an age that will see a public parks renaissance as local authorities across the country embark on restoration projects in the wake of the Heritage Lottery Fund's (HLF) Urban Parks Programme. But restoration needs to be based on meticulous study and a deep understanding of each site — an understanding not only just of how to bring parks back to a good state of repair in a way that respects their historic character and the spirit of the place, but also of how to tackle the underlying causes of dereliction such as lack of investment and the demise of the management structures by which they were formerly run.

Studying a park in detail involves a number of stages, the first and best known of which is historical research. However, if the aim is to try to conserve or restore a park, research in itself is not enough. All important is the art of analysis, of

comprehending the meanings of the landscape, of making informed judgements about the effects of change. This requires an ability to 'read' the landscape, an understanding of historic landscape design principles and a recognition of complex political, social and cultural contexts. If these skills are brought to bear on a restoration scheme, the resulting proposals are likely to be balanced and of a breadth and depth appropriate to the conservation of a park's character. The research, analysis and proposals need to be recorded and the accepted means of doing this is to prepare a 'plan'. This is an illustrated document with a history of the park, a vision for its future and some practical guidance on how to achieve the vision, including an estimate of costs.

There is no one universally accepted term for a plan. The HLF uses the term 'historic landscape survey and restoration plan', or 'restoration plan' for short, and for the purposes of this chapter its terminology is used. Restoration plans can be bland and timid, or overwhelming in the amount of information they contain. The best way to get a feel for the type and amount of information to include in a plan is to read a good one. In the absence of a central repository for plans, this is probably best done by contacting a local authority that has received a park restoration grant — lists are published by the funding agencies — or through the Urban Parks Forum.

Restoration plans for parks and gardens were first produced in the late 1970s, with early examples commissioned by the National Trust and the Royal Parks Agency. Many were produced after the great storms of 1987 and 1990 with financial assistance from English Heritage and the Countryside Commission. More recently the HLF has funded the production of over 100 plans as part of its Urban Parks Programme. As a result of over 20 years' experience, what is expected of a restoration plan has been tested and refined into a commonly accepted code of best practice, and the funding agencies demand the production of plans to similar 'model briefs'.

Whatever they are called, the aims of a plan are similar and they tend to contain the same types of information:

◆ Research: documentary sources and fieldwork.

◆ Analysis: commentary and judgement on change.

◆ Proposals: recommendations designed to conserve, repair, restore and enhance the park.

Before examining these stages in more detail, it is worth noting the recent promotion of the conservation plan. A conservation plan contains only the first two stages — research and analysis — and aims to draw up a 'statement of significance' about a site. It is generally accepted that conservation plans are inadequate for public parks because they fall short of established best practice in this field. In particular, they do not contain proposals drawn up by the same people who did the research and analysis, and hence the same level of expertise is not brought to bear on all three stages.

Who writes the plan?

A plan needs to be written by historic landscape experts. They will need to work closely with local authority officers and will typically need to consult other experts such as park managers, conservation architects, civil engineers, arboriculturists, horticulturists, hydrologists, ecologists, metalwork specialists, stone conservationists, archaeologists, health and safety officers, access officers, quantity surveyors and business planners. Statutory agencies can give names of historic landscape consultants who have a good track record in this type of work.

The value of restoration plans is recognized in the willingness of funding agencies to provide up to 75 per cent of their cost. Relatively high levels of grant are justified to help overcome occasional resistance to plans among owners who do not see their need. Experience suggests that it is these owners who often value the plans most highly once they are produced. Local authorities sometimes have an anti-consultant culture, but it is not to be expected that in-house staff will have the same level of specialist training as experienced consultants in producing landscape restoration plans. There needs to be a good working relationship between consultants and council officers in drawing up the plan together.

The benefits of preparing a plan

As well as a springboard to grant applications, there are very real and direct benefits from producing restoration plans. They are academic records and practical project blueprints. They provide site owners and managers with the key to understanding a park's heritage importance and present day value, and are a definitive record of a park's history, providing a sound basis for future management. A plan can provide the only element of continuity in the management of a park as staff and local authority policies and priorities change. Plans can also provide the means by which parks move up the political and social agendas. In Liverpool, for example, the production of restoration plans was important in raising the profile of historic parks within the local authority, and resulted in their becoming a political priority and winning a major commitment from the city's capital programme. For local authorities with a large number of historic parks a set of plans can be invaluable for helping to prioritize those parks where urgent attention is needed.

Writing a brief

The first step in commissioning a plan is to write a brief to the landscape consultants.[1] It is essential that time is invested in making the brief as clear and detailed as possible, to ensure that both those commissioning the plan and the consultants are clear about each other's requirements and expectations. Those preparing the brief should familiarize themselves with any existing research and surveys, and make these available to the consultants at an early stage to avoid duplication and unnecessary cost. The brief should also specify any specialist surveys that might be needed, for example, if there are problems with statuary, metalwork, water features or buildings, so that the estimates can be obtained at an early stage.

Research

Research needs to be of sufficient depth to permit a full understanding of the nature and character of the park, both historic and modern, and evidence of that research must be included in the restoration plan. Any deficiencies in gathering evidence should also be noted. This can be due to lack of time or resources, in which case the researcher needs to note the document reference and state that it was not looked at, or because documents have been destroyed, which is often the case with local authority committee minutes. The researcher needs to state which documents are missing, for example years 1898–1900 from an otherwise complete run of accounts. Research into documentary and published sources will need to be compared with the most important surviving record, the park itself.[2] Sources may include:

◆ Maps and plans — a sequence of maps and plans, studied chronologically, will reveal much about the design, layout and evolution of a park, including entrances, paths, buildings, structures and features, trees, shrubberies and flower beds. They can also reveal whether any of the original sites has been lost to development or added at a later date. The Ordnance Survey 25- and 6-inch

Figures 2 and 3: Views of Falmouth (top) and Rochdale (bottom) show the original form of ornamental structures. Such visual records can be invaluable in preparing restoration plans. (From the collection of Nigel Temple)

35

Figures 4, 5, 6 and 7 (left to right): Views of Cheltenham, Lowestoft c.1912, Ipwsich and Bromley. (From the collection of Nigel Temple)

maps are often the most useful — the 6-inch survey was a scaled-down version of the 25-inch, which was started in the 1850s. A copy of all editions, particularly the first and second, should be included in the restoration plan. The Ordnance Survey also produced between 1855 and 1894 detailed surveys of towns with a population in excess of 4000 at a scale of 1:500. Copies of maps, plans and illustrations should be incorporated into the main body of the restoration plan in chronological order rather than in the appendices. It is useful to present maps at a similar scale, and to the same orientation. Always include a north sign, a caption and a date. Where possible, the map series should include at least one map that predates the park.

◆ Local authority committee papers — if these were not thrown out during local government re-organization in the 1970s they are likely to contain details of park acquisition, layout, designers and management. They may also contain lists of plants and information on design details such as path surface finishes and furniture designs.

◆ Contemporary publications — from the mid-19th century there were popular gardening magazines, of which the best known is the *Gardeners' Chronicle*.[3] These contained articles on individual parks and public park design and management, often with illustrations and plans. Newspapers would sometimes report on park openings and special events — the opening of Birkenhead Park was reported in the *Liverpool*

Mercury (8 April 1847) and it described the layout of the park, which was used for no less than 11 'old English sports' including climbing a greasy pole and catching a greasy pig![4]

◆ Picture postcards, drawings, engravings, lithographs and photographs — as well as depicting features of civic pride such as bandstands, rockeries and water features, such images can reveal details of path surfaces, edging treatments, seating and lighting. It is useful to include copies of images in the plan next to modern photographs of the same view.

◆ Modern garden history reference works.

Reference should be made to modern published strategies relating to the park. These might include a park, landscape, environment or leisure strategy, or a Local, Structure or Unitary Plan, which has been adopted by the local council.

If the park was a pre-existing estate or landscape that was taken into municipal ownership and adapted for use as a public park, the researcher will need to establish whether any private papers survive. These may have been deposited in the county record office, local archive collection, one of the national repositories or held by a previous owner's family. Sources may include accounts, surveys, inventories, estate papers and personal papers such as sketchbooks, letters, diaries and notebooks. For example, Heaton Park, Manchester, is the former country house estate of the Earls of Wilton. It had an early 17th century

formal garden, was re-designed and enlarged by William Emes in 1770, further improved by John Webb in 1807 and brought into municipal ownership in 1902. The Historic Landscape Survey and Restoration Plan[5] for the park is based on detailed research into sources held at the following repositories:

◆ Greater Manchester County Record Office — where valuable manuscript evidence, particularly in the form of the extensive Egerton family estate papers, included accounts, letters, legal agreements and maps.

◆ The British Library and Map Room — in particular for a complete set of Ordnance Survey 1st edn 25-inch maps unavailable elsewhere, and for a set of plans for Lancashire from the mid-sixteenth century.

◆ Manchester City Library — for various surveys and a large collection of photographs and illustrations from the local studies unit.

◆ The Town Hall — the Corporation minutes were found in the basement and provided information relating to the purchase of Heaton Estate and the subsequent alterations that took place during its transformation into a municipal park.

◆ Heaton House Archive Collection — the house contained useful paintings, maps and photographs.

◆ Cheshire and Lancashire County Record Offices both held limited amounts of historical information.

◆ Site surveys.

A historic understanding of the site needs to be linked to an understanding of the physical fabric. A survey of the park is therefore essential to identify and describe existing and past landscape features and buildings. Walking the park with a copy of a 25-inch Ordnance Survey map and noting on it surviving structures, features and planting is the most commonly used method. This can be done using a modern Ordnance Survey map, but as these no longer include individual trees, earlier editions are more useful. Details of features known to have existed from earlier maps or from local knowledge but which no longer survive can also be sketched on. If a more detailed landscape survey is required from a surveying company, this must be specified in the brief, along with any other types of specialist work. This might include:

◆ Hydrological survey — to ascertain causes of problems with lakes and water features.

◆ Ecological surveys — if Phase 1 habitat surveys are available they will show whether the park has any areas of ecological interest and the distribution of habitats. This can form the basis for deciding whether a more detailed survey is needed.[6]

◆ Tree survey — if a tree survey has already been prepared it should be updated with any additions or losses.

◆ Archaeological survey — this is usually a visual assessment of 'lumps and bumps' to help locate lost items such as paths or water features. In parks of national historic importance a survey might include more specialist archaeological investigations, for example to confirm path layouts and levels or to inform the re-establishment of original planting mound profiles.

◆ Condition reports on statuary, stonework, metalwork and buildings.

In addition to documentary research and fieldwork, the recollections of local people and those who used to work in the park should not be overlooked when researching a park's history.

The results of research should be presented as an illustrated narrative that summarizes the historic evidence chronologically. In addition, a chronology of the development of the park should be produced. This should include dates for all the key phases of activity from the opening to the present, dates for different owners, designers and managers, dates for the built features and structures, dates for planted features and also for the key sources of information about the site such as visitors' descriptions, maps, plans and published articles. The source of each fact should be cited. The chronology can be included in the main text or the appendices.

Analysis

Gathering historic information is only useful if it leads to an understanding of the original purpose of the design, the way the landscape and buildings worked, and how they have changed. All the elements that contribute to the significance of a park need to be identified, described and assessed — how important and valuable is the contribution of each in its own right, and in terms of the park as a whole? For example, the landscape design, horticulture, historic buildings, ecology, archaeology or contribution to a townscape. Do any of these elements conflict and, if so, which is the more important? What is the primary importance of the park? The analysis should be explicit enough to allow a reader to follow the relationship between the history of the site and the restoration proposals with ease. This is the part of a restoration plan that is most commonly inadequate because it is poorly explained, and the need to make specific value judgements about the significance of the park is avoided.

There are various ways of presenting the analysis. One of the most popular is to divide the park into different character areas, such the bandstand, bowling green, play area, flower displays, woodland, boating lake, etc. The boundaries of these areas can be plotted on a map and their historic and current use, and condition described. Care should be taken to avoid omissions or too many repetitions. This allows a reader to gain a good idea of how the park appeared at different stages in its development and how it was intended to work.

The analysis will need to include an assessment of practical design features that were often highly sophisticated and subtle, allowing a wide range of activities to occur within a park without conflict. For example, were there different entrances and circulation routes for pedestrians, horses and through-traffic? How was the landscape shaped to influence behaviour and to evoke different moods? The design of many parks included a wonderfully rich assortment of prominent and grand formal terraces, more secluded and informal woodland walks, flower gardens, open grassed areas for recreation, naturalistic lakes, pastoral parkland, and geological specimens, alpine rockeries and ferneries to excite and educate. Great care was often taken with the detailed design of built features resulting in a cohesive and consistent design vocabulary which reveals itself in architectural detailing, use of materials, boundary railing finials, and path and flower bed edgings.

Once the original design intentions have been understood, changes to the landscape need to be considered and an assessment made about whether they enhanced or detracted from the original design. At this stage the most significant elements of the park should be becoming clear and a statement of aims and objective can be drawn up. These should be overall principles that will guide the restoration proposals, rather than the proposals themselves. For example, the restoration plan for Heaton Park summarizes the aims and objectives as follows:

Heaton Park represents a remarkable survival of an 18th/19th-century park with sensitive Edwardian additions and the overriding aim is to restore, preserve and enhance the scheme as completed in 1914. The heritage merit of the park ensures that this project is very definitely based on restoration rather than on a radical reappraisal and the introduction of new features. However, this restoration must seek to incorporate existing, much-valued facilities along with issues that have arisen since the park's purchase by the Corporation, e.g. the growth in vehicular traffic.

Figure 8: Carpet bedding at Vale Park, New Brighton. (From the collection of Nigel Temple)

39

In seeking to achieve this aim the proposals should be based on the following objectives:

To secure and enhance the unique heritage value of the park by restoring the historical features of both the soft and hard landscape in accordance with the particular historic character of the place.

To ensure the park continues to offer a variety of opportunities for both active and passive recreation, which do not threaten the particular quality which so characterizes the park.

To restore the tradition of horticultural interest and excellence for which the park was renowned prior to World War II.

To increase the quality of the park's presentation by ensuring that adequate resources are made available for long-term maintenance and management regimes, following successful implementation of the proposals.[7]

Figures 9, 10, 11, 12 (left to right): Views of
Reading, Harrogate, Liverpool and Handsworth.
(From the collection of Nigel Temple)

Proposals

This section of the plan outlines the specific
proposals that need to be carried out to achieve the
successful implementation of the aims and
objectives. In general, proposals should preserve,
restore or enhance the special character of the park
and increase the public's enjoyment of it, in terms
of capital projects, and improved management and
maintenance. Again, the continuity between the
research, analysis and proposals must be explicit
— a reader should be able to understand in an
instant why a particular proposal has been
recommended. If there is a need to ask 'why?'
then either the research and analysis are
inadequate or the proposals are inappropriate. A
good plan exhibits ruthless logic. An inferior plan
usually suffers from '*post-hoc* justification' where
research and analysis have been done in an
attempt to obtain support for a pre-existing set of
proposals. This results in a plan where there is no
clear relationship between the proposals and the
historic character of the site.

Proposals for structures and features

The restoration or re-creation of structural
elements should be as accurate as possible unless
a reasoned and convincing justification for
departures from the original design can be put
forward. The re-creation of lost features should be
justified and the current and future use of any
structure to be restored or recreated should be
considered. The opportunity should be taken to

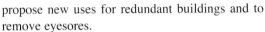

propose new uses for redundant buildings and to remove eyesores.

Planting proposals

Planting is an aspect of restoration schemes that is frequently misunderstood. In particular, there is a tendency to propose short- or long-term replacement of non-native trees and shrubs by indigenous species. While there may be some parks or areas of parks that lend themselves well to this approach, habitat creation is best kept away from areas with distinct historic character unless it can be incorporated without adverse effects. Nature conservation is too often used as an excuse to lower standards of care and maintenance, neglect being cheaper in the short-term than good husbandry.

Structural planting proposals (i.e. trees and shrubs) should be designed to maintain the historic character of the landscape with species appropriate to the site, in locations which respect the original (and later) design intentions. Attention should be paid to planting style, particularly the grouping of trees, placing of specimens and planting distances. Municipal planting of trees along every path and drive, thus fragmenting the landscape, and dot planting in open grass areas are common problems and should be considered for the effect they have on the character and appearance of the park. The opportunity to remove past examples of ill-conceived planting — wrong species, wrong place — should be taken.

Particular attention should be paid to the management of shrubberies — often all that is needed is remedial pruning and feeding where shrubs have grown much larger than intended. If they are properly tended, shrubberies remain a cost-effective way of managing difficult areas and of controlling circulation. Yet proposals to grub them up and grass them over are surprisingly common, and invariably justified by a strange logic that they are overgrown and attract flashers — do not blame the shrubs!

Park furniture

Poor quality, ill-sited and uncoordinated park furniture — seats, signs, notice boards, bollards, boundary railings and fences, litter bins, lights — can have a disproportionately strong negative effect on the overall appearance and public perception of a park. Proposals should aim to retain historic and local character in park furniture — suppliers can often be traced and they may retain copies of original catalogues.

Once the proposals have been drawn up they should be presented with a time-scale for implementation and an outline schedule of costs. It is useful to present proposals in order of urgency and priority, with a view to implementing them in stages, as funding becomes available while working towards a long-term goal.

Innovation

Innovation may be necessary to redesign areas of a park that no longer function for various reasons, or to provide facilities for which a need can be

41

demonstrated. There also needs to be an assessment of whether associated maintenance costs can be met. In all cases, proposals for new facilities should be of high quality and sufficiently imaginative to add to the overall quality of the park. Innovation should neither be seen in isolation nor at the cost of the conservation of the park, and new facilities should enhance people's enjoyment of the park itself (playgrounds, cafes, restaurants, toilet facilities) rather than being a destination in their own right that could just as well be placed anywhere (cinemas, ice-rinks, leisure centres, shopping malls).

Presentation and layout

The restoration plan should be presented as a spiral bound A4 document, and is likely to be of either one or two volumes, depending on the size and complexity of the park. Although presentation of the final report can vary the following list can be a guide to its contents and sequence.

◆ Contents and list of figures.

◆ Acknowledgements — who assisted in the preparation of the plan.

◆ Introduction — how the plan came about, who funded it, who prepared it and for whom. It should be dated.

◆ Executive summary — should give details of location, size in hectares, ownership, conservation designations, an outline of the park's history and condition, and restoration aims. Always include an up-to-date map to show the location of the park at the start of the plan.

◆ Planning context — a summary of published strategies, policies and designations relevant to the park. It is useful to quote extracts that give strong endorsement to the protection and enhancement of the park. How many parks does the local authority manage, and how many are historic?

◆ Consultations — a summary of any public consultation exercises and organizations consulted on the plan.

◆ Methodology — should give details of the documentary survey and site survey methods, a summary of the sources consulted, and whether any other surveys have been undertaken or consulted.

◆ Historical development of the park — an illustrated, factual narrative presented chronologically.

◆ Historic landscape analysis.

◆ Appraisal of the existing park — some consultants include as a matter of course a photographic survey, or artefact schedule, of all surviving structures and features. This provides an excellent record of the current condition of the park and is useful for those consulting the plan who are not familiar with the site.

◆ Visitor use of the park including access arrangements.

◆ Ecology, if applicable.

◆ Landscape management and maintenance.

◆ Statement of key issues and aims/vision for the future.

◆ Proposals for conservation, repair, restoration and enhancement.

◆ Estimate of costs and time-scale for implementation.

◆ Bibliography — all sources of published and unpublished information that has been located.

◆ Appendices.

◆ Large-scale plans — there are two essentials: a plan with annotations of the current situation and condition, and an overall masterplan showing the proposals (see colour section). It is useful if the latter can show details of trees to be retained, removed and planted. It should be folded and bound into the inside back cover.

People

Frederick Law Olmsted visited Birkenhead in 1850 and was persuaded by a baker not to leave without seeing the new park. Olmsted enthused that 'all this magnificent pleasure-ground is entirely, unreservedly, and forever the people's own. The poorest British peasant is as free to enjoy it in all its parts as the British queen. More than that, the baker of Birkenhead has the pride of an owner in it. Is that not a grand good thing?'[8]

The owners and users of a public park also need to have a sense of ownership of the restoration plan. Local community support is crucial to the long-term success of restoration schemes and can be one of the best ways of ensuring that works are carried out to a high standard and maintained in the long-term. Once a team has been selected to prepare a restoration plan it is useful to invite local residents to a meeting to share ideas and voice concerns. One or two public meetings will also be needed to present the draft plan so that the results of the research can be shared, the aims of the restoration explained and the suggested proposals discussed.

It is useful to include the following information in a restoration plan:

◆ Estimated or counted annual visitor numbers to the park.

◆ Evidence of community support for the proposals — the results of public consultation exercises and visitor surveys are often lengthy documents. If available, they should be summarized in the plan with details of how to obtain a full copy.

◆ Is there a Friends' Group and, if not, should one be set up?

◆ Access arrangements — is the park locked at night and, if not, does this present security problems that need to be addressed?

◆ Current security arrangements — the most common concern voiced in public consultation exercises is that of feeling unsafe and insecure in a park. The most common request is for a park keeper or manager to be a permanent on-site staff presence. Do the proposals include for this: if not, why not?

Management and resources
The restoration plan should contain a review of all existing financial and staffing resources, an assessment of future requirements and suggestions for an enhanced programme of maintenance and care. Contract management responsibilities should be described and current annual maintenance budgets noted with a summary of the works these are expected to cover. Any significant omissions from the contract should also be noted — it is not uncommon to find parks where the grass is cut but not the edges, because this task was not specified in the contract! Describe who is currently responsible for the management and maintenance of the park — a chart is useful to show the relationships between different local authority departments and individual staff, whose names and job titles should be shown. If there are conflicts between different departments, for example where special events are undoing grounds maintenance, these should be noted.

Where management and maintenance arrangements are unsatisfactory, improvements should be suggested. These could focus on more sympathetic and detailed contract management, closer supervision of contracted work, the use of dedicated, on-site parks staff and voluntary wardens, alterations to management regimes, enhanced security provision and increased responsiveness to the public. Where there are opportunities to raise funds from the park through the provision of facilities or staging events, at least some of the income should be ring-fenced for use in the future management of the park.

Management and maintenance plans
The funding agencies usually request that grant recipients prepare a management or maintenance plan within a year of works commencing. This is a separate document to the restoration plan and its purpose is to establish a strategy for managing and maintaining the park over a period of at least 10 years on a day-by-day, month-by-month basis. The restoration plan contains the vision for the park; the management plan is about putting together the details of how to get there. It should be a working document that can be easily understood by all those involved in site management and maintenance and should contain a comprehensive coverage of management issues. It should be reviewed and updated annually and, as with the restoration plan, should ultimately become part of the park's archive.[9]

43

Other sources of funding for historic urban parks

Funding programmes come and go rapidly and it is worth making contact with individuals and organizations in the locality who keep up to date with the latest schemes and eligibility criteria. Local authority Lottery Officers and regional Government Office European Funding Officers are good sources of information. The funding agencies have mailing lists and most produce regular newsletters. The Urban Parks Forum is a melting pot of ideas and wisdom on how to tap into the latest sources of funding.

The HLF's Urban Parks Programme is currently the major source of funding for historic public parks and will probably remain so for the next few years. Grants are available for capital works, fixed-term park manager posts and restoration plans. There are a few other possible sources of funding, such as the Landfill Tax. This was introduced in October 1996 and allows for up to 20 per cent of the tax on each tonne of waste deposited by a landfill operator to be applied locally towards environmental projects, instead of going to the Treasury. This is achieved by a landfill operator donating money to organizations called Environmental Bodies who must be registered with a regulator called Entrust. Entrust can provide information packs on how to apply for Landfill Tax in each locality.[10] There are grant programmes involving European funding, each with its own criteria and priorities, and information on these can be obtained from the regional Government Offices. English Heritage has a small amount of funding available for parks included on the Register of Parks and Gardens of Special Historic Interest in England at Grade I or II*, for both capital works and restoration plans. Finally, the New Opportunities Fund (NOF) has announced that it will be launching a grant programme in early 2000 for 'Green Spaces in Sustainable Communities', although it is not yet clear whether it will be of relevance to urban park projects.[11]

Acknowledgemends

The author thanks Stewart Harding, Alan Barber, Adrian Wikeley and Lorna McRobie for their ever-generous advice.

Notes

1. Guidance on preparing a restoration plan brief is available at no cost from the funding agencies. A model brief is included in every HLF Application Pack.

2. The essential guide is David Lambert, Peter Goodchild and Judith Roberts, *Researching a Garden's History: A Guide to Documentary and Published Sources* (Reigate: Landscape Design Trust, and York: University of York Institute of Advanced Architectural Studies, 1995). There is no equivalent publication for fieldwork, but see John L. Phibbs, 'An approach to the methodology of recording historic gardens', *Garden History*, 11/2 (1983), 167–75.

3. Some Victorian gardening magazines have been indexed in Ray Desmond, *A Bibliography of British Gardens* (Winchester: St Paul's Bibliographies, 1988).

4. Clifford E. Thornton, *The People's Garden: A History of Birkenhead Park* (Birkenhead: Metropolitan Borough of Wirral, n.d.), 10.

5. 'Heaton Park Historic Landscape Survey and Restoration Plan' (London: Land Use Consultants, 1997), 13.

6. *Field Manual for Phase 1 Survey: A Method for Environmental Audit* (London: Joint Nature Conservancy Council, 1993).

7. 'Heaton Park Historic Landscape Survey and Restoration Plan', 40.

8. Frederick Law Olmsted, *Walks and Talks of an American Farmer in England* (1852), quoted in Thornton, *The People's Garden*, 15.

9. A brief on preparing a management plan has been prepared jointly by English Heritage and the Heritage Lottery Fund and is available at no cost from these organizations.

10. Entrust, Profex House, 25–27 School Lane, Bushy, Hertfordshire WD2 1BR; tel.: 0208 950 2152.

11. New Opportunities Fund, Heron House, 322 High Holborn, London WC1V 7PW, tel: 0845 0000 120.

Buildings and monuments

by Hazel Conway and David Lambert

Figure 1: Remains of
St Mary's Abbey,
Museum Gardens, York.
(Photo: Hazel Conway)

In 1873 the *Illustrated London News* published a page of views of Victoria Park, London, praising it as the best people's park in London because of the facilities it offered.[1] These views included a Chinese pagoda, which had stood at Hyde Park Corner, a bridge, a boat house and a refreshment saloon, but omitted the Moorish arcade (designed by Sir James Pennethorne) and the Victoria drinking fountain (designed by Henry Darbishire).[2] In general, park buildings fall into four main categories: those needed for maintenance and for the keepers and superintendents; those intended for the users; commemorative buildings; and monuments and inherited buildings that existed on the site before a park's creation. Park buildings intended for users is the largest category and might be subdivided to include structures as well as buildings, for example buildings for displaying plants (palmhouses, conservatories, chrysanthemum houses, etc.), for displaying animals (aviaries, animal houses, etc.), for entertainment (bandstands, theatres), for refreshment (cafés, kiosks), for sports (pavilions,

gymnasiums), mainly functional (shelters, bridges, lavatory blocks), for viewing (temples, pavilions, pagodas, terraces, etc.), for ornament only, and buildings and structures associated with water (rock features — cliffs, grottoes, wishing wells, etc. such as those in Pulhamite — bridges, drinking fountains). Parks also became the resting place for structures moved as a result of development or road building. The role of these buildings and monuments and the meanings that they communicate today are very different from those when parks were created in the 19th and early 20th centuries and this changing role will be explored in this chapter.

The prototype for many public park buildings such as the lodges, shelters, boathouses, pagodas, monuments and sculptures lay in the private parks of the 18th century. Other building types such as palmhouses and winter gardens developed in the early years of the 19th century before the public park came into being. Refreshment rooms and early forms of the bandstand had their precedent in public pleasure gardens such as Vauxhall, London, while the aviaries and animal enclosures added to public parks in the last decades of the 19th century drew on earlier precedents both in zoological gardens and the menageries in private parks. Of all the buildings found in parks the one that became most closely identified with them, to the extent that it became the symbol and signifier of the public park, was the bandstand. Perhaps because it was such an important symbol, the bandstand clearly illustrates the changing role of park buildings today. Designed originally for bands to play in, they were a popular focus for entertainment, but most were removed or destroyed after the Second World War. The few of these light airy structures that remain have in a sense become memorials to their original role, punctuating the landscape and acting as a focal point.

Some parks were created out of sites of great antiquity. In Dane John in Canterbury, Kent, stands a Romano-British burial mound of the first or second century AD. Two sides of the park are also bounded by ancient ramparts, now part of the city walls. The gardens and the walk along the walls were formed in 1790 by Alderman John Simmons who is commemorated by a monument (1803) erected by public subscription on top of the mound. Dane John became a public park in 1836 and the historic layout that existed before the creation of the gardens and the walks along the walls has been retained to this day.[3] The Heritage Lottery Fund (HLF) restoration has recently been completed (1999).

The extension to Abbey Park in Leicester, which opened in 1932, was intended as a sports area and recreation ground. This may be one of the reasons why so little attention is drawn to the remarkable historic features of the site. In the north-west corner are the ruins of Leicester Abbey, founded in 1143 and one of the major monastic establishments in the area. Today the footings of this complex structure remain, but there is little interpretation. Similarly, little attention is drawn to the western boundary wall along Abbey Lane and Abbey Park Road, a long stretch of red brick diapered with blue that dates from $c.1500$. In York the Museum Gardens laid out by Sir John

Naysmith (1844–50) are a Scheduled Ancient Monument containing five Grade I-listed buildings and six Grade II buildings. The gardens, designed for the York Philosophical Society as a setting for these historic buildings (figure 1) and for the York Museum, also provided a scientific and botanic garden. It has been a public park since the 1960s. Some of the problems of such sites concern the amount of interpretation that should be provided without generating a feeling that the park is a museum of building, and the degree of security necessary to secure the historic remains.

Siting the buildings

The central feature of most private parks is the main house, the largest building on the estate. The house either formed the focus of the surrounding landscape or could be picturesquely sited so that it was ensconced in the landscape. In most public parks, however, there were no such major buildings unless the park was created out of a private estate that included the main building. In Peel Park, Salford, and Queen's Park, Manchester (both by Joshua Major, 1846), major buildings existed before the decision was taken to create parks. The problem then was what to do with them. In Peel Park the mansion was used for refreshment rooms, a library and a museum, and in Queen's Park a museum was developed in 1864. In Glasgow, Tollcross Park was created out of the estate in which an extensive baronial mansion (by David Bryce, 1848) formed the focus. This building is now used for sheltered housing.

In some parks major buildings formed a central part of the park development. The largest of such buildings must surely be the Crystal Palace, London (by Joseph Paxton, 1851), which was enlarged when it was moved from Hyde Park to Sydenham where it was sited at the top of an imposing series of Italian terraces. Similarly in North London the grounds of Alexandra Park, laid out by Alexander McKenzie in 1863, were dominated by the Alexandra Palace exhibition building. The palmhouses and winter gardens added in the late 19th century were also large buildings, but most other park buildings were small in scale. Despite their small scale they could nevertheless be positioned in a variety of ways. In Sefton Park, Liverpool (by Edouard André, 1872), part of the competition brief was to preserve the longest vistas in the park in order to enhance its apparent size. The brief also suggested that bandstands and refreshment pavilions should be positioned as points of interest to terminate some of the vistas within the park, and outside the park significant points of interest such as church spires should be used to terminate vistas.[4]

Today historic parks cannot be viewed in isolation from their surroundings, for the impact of proposed new buildings outside parks can be most detrimental. Unsympathetic adjacent developments not only alter the envelope of the park, but also can intrude on existing sightlines and also have a damaging effect on the park's character and appearance. Planning Policy Guidance Note (PPG) 15, *Planning and the Historic Environment*, is clear in its advice that 'planning authorities should protect registered parks and gardens in preparing development plans and in determining planning applications'. Furthermore, it states clearly that 'The effect of proposed development on a registered park, or garden, or its setting is a material consideration in the determination of a planning application'.[5]

Lodges

The first building that the park visitor sees is often the lodge by the entrance gate, the home of the superintendent or park keeper, with the park bylaws prominently displayed nearby. The entrance gates and lodges set the scene for the park within. Their message was that the park was a special place, protected, well-maintained and different from its urban surroundings. Lodges were included in public parks from the earliest stages of the park movement. When Paxton suggested that Edward Kemp be retained as head gardener of the newly designed Birkenhead Park it was on the understanding that he should have free accommodation in one of the lodges, as this was 'the almost invariable custom'. Paxton also suggested that it would be useful to have the park overlooker living in the lodge in the middle of the park 'and it is the usual practice in good gardens'.[6]

Thus, the standards appropriate to private parks should be applied to public parks.

The lodges in the early parks of the 1840s illustrated the picturesque demand for variety. The main entrance lodge in The Derby Arboretum (a semi-public park when it opened in 1840) was 'in the Elizabethan style', the East lodge in the Tudor style, while the two pavilions were in a classical style. Edward R. Lamb designed them all.[7] In Birkenhead Park (1847) the lodges designed by Lewis Hornblower and John Robertson were in an even wider range of architectural styles. The main entrance was in the form of a triumphal arch with giant unfluted Ionic columns. In the two wings were lodges linked by a triple arcaded screen. It was to remain among the grandest park entrances. There other lodges whose names belied their style. The Gothic Lodge was Tudor in style, while the Norman Lodges was a pair of symmetrical Greek Revival buildings on either side of the entrance. Both the Castellated Lodge and the Italian Lodge were more aptly named, while the Central Lodge featured a number of classical references.

The bridges in Birkenhead Park included a Chinese bridge, a Swiss bridge and a rustic bridge, so picturesque variety was achieved by adding exotic geographical imagery from around the world.

An examination of lodge building during the 19th and 20th centuries shows that their style either tended to reflect what was happening in the domestic architecture elsewhere or else showed strong local references. The lodge in Baxter Park, Dundee (by Paxton, 1863), which no longer exists, showed the influence of the Scottish baronial style. In Grosvenor Park, Chester (by Edward Kemp, 1867), the black-and-white half-timbered entrance lodge (by John Douglas) deferred to the town's past architecture and included coloured statues of the Norman Earls of Chester. Some lodges featured a bell that was rung to announce the imminent closing of the park, and an example of a bell housing can still be seen on the side of the main lodge in Abbey Park, Leicester.

In the great suburban expansion of the 1920s and 1930s some 4 million houses were built on

47

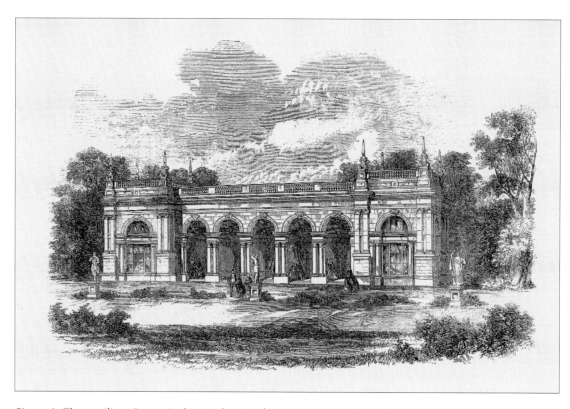

Figure 2: The pavilion, Baxter Park, Dundee, is a large two-storey classical structure in the centre of the park. Originally it housed a refreshment room at one end and a gardeners' tool shed and ladies' toilet at the other. In the open arcade linking the two ends stood a statue of the donor, Sir David Baxter. The building has been derelict for years but there are now hopes that it will be restored with an HLF grant. This drawing is taken from *Illustrated London News* (19 September 1863), the year the pavilion was built.

greenfield sites. The Open Space Standard of 5 acres of open space per 1000 population meant that parks and recreation grounds were included in these new developments. The park lodges generally tended to be in a similar style to the surrounding housing.

In the recent 20 years of the decline of parks, lodges became one of the first signs that all was not well. With the introduction of Compulsory Competitive Tendering (CCT) in 1988 park maintenance was put out for tendering so dedicated park keepers were no longer required and the lodges became redundant. Boarded up and derelict, the lodges signified decay and neglect, the opposite of

the message that they once gave. In some areas lodges were sold to private owners, for when the government gave local authorities permission to sell council housing the sale of park lodges was seen as an opportunity for hard-pressed authorities to increase their finances. The new owners wanted to enhance their privacy with high fences and to add car parking facilities. They certainly did not wish the public to knock on their door, so again the message on first entering the park changed. CCT has now been replaced by Best Value, and while some local authorities are introducing park rangers as a presence in their parks, the problem of what to do with the lodges remains.

Other park buildings

Parks provided the opportunity for people to relax in green surroundings and to breathe fresh air, but they needed access to shelter from bad weather. Furthermore, if people were to spend some time in the park, then refreshments, drinking water and toilets were necessary. The range of park shelters and pavilions varied widely in scale and in the sources of inspiration for design. The pagoda in Victoria Park was placed on an island in the ornamental lake in 1848 and it was intended either as a boathouse or for the Eastern Literary and Scientific Institution. It was removed after damage in the Second World War.[8] In Birkenhead Park the pagoda, also sited on an island, served as a shelter. Peasholm Park, Scarborough (1919–29), was designed completely in the Japanese style with a pagoda on the top of the hill and it represented a last, final flourish of the genre.[9]

Generally shelters were small-scale buildings of brick or wood. The shelters in Sefton Park, Liverpool included a delightful tiny half-timbered thatched building set among the trees, as well as a brick and wood shelter positioned by the lake to take full advantage of the views. These small-scale structures are particularly vulnerable to arson and to vandalism, and one local authority was advised to reduce the number of buildings in its parks for this reason and to retain only those that were listed.

Refreshment rooms could be temporary structures that were open only in the summer, or they could take the form of substantial buildings that acted as the focus of the park. George Stoke's pavilion (1863) in Baxter Park, Dundee, is a large two-storey classical structure in the centre of the park (figure 2). Originally it housed a refreshment room at one end and a gardeners' tool shed and ladies' toilet at the other. In the open arcade linking the two ends stood a statue of the donor, Sir David Baxter. The building has been derelict for years. In the plan for its restoration the arcade will be glassed in, a Registry Office will occupy the former restaurant area and the former toilet area will be a café. When the new extension to Abbey Park, Leicester, opened in 1932 on the opposite side of the River Soar from the original park, the first building

that visitors saw as they crossed the bridge was an elegant two-storey Arts and Crafts building with refreshment rooms on the ground floor. The building is still in use and is very popular. In Preston Park, Brighton, a new circular tea pavilion with sunken rose garden was added to the existing Victorian park in the 1930s, while in Roundhay Park, Leeds, the recent café/restaurant is open all year round and is a popular attraction.

The new parks of the 1920s and 1930s also featured a variety of shelters and pavilions. The grandest of these is in Norwich where the Parks Superintendent, Capt. A. Sandys-Winsch, a gifted horticulturalist who had trained at Wisley, Surrey, and then worked with Thomas H. Mawson, designed some seven parks in Norwich.[10] Sandys-Winsch's most prestigious projects were the 80-acre Eaton Park (1928) and Waterloo Park (1933). Eaton Park was designed as a sporting and recreational park and was opened officially by the Prince of Wales in 1928. The central focus of the park is the domed, concrete bandstand surrounded by a great circular, colonnaded concrete pavilion housing changing rooms and refreshment facilities. This great rotunda and colonnade were built not to honour some deity or to express the wealth or position of some magnate, but for visitors and those who were playing football, tennis or cricket in the park. Waterloo Park at its opening was considered the finest park in East Anglia. In the centre is a concrete pavilion with a balustraded roof terrace. On the lawn in front of it is a concrete bandstand with pools and rills of water flanked on the north and south sides by pergolas. Both parks are being restored with Heritage Lottery Fund grants.

The first park to be completed under the HLF Urban Parks Programme was the Emslie Horniman Pleasance, North Kensington, London (originally completed in 1914). The walled garden, designed by C. F. A. Voysey — one of the few public parks designed by a well-known architect — with planting designed by Madeline Agar, featured a pergola and Japanese bridge by J. P. White and Sons. The garden has been meticulously restored and a new park and playground designed around it (figure 3). Butting the walls on the north side of the walled garden, an extension

Figure 3: Emslie Horniman Pleasance, North Kensington, London, at the opening in 1998. This was the first park to be completed under the HLF Urban Parks Programme. The walled garden, designed by C. F. A. Voysey, has been meticulously restored and a new park and playground designed around it. (Photo: Hazel Conway)

has been added for a park keeper's office and a kiosk for serving drinks and snacks.

Imposing terraces also offered views over the park as well as shelter. Belle Vue Park, Newport, Wales (by Mawson, 1898), is built on a steep slope and at the highest point are a glasshouse, a terracotta pavilion and a terracotta terrace from which there are magnificent views of the estuary and the transporter bridge. The dramatic red sandstone terrace at Stanley Park, Liverpool (by Kemp, 1870) offered views of the park, while from the terrace in People's Park, Halifax (by Paxton and E. Milner, 1857) there were views of the moors beyond Halifax. Positioned along the edge of the People's Park terrace (by G. H. Stokes), were 6-foot-high vases of Carrara marble

and sculptures of mythological figures. The latter included Hercules, Venus, Diana, Telemachus, and the Neapolitan or Music girl, and they were intended to introduce working men and women to the works of high culture. In 1992 the statues were encased in tall, green, rectangular plywood boxes to protect them from vandalism and destruction, and this image became a potent symbol of the state of public parks (figure 4). The park is now being restored with an HLF grant.

Monuments and sculptures

Monuments, drinking fountains, sundials, war memorials and statues commemorated local and national heroes as well as local achievements and international events. They were thus part of people's pride in their town and they added to the

Figure 4. The terrace, People's Park, Halifax, 1993. Positioned along the edge of the terrace (by G. H. Stokes), were 6-foot-high vases of Carrara marble and sculptures of mythological figures. They were intended to introduce working men and women to the works of high culture. In 1992 the statues were encased in tall, green, rectangular plywood boxes to protect them from vandalism and destruction, and this image became a potent symbol of the state of public parks. The restoration of People's Park with an HLF grant and other funding is now under way. (Photo: Hazel Conway)

individual character of each park through their variety. Monuments and sculptures were acquired *ad hoc* over many years, and this process continued until the Second World War. However, unlike 18th-century private parks there appears to have been no deliberate programme or plan, nor do they have any consistent theme.

Donors

The 'grandest monument in England', according to Nikolaus Pevsner, is the 45-foot-high Ashton Memorial in Williamson Park, Lancaster — it is a landmark for miles around.[11] A flamboyant Edwardian baroque design in granite and Portland stone by John Belcher and J. J. Joass (1909), it commemorates James Williamson, the donor of the park who made his fortune from the manufacture of linoleum. Donors naturally wished to be remembered for their generosity and the ways in which they were is most revealing. Sir Francis Crossley, MP, owner of Dean Clough Mills and donor of People's Park, Halifax, sits under the shallow dome of the central pavilion. His statue by Joseph Durham (1860), erected by public subscription, rests on a plinth inscribed: 'As a tribute of gratitude and respect to one whose public benefactions and private virtues deserve to be remembered'. Outside the façade is inscribed with somewhat equivocal Biblical texts: 'The rich and poor meet together — the Lord is the maker of them all', 'Let no man seek his own, but every man another's wealth' and 'Bless the Lord, who daily loadeth us with benefits'. Today the statue is imprisoned behind railings and a scaffolding cage for protection.

52

Figure 5: Frank M. Taubman's statue of Sir Sydney Waterlow (1900), who gave his house and land to form Waterlow Park, London, stands modestly in a soft hat and overcoat, an umbrella in one hand and a key in the other, symbolizing his gift of the park to the public. (Photo: Hazel Conway)

By contrast, Frank M. Taubman's statue of Sir Sydney Waterlow (1900), who gave his house and land to form Waterlow Park, London, stands modestly in a soft hat and overcoat, an umbrella in one hand and a key in the other, symbolizing his gift of the park to the public (figure 5).

Some donors were surrounded by controversy in their lifetime, which is not always evident from the statues commemorating their generosity. The figure of Samuel Cunliffe Lister (later Lord Masham) is set directly in front of the main entrance to Lister Park, Bradford (1870), which he donated. The 10-foot-high figure on a 13-foot-high plinth (by Matthew Noble) is shown holding a rule and a scroll of drawings, the symbols of his inventiveness. Around the plinth are bronze bas-reliefs by Alfred Drury showing the progress of yarn manufacture from the cottage industry of handcombing to the power wool-combing machine and Lister's 'velvet loom' used for processing silk waste. A third panel shows the sources of the raw material: a sheep, an Angora goat and a llama set in a romantic, picturesque landscape. The whole was intended to demonstrate Lister's 'inventive genius and philan-thropic spirit' and the benefits he produced for 'employers and employed' in bringing to an end 'a most unhealthy and demoralising occupation', rather than starting it up.[12] The reliefs ignore the bitter acrimony over Lister's theft of the idea of the machine from Richard Arkwright. Indeed, the naming of the new art gallery built in the park after Arkwright has been interpreted as an act of contrition by Lister. There was strong resistance to his statue being placed in the town hall and even the romantic story of his career alludes to the 'years of opposition' from his fellow townsmen to acknowledging him as a public benefactor. The statue can, therefore, be read as an attempt to close a particular version of this history.

Civic pride

The civic sculpture that appeared in the parks often employed the iconography of the aristocratic patrons of the previous century. So the massive Wilberforce memorial overlooking Queen's Gardens, Hull, celebrates Samuel Wilberforce's role in the abolition of slavery with a figure in senatorial costume atop a mighty classical column, the whole reminiscent of 18th-century Augustan imagery. One of the grandest illustrations of civic pride is the Stewart Memorial fountain (by James Sellars), erected by the Water Commissioners in Kelvingrove Park in 1872 as a tribute to Robert Stewart who had led the fight to bring clean water from Loch Katrine to Glasgow. The whole fountain was based on the iconography of Sir Walter Scott's poem *The Lady of the Lake* (1810) and its crowning figure was the Lady herself in gilded bronze.[13] The campaign to provide free, clean drinking water in the years following the mid-19th century cholera epidemics found its expression in the drinking fountains built in many parks. While some proclaimed the values of temperance — 'Water is Best' — others such as the drinking fountain in Roker Park, Sunderland, proclaimed that the water was for 'the people of Sunderland' and 'free' forever. The words still ring out. To avoid any misunderstanding the chosen virtues were literally spelled out on the plinths or around the structures. Sundials, for example, warned against laziness: 'First the moments, then the day, time by moments, melts away' proclaimed the sundial in People's Park donated by the Mayor of Halifax in 1878.[14]

Parks often included objects of local pride and *objets trouvés* such as the fossil grove in Victoria Park, Glasgow, discovered in the quarry, which subsequently formed part of the park, or the cupola of Hull's old town hall, which was salvaged and placed in Pearson Park. In Lister Park, Bradford, a miniature waterfall, a version of a local beauty spot the Thornton Force, was created at the top of the lake in the park.

Nationalism and imperialism

Behind many of these monuments and sculptures lay an explicit ideology of patriotism, deference, hard work, temperance and civic pride. Many of the statues of Queen Victoria were erected to celebrate a royal visit, for in the 1850s and 1860s the Queen travelled widely throughout Britain visiting towns and opening new parks and buildings. After the death of Prince Albert in 1861, Victoria retired from public life and was rarely

seen. In the 1870s she began to resume public life, but it was not until her Golden and Diamond Jubilees of 1887 and 1897 that interest in commissioning statues of her was renewed. The Doulton Fountain designed by E. A. Pearce for the International Exhibition of 1888 now stands on Glasgow Green. At 14 metres high it was the largest terracotta statue in the world and its subject is the Queen, with the Imperial crown, orb and sceptre, ruling over the Empire. Above the lowest basin are four groups of personifications of India, South Africa, Canada and Australia, and the peaceful contributions of the Empire, while above the middle basin are the figures of a sailor and of Scots, Irish and English soldiers that made such conquests possible. It is now in a dreadful condition with most of the figures so broken as to be almost unrecognizable.

The most common emblem celebrating Britain's Imperial role was the cannon from the Crimean War (1853–56). Between 1857 and the early 1860s many parks acquired two cannons and displayed them with pride. In the Nottingham Arboretum in 1857 two original plus two replica cannons, as well as piles of cannon balls, stood around a pagoda which housed a silver bell taken from a temple at Canton. Other wars were commemorated, but not nearly so widely. It is not until the memorials to the First and Second World Wars that one finds the names of individual soldiers being recorded. The majority of these monuments and memorials represented the existing order, by celebrating the bravery and patriotism of regiments, but there are also memorials that pay tribute to the contribution of the individual, of the soldier, to the sense of duty of the engineer and to the working man's loyalty to the Queen.

In Weston Park, Sheffield, are two extraordinary war memorials commemorating soldiers, rather than particular regiments and their officers (figure 6). One is dedicated to Sheffield men lost in the Crimea and states: 'This memorial was erected by their comrades'. The other, dedicated to those lost in the First World War, stresses the reality of modern warfare with an ammunition box of '.303 inch bandoliers', and the difference, but at

53

Figure 6: In Weston Park, Sheffield, are two extraordinary war memorials commemorating soldiers, rather than particular regiments and their officers. This one was erected 'To the everlasting honour and glory of the 8814 officers, non-commissioned officers and men of the York and Lancaster Regiment who fell in the Great War 1914–1919'. (Photo: Jan Woudstra)

Figure 7: Titanic — Engineers' Memorial (1914), East Park, Southampton. This memorial, by F. V. Blundstone, 1914, in East Park, Southampton, was dedicated to the Engineer Officers 'who showed their high conception of duty and their heroism by remaining at their posts, 15 April 1912'. The dedication also states: 'This memorial was erected by their fellow engineers and friends throughout the world'. (Photo: Roger Greenwood)

55

the same time the equality, between the officers and the soldiers.

The monument of Queen Victoria that stands in Endcliffe Wood, Sheffield, was as much a tribute to the people of Sheffield and the Sheffield Workmen's Tribute Committee who paid for it as it was to the Queen herself. On the plinth are two heroic bronze statues of Labour and Maternity, commemorating the working man and working woman, and the official Opening Programme gave as much emphasis to working-class dignity as it did to the Queen, in effect linking her to working-class emancipation:

> During the period of her reign a great development has taken place in the organisa-

tion of the working classes, and much of the improvement of their condition is due to the efforts of Trade Unions, Friendly and Co-operative Societies, and knowing that nothing was so dear to the late Queen as the happiness and welfare of her people, the Committee determined that the working men should have an opportunity of paying a public tribute of respect for her noble life and services as a Queen, a Mother and a Friend.[15]

In a period predominantly associated with deference there were monuments that evinced a strong democratic emphasis. In Weston Park, Sheffield, stands a statue to Ebeneezer Elliott, the Corn Laws rhymer and campaigner against the Bread Tax of the period of the Napoleonic War and the subsequent depression of the early 19th century. The memorial to the loss of the White Star Line *Titanic* (by F. V. Blundstone, 1914) in East Park, Southampton, was dedicated to the Engineer Officers 'who showed their high conception of duty and their heroism by remaining at their posts, 15 April 1912'. The dedication also states: 'This memorial was erected by their fellow engineers and friends throughout the world' (figure 7). The bronze bust of Samuel Plimsoll in Victoria Embankment Gardens, London, is flanked by two supporters, one a representative of the seamen whose welfare he devoted so much of his parliamentary life to. The inscription reads: 'Erected by members of the National Union of Seamen'.

According to some views these buildings and monuments were there to promote an authoritarian, paternalist agenda: part of a programme by those in power to create an environment in which dissent was limited and anti-social actions prohibited. Another view sees such structures as part of the lost world of communitarian ideals to which most people subscribed. In yesterday's deferential and patriotic society they were seen as objects of pride. Today the context of these memorials and sculptures has changed radically. Many parks are unpoliced territory and the opposite of an orderly environment. Indeed, a drunk commented how he was ordered off the street by Metropolitan Police officers and told to go and do his drinking in Victoria Park! Small wonder that certain parks gained a reputation of being a haven of abusive winos, rapists and muggers. Despite neglect, these semi-ruinous landscapes have now gained a new power and meaning. In a society such as ours today, still splintered after years under a Conservative government that believed that 'There is no such thing as society', these memorials and sculptures with their inscriptions can still deliver inspiring messages. Although the original authoritarian overtones have been lost, nevertheless the remaining monuments and sculptures evoke an era of civic identity and commitment that can be very moving.

Many of these monuments and sculptures have either been removed for safe-keeping or have been boarded up pending a decision on what action to take. The Stewart Memorial fountain in Kelvingrove Park was restored in 1988, only to be re-vandalized and boarded up again. The once derelict palmhouse in Stanley Park, Liverpool (by Mackenzie and Moncur, 1899) was renovated in 1989, reopened as a club which subsequently failed, and again fell into ruin. Several palmhouses have received funds for restoration from the HLF and both the Sefton Park palmhouse and that at Tollcross Park, Glasgow, will reopen as combined restaurants and palmhouses. It is now recognized that the restoration of a single building within a park — and in isolation from the rest of the park — will not work, and now both Sefton Park and Tollcross Park are being restored. Moreover, it is most important that the adjacent community is consulted and engaged in the whole process.

In some parks replicas of buildings that were once removed have been reinstated. In Victoria Park, London, the meticulous restoration of the bandstand (by Robert Matthew, Johnson, Marshall) was based on the original drawings in the park archive. Only if such drawings exist or if there are sufficient details from other sources should such buildings be recreated, otherwise there is a strong risk that a pastiche may result.

Finally there is the question of innovation. Parks have had buildings and monuments added to them for most of their lives and there is no reason why new buildings and monuments should not be added, provided their location, design and scale respect the historic fabric of the park. In Victoria Park RMJM built a new single-storey café by the lake that fits well into its setting. In Lister Park, Bradford, as part of a successful HLF application to restore the park, a new Mughal garden with a pavilion is being added to a once-derelict area. Each park has its own individual character and, therefore, there are no general rules, and each case must be treated sensitively on its own merits.

56

Figure 8: The aviary at Clissold Park, London (Photo: Jan Woudstra), is an updated version of the 19th century rustic aviary shown below, Figure 9. (From the collection of Nigel Temple)

Acknowledgements

The authors thank Fiona Jamieson for supplying the image of Baxter Park, and Roger Greenwood for the image of the Titanic — Engineers' Memorial, East Park.

Notes

1. *Illustrated London News* (12 April 1873), 349.

2. The pagoda was for sale at £800 and Pennethorne, the designer of Victoria Park, thought that if it was moved and installed on an island in the lake it would be 'extremely useful and ornamental'. Victoria Park Papers, III (London Metropolitan Archives, 1847–52), entry for 17 September 1847.

3. *The Dane John: Canterbury's Historic Garden* (Canterbury: Canterbury City Council, 1993).

4. 'Report on Sefton Park, April 1867', in *Proceedings* (Liverpool: Liverpool Council, 1868–69), 637.

5. Planning Policy Guidance Note (PPG) 15, *Planning and the Historic Environment* (September 1994), para. 2.24.

6. Birkenhead Road and Improvement Committee, *Minutes* (1845–47), 118–19.

7. John Claudius Loudon, *The Derby Arboretum* (London, Longman, Orme, Brown, Green & Longmans: 1840). The public was admitted free to the arboretum on Sundays, except during morning service, and on Wednesdays, from dawn to dusk. It was not until 1882 that there was free access.

8. Hazel Conway, *People's Parks* (Cambridge: Cambridge University Press, 1991), 84.

9. Patrick Eyres, '"Naval Warfare": the battle of Peasholm Park', *New Arcadian Journal*, nos 39/40 (1995), 33–48.

10. Denise Carlo, 'Development of public parks and open spaces in Norwich, 18th–20th centuries', unpublished diploma thesis, Architectural Association, London, 1989.

11. Conway, *People's Parks*, 147.

12. *Lord Masham: Story of a Great Career, An Industrial Romance* (Bradford: Bradford & District Newspaper Co., 1906).

13. Conway, *People's Parks*, 154.

14. Tiffany Thomas, *A Complete Illustrated History of the People's Park* (Halifax: Womersley & Stott Bros, 1907).

15. Opening Programme (Sheffield: Sheffield Workmen's Tribute Committee, 1901).

The use of iron

by Edward Diestelkamp

The public park, as it evolved during the 19th century, was related to garden design and to the ideas found in 18th-century pleasure gardens, gardens of botanical and horticultural institutions that became very popular and widespread during the early 19th century, and to ideas found in so-called public gardens which made a charge for admission.[1] As the design ideas were borrowed from other types of gardens, it is not surprising that garden features were too. Of course, those in public parks were not necessarily exactly the same in form or scale as the examples that inspired them, but they often were very close in concept and in the materials used.

The introduction of iron as a constructional building material may have begun in the 18th century, but in the 19th century its use became more widespread when adopted for many more different purposes. Iron was *the* material of the 19th century and in the early part of the century it was, in a way, seen as the wonder material of the day. This was really before the structural potential of the material was understood fully, which did not happen until the later part of the century. In the 18th century the decorative potential of iron was adopted in traditional forms, such as in the construction of railings and gates, but towards the end of the century there were experiments in the substitution of iron for other materials, such as timber, which displayed the structural use of the material, even if its potential was not fully appreciated at the time.

Writers have considered the development of structural iron during the later 18th and early 19th centuries, but the most recent collection of papers on the subject offers a well-rounded basis for further investigations.[2] Early 19th-century writers on gardening and horticulture, such as Humphry Repton and John Claudius Loudon, were enthusiastic about the potential of iron.[3] Its introduction to gardens was rapid during the first two decades of the century, and the ways in which it was utilized were to a large extent not unlike the uses to which it would be put in public parks about 30 years later. A review of Loudon's *An Encyclopaedia of Gardening* (1822 onwards) shows the enthusiasm he had for the material and displays the forms of its use that he promoted through the small woodcut illustrations peppered extensively throughout the text.[4]

One feature of the material that Repton and Loudon praised was its great strength in relation to the size of member when compared with other materials such as wood or stone. An iron scantling could be much slighter than its equivalent in these other materials and so had a certain lightness of effect that was particularly suitable to the Regency taste for eclectic styles of design. This lightness of effect was particularly appropriate to the world of the garden, which was concerned primarily with buildings and features in the landscape rather than the more architectural application of iron to buildings, and, more dramatically, to great engineering works. Iron offered to garden designers and horticulturists a strong, durable material that could be used for many different purposes, but which physically would not appear as large as objects made of more conventional materials. So structures, railings, gates and other objects of cast and wrought iron, because of their lightness of form, offered a more sympathetic relationship with the natural world of the garden.

Another characteristic associated with iron by early enthusiasts for its use was its supposed infallible strength. The dramatic failures of strength and collapses of large structures that occurred during the 19th century were not anticipated early in the century. The strength of the material was to be one of the main pursuits of investigation for many designers and engineers during the remainder of the century. These often were directly related to design proposals and constructional problems. There was a tendency to undersize structural iron members for their intended purpose, particularly in the first half of the century. This is probably due to the general desire for a 'lightness of effect' in structures so admired by Repton, Loudon and others.

In one particular area, that of glazed structures for the growth of plants, such as glasshouses, conservatories and forcing houses, this objective was considered to have a direct benefit to plants in so far as the structural material in its slighter form afforded less obstruction to the rays of sunlight penetrating the glazed structure.[5] The quest for the perfect shape and form of glazed surface that would result in the maximum benefit to the plants inside the glasshouse was debated by horticultural writers at the beginning of the century, some of whom were very active in promoting the benefits of iron, both wrought and cast. Scientific theories surrounding this debate resulted in different forms of glass buildings for plants, and these experiments in their own way had an effect upon the design of glasshouses throughout the rest of the century.

The decorative advantages of iron were also an important factor in its widespread adoption in gardens during the 19th century. Both wrought and cast iron presented advantages over other materials. Wrought iron could be worked into different shapes while hot, and through repeated heating, and beating or rolling could take on shapes, which could be used for constructional or decorative purposes. The real discovery of the early 19th century was the recognition of the potential of wrought iron for constructional

purposes, but the potential of cast iron was also more widely understood during the century. Cast iron was very important for decorative purposes, and able to adopt the form and relief surface of the moulded shape into which the molten cast iron was poured, and so offered the possibility of replication and repetition with little additional need for craftsmanship beyond the making of the initial pattern. This was in contrast to wrought iron, each member of which would have to be worked by hand, first having been heated to a temperature where it was malleable when it could be worked by beating and other tools, to bend, twist and cut the material to the desired shape. The characteristics of the two different materials can be very clearly seen in the ways in which they were used.[6]

Cast iron

The raw material from which cast iron is made appears in nature as iron ore, is rarely in a pure state and is usually found in association with carbon. The raw material has limited resistance to compression, characteristic of other ores, and is of little practical use. It is through the heating of the ore that the material becomes a more useful material.[7] Heating the ore to a molten state releases much, though not all, of the carbon. In this form it can be poured into sand moulds of standard size. Known as pig iron, the 'pigs' or cooled masses of iron were in their first refined state, which could be traded or exported to others for further working into a more refined state or into a practical, useful shape. Further working of the pig iron by heating and hammering led to the creation of wrought iron, but the pig iron could also be reheated to molten state and as cast iron could be used for many purposes.

Casting at a foundry could be carried out in a number of ways, the most common of which during the 19th century was casting in sand. This was a very old means of creating a replica of the model. Known as greensand moulding, it was developed to a highly sophisticated technique by some foundries, using a mixture of naturally bonded moist or green sand and coal dust. Another method for making a mould involved the use of sand that had been baked or treated with heat to

Figure 1: Foundry and smithy, Dinorwic Quarry, North Wales: wooden moulds for window frames, decorative castings and other architectural hardware. (Photo: the author)

61

make it harder and more resistant to deformation by the action of the molten metal. Known as dry sand moulding, it and the greensand method were the two traditional methods of the 19th century.[8] The moulding shop of iron foundries included a model-maker's shop, where there were often stores of models, many of wood, that were used to form the sand moulds (figure 1). This simple method would not be used for columns and other hollow cast members which involved a more complicated process.

Under the microscope the composition of cast iron is granular, which explains an important element of its character, namely its greater strength in compression rather than in tension.[9] Cast iron is brittle and can break or snap when subjected to significant lateral forces. Its use, therefore, for columns was ideal where the forces to be resisted were applied at one end or the other. Where the cast iron was vulnerable to forces or strains on its side, including those of its own weight, it has much less strength and, therefore, had more limited uses. So castings of a thin light section might sustain vertical forces of some size, but they would be vulnerable to the horizontal forces of wind or lateral strains.

Wrought iron

Wrought iron is a more refined state than cast iron with more of the carbon removed. Heat and the application of hammers, coupled with the passing of the pig or 'bloom' through rollers, helped further to refine the iron and to remove carbon impurities from the material. This hammering and rolling brought about a change in the nature of the composition from the more granular form of cast iron to one of thin strings or fibres arranged in a linear form parallel to the length of the bloom. This physical form is suggestive of the properties of the material, namely its significantly greater tensile strength than cast iron, which affords greater ability to withstand lateral forces as well as forces in compression. Wrought iron has nearly the same strength in compression as it has in tension and so was exploited throughout the 19th century as a structural material in both ways.

The 'lightness of effect' so admired by writers and inventors was particularly possible through the application of wrought iron. Loudon was fascinated by this material and was involved in its development as a material for glazed horticultural structures. He recognized the significance of its greater tensile strength, where a smaller section of wrought iron could more effectively support and withstand lateral forces than its equivalent in cast iron. This advantage was particularly revealed in the shape and thickness of vertical and horizontal members, affording much more slender profiles than might be possible in cast iron. In the first decades of the 19th century the use of wrought

Figure 2 (left): Design for a bandstand, from the illustrated catalogue of *Macfarlane's Castings*, 7th edn, vol. i, no. 279. Figure 3 (above): Shelter, Victoria Park, Stafford, Staffordshire, 1904, Walter Macfarlane and Co., Saracen Foundry, Glasgow. (Photo: the author)

iron was often more widespread than is often believed and many structures considered to be of cast iron were often primarily of wrought iron, or were structures combining both materials. This applies to structures such as garden buildings as well as to more decorative features, such as railings. Edward Kemp preferred wrought iron railings as their thinness rendered them much less visible in natural parkland settings.[10]

During the 18th century, wrought iron was primarily considered a material that was to be worked by hand, over the forge, and with hammers and tongs at an anvil, but by the mid-19th century the ability to work or shape wrought iron to the desired form by water- or steam-powered machinery, such as hammers or sets of rollers, was well established. Many different shapes were widely available, from different sizes of plate iron to bars or rods, angles, tees and more elaborate shapes, all of which could be extruded through the rollers. This change from a craftsman's approach to one of more industrial processes resulted in a distinct change in the apparent form of the material which adopted the shapes described above. These basically simple forms were in contrast to the individual hand-crafted shapes commonly associated with the

material as it was used in the 18th century. The rolling process also produced a different surface finish, smoother than the hammered surface of hand-wrought iron.

The early decades of the 19th century were innovative in many respects: first, in the application of iron to new purposes; second, in the development in the understanding of the structural potential of both cast and wrought iron; and third, in the development in the fields of gardening and horticulture, as well as in architecture and construction. Many new ideas and concepts were introduced at this time, some of which were not fully expressed until mid-century. Certainly by then there were iron foundries throughout the country specializing in the manufacture of cast and wrought iron decorative ironwork for private and public gardens, many of which specialized in the design and construction of horticultural and ornamental buildings that became associated with public parks.

Different applications of iron in public parks

The different uses of iron as a decorative and structural material in public parks were many and included such diverse applications as railings,

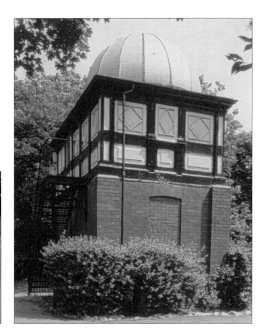

Figure 4 (left): Design for a drinking fountain, from the illustrated catalogue of *Macfarlane's Castings*, 7th edn, vol. i, no. 8.
Figure 5 (right): Fernley Observatory, Hesketh Park, Southport, Lancashire, 1871, with a sheet of metal dome over the telescope (photo: the author)
Figure 6 (below): railings, Stanley Park, Liverpool. (Photo: the author)

gates, conservatories, bandstands (figure 2), pavilions, shelters (figure 3), sanitary conveniences (urinals), bridges, seats and benches, light standards or pillars, ornamental vases, fountains, drinking fountains (figure 4), and other sculptural purposes. Iron was also used on buildings within public parks in many of the same ways then common in building practice, such as for external and internal stairs, balconies, verandas, handrails, windows and window frames, gutters and downpipes, roof coverings (figure 5), skylights and ornamental cresting on roof ridges, eaves and along gutters, and for heating boilers, kitchen ranges and ovens. The extensive range of iron fittings and building materials available can be quickly appreciated by examining a catalogue of an iron foundry such as Walter Macfarlane's Saracen Foundry in Possilpark, Glasgow, which manufactured a very wide range of iron hardware and building components. Not all iron works were on the same scale and many specialized in certain ranges of products. Several firms, for instance, were renowned for the design and fabrication of glasshouses and conservatories, while others were better known for very high-quality decorative castings and the manufacture of ornamental fittings.

Railings

Iron railings often surrounded public parks (figure 6). These afforded security of the park during hours when it was closed and helped to control access by the public. Where railings in earlier centuries may have been of timber and sometimes were provided to restrict the movement of animals within the park, the railings around a public park were intended to keep the public out during closed hours. Railings afforded some security also against vandalism where there was no supervision.

The design of railings often responded to the particular situation. Where an ornamental character was desirable, decorative finials could be attached to the top of the railings. Their sharp points were intended to deter those who attempted to climb over. The extent of ornament considered appropriate depended on the character of the surrounding area, and additional decoration could be added to the tops of the vertical rods as well as to their bases. Ornamental braces regularly disposed along the length of railings to help stiffen and hold them vertical were often cast in the shape of scrolls or brackets. Throughout the century railings were often of cast iron, including vertical rods, horizontal bars and decorative finials, but in many cases they were of combined cast and rolled

63

wrought iron pieces. The bottoms of railings were sometimes let into stone curbs, with individual holes drilled for letting the vertical rods into. These were inserted into the hole and the void around run with molten lead to secure the stone and iron together.

Many railings were removed from public parks in this century. The most widely cited reason was their use as scrap iron for the war effort, but there was also a philosophical reason in some cases, to liberate enclosed spaces and remove barriers in the pursuit of greater access for all.[11] In many cases the removed railings have been replaced with expedient substitutes that are not of appropriate character. Concrete posts with wire netting or inferior industrialized fencing have been adopted with a resultant loss of character. Restorations of railings are numerous, and often small sections of original railings may survive to serve as a model, or old photographs can offer good evidence. Substantial bases for railings such as curbstones may survive embedded in the ground, or they may have been removed and stored, and where possible these should be incorporated in restorations.

The restoration of lost or damaged railings around a public park should be a priority, which is as important as providing a physical presence to help deter vandalism and theft. If the adverse effects of these threats can be minimized, the character of parks will not be eroded. As the historic features of public parks are important elements of their character, these should not be overlooked when considering the significance of a place. The design of any railings to be renewed should be carefully considered so that they are sympathetic to the character of the park. Designs should include more formal considerations such as the height and proportion of the railings; the length between regular vertical stanchions or standards; and, most importantly, the gradient or slope of the intended site and how it relates to the general layout, as well as to details of the ornamental elements such as finials or supporting brackets, and the shape and design of the base or bottom rail. A careful study should be carried out before any changes to previously existing railings are entertained. Modern railings, which are available

in standardized sections, of varying lengths and heights, in many cases are not appropriate to the historic setting of public parks. These are made of mild steel and the horizontal members at the bottom and top are of rectangular section while the vertical members are often round or circular in section. Their most unfortunate aspect is their square, regular construction that cannot take account of the form of the land. They often look rigid and inflexible in natural settings as it is not possible to adjust them to the land's contours. Stanchions or standards between the bays of railings are often simple industrial 'u'-shaped sections of mild steel, which in many settings would not be historically correct, especially around the perimeter of parks where more ornamental railings would have been used. One major problem with modern replacement railings, and an important factor to consider when restoring railings, is the appropriate thickness of the individual members of iron or mild steel. Sections of contemporary manufactured railings are often too slight and do not have the same visual weight as historic examples. This is crucial to the historic character of railings and poor reproductions are usually easily identified.

Many specialist firms, companies and foundries around the country can carry out careful restorations and reproductions.[12] The repair of like with like, using cast iron where it originally was used, can be done using both traditional methods or newer, more recently developed methods of casting.[13] The replacement of wrought iron with like is also possible, but the commercial production of wrought iron ceased in the UK in the 1950s. The recycling of used wrought iron is possible but the rolling of wrought iron is both expensive and difficult. Repairs of wrought iron railings, however, might be possible from basic shapes such as rounds or flats of wrought iron which are available. The temptation to substitute readily available standard sections of mild steel should generally be avoided if a source of appropriate wrought iron can be found. The size of the mild steel members is rarely identical to the size of historic members and the surface is usually smoother, but, most importantly, the square or rectangular members do not have sharp and

64

Figure 7: Entrance gates, Prince's Park, Liverpool, designed by Sir James Pennethorne, 1840s. (Photo: the author)

pointed corners, but are rounded off.

Railings must be regularly painted to ensure that corrosion and rust are minimized. Painting should be carried out as part of an on-going quinquennial programme of maintenance works, much in the same way that it would be carried out on buildings. Vegetation should not be allowed to enclose or cover railings, particularly at their base where damp and moisture can be trapped. Self-seeded saplings and other hardy plants should be regularly removed from around the bottoms of railings, particularly those with stone base curbs, which might be disturbed by the growth of trees. Painting should be carefully undertaken so that excess paint is not spread over other surfaces nearby, particularly porous ones such as stone, which might be difficult and expensive to clean. Colour is a very important consideration. Black is the colour usually associated with iron railings and gates, particularly in cities, but in the 19th century other colours were common. In the early part of the century ironwork was sometimes painted a bronze green to simulate the more expensive metal. Chocolate or rust brown, endorsed by John Ruskin as a colour which the material naturally adopts, was used in mid-century, but shades of other colours were also used. It was common prac-

tice to apply several coats of red lead initially as a preserving coating onto which the colour coats of paint were applied. Scrapes and paint sections can be very informative, but it is likely that evidence may be elusive in some cases as it was usually general practice to scrape down the iron with the result that historic colours may no longer be easy to locate or identify.

Gates

Both pedestrian and vehicular gates were usually associated with railings, incorporating similar decorative elements and designed to be seen in connection with each other. Like railings, they played an important function in the security of public parks, which could be closed to the public at night and at other times. Gates were often associated with architectural features such as lodges or gateways, which were sometimes constructed of more solid materials such as stone or brick (figure 7). These often included living accommodation so that a keeper or warden would be on hand to open and shut the gates. Early public parks, such as Birkenhead Park or Queen's Park, Glasgow, were on a large scale and incorporated carriage drives around the perimeter so that large openings were needed at entrances to parks. Vehicular gates were often more ornamental than railings, and their style frequently reflected the architectural style of the lodge or gateway of which they formed a part. The historic tradition of 17th- and 18th-century gates and gate lodges belonging to private landed estates was an important influence, and, while the design of some gates may not have been directly based on earlier examples, the basic form and mode of fabrication owed much to tradition. This tradition was largely one of wrought iron and based upon the craftsman rather than industrial processes.[14] The structural frame, usually composed of straight or curvilinear members of rectangular section, and the more decorative repoussé work which was applied, were all usually made by hand. From the early 19th century cast iron decorative elements came into use as they were less expensive to produce than hand-wrought repoussé details. During the mid-19th century, firms such as the Coalbrookdale Ironworks, which specialized in very fine castings, manufactured highly decorative ornamental gates to public acclaim, marking a fashion for gates with pierced relief panels of cast iron. The repeating motifs of decoration, often elaborate and highly sculptural, were produced from moulds that were often used more than once.

The quality of the decorative castings was crucial to the design, and this factor must be remembered when considering repairs or restoration. Surviving fragments, if clean of layers of paint and in good repair, can serve as a model to replace missing features. Making a cast of existing elements is not a complex procedure and can be carried out by foundries that produce the replica castings. However, where original castings do not survive, poorly modelled elements can detract from the integrity of the design. Careful study of photographs or drawings can help to establish the correct scale, but the creation of a new mould requires skill and should be entrusted to a craftsman who can make an accurate model. In some instances gates are no longer in use as carriage drives have been given over to walks. Maintenance and care are very important, and like railings they should be treated to remove rust and painted regularly. Where gates are not in frequent use hinges should be regularly lubricated. Where they are in use, large vehicles can cause much damage. Damage

caused by the impact of a vehicle can affect the gates as well as their fixings and mountings and can be very expensive to repair. Precautionary measures such as discreet curbs or bollards placed on the vehicle approach can help to direct traffic to the centre of the opening. Where gates have overthrows, access should be carefully restricted or monitored so that tall vehicles are not allowed to enter or exit through the gateway.

The repair of gates and of ornamental railings, both cast and wrought iron, should be entrusted to specialists firms or metalwork conservators who have experience in the different repair techniques of the two materials.[15] Damaged work very often can be repaired and suggestions of wholesale or even partial renewal of damaged parts should be carefully analysed to determine if this is absolutely necessary. Methods of replacing of missing elements should also be considered to ascertain if the profile of the iron member in question would be the correct size so that the composition of the whole is not affected. In the case of elaborate wrought iron gates with repoussé work of leaves, flowers, etc., detail may often be missing, such as extended forms, which are prone to being knocked or hit. Elongated forms of thin fragile sections are also prone to rust and corrosion, particularly in areas where members are connected and where water can be trapped. Repairs to wrought iron repoussé work should really only be given to ironsmiths with considerable experience in the repair of delicate ironwork such as this.

Conservatories and winter gardens

Conservatories and winter gardens in public parks offered the public the opportunity to enjoy plants of different exotic climates, and floral displays at all times of the year, but particularly in winter when there were no leaves on trees and plants, and when it was not possible to offer visitors arrangements of floral display outside (figures 8–10). Glasshouses provided a focal point for public parks, offering variety and interest to visitors. In many cases these were not large structures, but sometimes they were of very considerable scale such as the palm house in Sefton Park, Liverpool,

Figure 8 (above): Conservatory, Hesketh Park, Southport, which was originally part of Brunswick Villa on Lord Street, and was purchased by the Corporation for £200 and moved to the park in 1878. (Photo: the author)

Figure 9 (left): Conservatory, Hesketh Park, Southport, detail of awning on the front of the building. (Photo: the author)

Figure 10 (below): Interior of the Conservatory, Hesketh Park, Southport. (Photo: the author)

erected by Mackenzie and Moncur of Edinburgh in 1896, which was over 100 feet (30 metres) in width and 74 feet (*c*.22 metres) in height.

The 19th century was the great age of the conservatory and winter garden, and the use of iron was important in this development.[16] Both cast and wrought iron were often employed together, particularly in larger structures; the cast iron acting in compression and used for columns and vertical supports as well as for decorative features where repetition of ornamental detail was desired, while the wrought iron was frequently used for glazing bars and other members in roles where tensile strength or strength in bending was needed, such as for horizontal members which sometimes took the form of light lattice trusses or arched ribs.

The potential for the use of iron in horticultural structures was widely discussed in the early 19th century and some early experimental structures were built in Britain. Loudon advocated its use in many articles and in other publications. Iron was not the exclusive structural material for glasshouses and there was a lively debate over the advantages of iron versus wood throughout the mid-century. But iron was stronger in longer lengths than wood in proportion to its sectional thickness, and longer, larger continuous glazed surfaces could be achieved in iron. It is not possible here to consider the development of the use of iron for conservatories and glasshouses, which has been dealt with elsewhere,[17] but its application with glass produced some of the most elegant and innovative buildings of the century.

This fashion for conservatories and winter gardens was first established in the private gardens of noblemen and was followed by botanical and horticultural societies and gardens. Those that were built in public parks from the mid-to-late 19th century were very similar in purpose and were inspired by the structures erected in the botanical gardens of Liverpool, Birmingham, Regent's Park in London, Belfast, Glasgow and Edinburgh from the 1830s to the 1850s. The development of metropolitan authorities, with the associated growth of municipal pride and sense of

purpose, was in some cases expressed in the aim to emulate botanical gardens and to enhance the role of public parks to provide more than a landscape park, flower garden and recreation area, and to include an enclosed indoor garden for exotic and delicate plants.

The construction of conservatories and winter gardens was specialized and involved the combination of materials in an unusual way. These materials, iron and glass, are fragile and iron in particular is susceptible to decay from damp. Experienced specialists familiar with appropriate methods of repair should carry out the repair and restoration of structures such as these.[18] One important aspect of the expertise required is knowledge of structures. An able structural engineer experienced in the repair of historic iron structures should assess the relative strength of the structure and the implications for public safety. In the hands of someone with little experience, or unsympathetic to the attributes and qualities of the structure, inappropriate proposals might be entertained that would affect its appearance as well as the historic character.

The special qualities of iron and glass conservatories and winter gardens are found in the detailing of the glazing, which is often characterized by thin, light wrought iron glazing bars of elegant form and length, supporting quite large-sized panes of sheet glass or slightly thicker cast plate glass that was used sometimes on roofs and elevations. Another quality is the internal space associated with these structures that is directly related to the glazing, in the proportion, depth and width of the glazing bar in relation to the size of the glass pane; and in the general form of the glazed surface, whether curved or straight, and in the distance between supporting structural members. It would be inappropriate to attempt to identify a general or characteristic form, and the 'effects of lightness' referred to by Repton certainly could not be applied to all of the structures produced. But the general impression of the internal quality of space, and the limited obstruction of natural light by the structural frame, are important elements in describing the character of structures such as these. The significant characteristics of the particular conservatory should be identified and should guide decisions about any changes or alterations that may be considered necessary or desirable, such as proposed strengthening of the structure by the introduction of additional structural members. In some instances, such necessary interventions might not perceptibly alter the building's character, but in other instances they may introduce an inappropriate alteration. Knowledge and experience of working on similar structures and in identifying alternative ways of achieving acceptable solutions can be very valuable.

Iron and glass buildings were in some ways exceptional to the standard building trades and often relied upon quite precise principles of detailing and exacting proportions in the size of components that were adopted. The derivation of the wrought iron glazing bar was the metallic glazing bar used in the 18th century for rooflights, and later in the century within special window sashes made up of brass or other 'light' metal glazing bars. The method and material used to connect the glass and bar was linseed putty, commonly used for glazing windows. The arrangement of glazing bars and glass was carefully devised in many cases and directly related to the manufacture of the iron parts and to the glass. This could be more efficiently organized and less costly if it were identical to other parts of the same building and of other buildings. Specialist companies produced many of these structures, particularly as the century progressed. By the late 19th century there were hundreds of firms throughout Britain producing glasshouses either with iron or wood structural frames, and many provincial centres had one if not more larger firms capable of manufacturing quite good-sized iron-framed glasshouses and winter gardens.

As the 19th century progressed many new techniques and inventions were developed to improve the detailing of the junction of glass with the iron glazing bar, in the search to find a solution requiring less maintenance in the way of regular painting, and offering less chance of broken glass as a result of rusting glazing bars. Innovative developments included dry-glazed systems using no putty and in some cases no glazing bars where the glass was held on the structural frame by means of galvanized iron clips attached to wires. Alternatives to putty such as gutta-percha or rubber gaskets and seals were also devised. Details such as these, though once more common, are now quite rare and their importance and relevance should not be underestimated. The possibility of retaining, repairing or restoring such integral detail should be carefully researched before any decision to alter the original is adopted. Gardening and horticultural journals of the 19th century such as the *Gardeners' Chronicle* are often a good source of information about conservatories and winter gardens erected in public parks, and sometimes also of the constructional details developed by different firms. As mentioned above, the rolling of wrought iron is difficult and can be expensive, though the remodelling or refashioning of used wrought iron glazing bars has been successfully carried out as part of the restoration of the Curvilinear Range at the Botanical Gardens in Glasnevin, Dublin.[19] Health and safety regulations may in some cases preclude the retention of existing glazing and this may have implications for the reuse of existing methods of support and fixing.

Not all of the conservatories or winter gardens in public parks are necessarily included in lists compiled by English Heritage, Historic Scotland or Cadw: Welsh Historic Monuments as buildings of historic importance, though it is very likely that the most important ones have been already identified. English Heritage's guidelines for the conservation of historic buildings offer valuable guidance on principles to follow.[20] Buildings listed Grades II* or I may be eligible for a grant towards their repair. The appointment of an architect and structural engineer with experience in working on iron and glass structures is very important. Historic buildings such as these derive their architectural language from their constructional detail and its careful retention, repair and restoration, where missing, should be the aim. In many cases the material of construction, here either cast or wrought iron, may be of technological interest and of intrinsic importance to the concept and to

69

the realization of the design. The substitution of other materials should be questioned and should not be entertained without very good grounds. Likewise, mechanical inventions and arrangements for ventilation and heating such as sliding or swivelling sashes, or perhaps in the case of heating arrangements the use of humidification trays on top of heating pipes, should also be assessed for their importance.

Unlike other structures of iron found in public parks, conservatories and winter gardens have interiors that form an important and integral aspect of the building, and the internal arrangement of plants, beds, paths, galleries and plant shelves deserves the same attention as the repair and restoration of the structure and outer envelope of the building. While not all of these elements are necessarily made of iron, it is very likely that there will be fittings of iron such as cast iron grating over paths, hot water pipes, cast iron curbing around plant beds, iron plant shelves around the perimeter or in the centre of the building, iron galleries, and iron-winding gear and ventilation flaps for introducing air into the building.

Techniques for the repair of a structural iron framework of wrought iron may include the welding of steel plates onto sections of corroded wrought iron for additional strength. In the case of cast iron, a special form of welding or stitching can restore the integrity of the broken or split structural member. Perhaps the most damaging effect is that of corrosion from trapped water that can freeze and cause downpipes or other enclosed hollow members to split, or of condensation which can lie in areas and penetrate between two surfaces of iron and begin corrosive action with the lamination, expansion and break up of the surface.[21] Alterations or minor adjustments that can help to eliminate the trapping of water within, on top of or between surfaces can be desirable, but care should be taken to ensure that these changes do not detract from the overall appearance of the structure, thereby distorting the intended design.

Glass is an equally important element of these structures and, while this chapter is not intended specifically to cover that material, it is important that, where possible, care is taken to re-use old glass. 19th century sheet glass was not entirely smooth and imperfections give the surface movement that modern glass usually lacks, but, as mentioned above, health and safety are important considerations that should not be overlooked.

Bandstands, pavilions and other shelters or conveniences

The bandstand was perhaps the most common feature of public parks, reflecting the widespread interest and the popularity of bands throughout the 19th and early 20th centuries, and illustrating that public parks were places for public musical entertainment before the advent of gramophones and the radio. Like conservatories and winter gardens, bandstands and pavilions were often of iron (figure 11). In many instances cast iron was used, but wrought iron was too, particularly for light lattice rafters to support roofs. As with conservatories, cast-iron columns were a common feature of their design. Frequently these functioned as rainwater downpipes, so it is not unusual to find that these pipes are sometimes split from the action of freezing water inside. Decorative castings around the eaves, or cresting along the top of the gutter or the ridge, and a finial or weather vane at the centre of the roof were common elements, but these are now usually missing in some part and it is quite rare to see a bandstand with all of its ironwork intact. Bandstands were usually elevated on a platform for visibility and the decorative iron stairs, handrail and railings around the perimeter are often broken or missing elements because they are vulnerable to vandalism. The underside of the bandstand roof was frequently boarded to serve as a sounding board, like the tester above a pulpit, and the superstructure upon which the bandstand was raised was sometimes of masonry construction.

Pavilions in public parks offered a covered enclosed space where people could sit and rest, read, or talk in any kind of weather (figure 12), and sometimes refreshments could be purchased. These structures were sometimes of iron, made to a prefabricated system that allowed the constructional elements to be used in different ways to produce different forms or shapes of buildings.[22]

Figure 11 (above): Bandstand, Victoria Park, Southport, Lancashire, supplied by the Lion Foundry Co. Ltd, Kirkintilloch. (Photo: the author)

Figure 12 (left): Design for a pavilion, from the illustrated catalogue of *Macfarlane's Castings*, 7th edn, vol. i, no. 112.

Figure 13 (below): Design for a sanitary convenience, from the illustrated catalogue of *Macfarlane's Castings*, 7th edn, vol. i, no. 214.

Figure 14: Shelter, Marine Gardens, Southport, Lancashire, supplied to Wm Robson Ironmonger, Southport, by David Ling and Sons, Possilpark, Glasgow. (Photo: the author)

72

Macfarlane and Co. of Glasgow manufactured different building elements in iron that could be used for different types of structures such as pavilions, sanitary conveniences and shelters (figure 13). Cast iron columns could be combined with solid or partially glazed iron panels with decorative shallow relief patterns to form walls (figures 14 and 15). Roofs carried on light wrought iron trusses or lattice rafters might have been partially glazed by regular rows of rooflights, or solid with boarding beneath the roof covering of corrugated iron or another appropriate material. Structures such as these often incorporated verandas around the perimeter to offer shelter from the rain and the sun.

The structural frame of shelters, pavilions and covered seats is often more robust than the wall panels, which may have been badly affected by rust through lack of maintenance. In some instances frames have been adapted and the wall panels replaced by new ones in inappropriate materials and with inappropriate decorative finishes (figure 16). Additional timber framework with applied timber boarding or plywood may be attached to the iron frame, disguising or hiding it in some cases (figure 17). Evidence of the original arrangement and of the original iron components

may survive on other structures nearby, or may be seen in old photographs, so that the structure may be restored to its original appearance.

Park benches and ornamental ironwork

The park bench was a common feature of public parks, though today it may be difficult to find a place to sit and rest. Benches are prone to both vandalism and a lack of regular maintenance. Damage of the wooden slatted seats renders them useless and they are often removed from use. Security is also a real problem as they are desirable and of considerable value, due primarily to the decorative quality of the cast or wrought iron bench ends. Park benches were frequently placed in areas where people liked to meet such as in front of the bandstand (figure 18), or where there was a good view, like in the flower garden where one could enjoy looking at the floral displays, or in a place where people could rest sometimes in the shelter of a building or under a veranda. The tradition of iron park and garden benches is very rich, particularly in Britain with hundreds of different designs produced by foundries around the country.[23] There has been a revival of interest in benches for parks and gardens, and reproductions are available in many different designs. Most repro-

Figure 15: Detail of the base panel of the Shelter, Marine Gardens, Southport. (Photo: the author)

Figure 16: Shelter, Hesketh Park, Southport, by McDowall, Steven and Co. Ltd, Glasgow. The cast iron frame is made up of cast iron columns with light iron rafters supporting the roof. There have been alterations, though some of the seats around the base survive. Timber panel infill has been used on the walls, and the roof has been covered with felt. (Photo: the author)

Figure 17: Shelter, Hesketh Park, Southport, by McDowall, Steven and Co. Ltd, Glasgow. The cast iron frame is similar to the other shelter in the park (cf. Figure 16), but the walls have been renewed with inappropriate aggregate faced panels. (Photo: the author)

Figure 18: Iron benches arranged in a curve in front of the bandstand, Victoria Park, Stafford. (Photo: the author)

ductions are cast in aluminium, so they are lighter and easier to lift and carry. But the range available does not match that available in the 19th century, and many are very poorly modelled and scaled. Indeed, there are complete ranges of ersatz 'heritage' furnishings for street, garden and park that are very different to 19th-century examples. These furnishings should be avoided because of their poor character and quality of design. In some instances benches were individual to particular parks and, where appropriate, consideration should be given to identifying the type(s) of benches used and, if they no longer survive, thought given to reproducing them.

Other decorative and functional iron elements such as cast-iron vases, urns, fountains, drinking fountains and lamp pillars or standards were also popular, though few survive today. As with park benches, vandalism has claimed many, while the adverse effects of freezing water on fountains and drinking fountains have taken their toll. Municipal authorities regularly renew lamp standards or pillars with the result that it is quite rare for decorative lighting fixtures to survive in their original position (figure 19). All of these lesser, yet often highly decorative features, performed an important role in public parks. It is now remarkable to

find a drinking fountain in working order in many public parks, and almost too much to expect that the decorative late 19th-century versions once so commonly found might still survive (figure 20). It is a pity that those which do survive are sometime dragooned into symbolic use as 'heritage' furniture and found scattered on windswept sites or in the centre of a roundabout as a sad reminder of what was once a very rich past.

Notes

1. George F. Chadwick, *The Park and the Town* (London: Architectural Press, 1966); Hazel Conway, *People's Parks* (Cambridge: Cambridge University Press, 1991); Hazel Conway and David Lambert, *Public Prospects, Historic Urban Parks under Threat* (London: Garden History Society and Victorian Society, 1993).

2. R. J. M Sutherland (ed.), *Structural Iron, 1750–1850*. Studies in the History of Civil Engineering, vol. 9 (Aldershot: Ashgate, 1997).

3. John Claudius Loudon, *Sketches of Curvilinear Hothouses* (1 March 1818); *idem*, 'Letter to the Editor', *New Monthly Magazine*, 9 (May 1818), 313-15; Humphry Repton, *Observations on the Theory and Practice of Landscape Gardening* (London, 1803), 105–6.

Figure 19 (top): Entrance to a public park or garden, from the illustrated catalogue of Macfarlane's Castings, 7th edn, vol. i.
Figure 20 (right): Drinking fountain, Clifton Green, Bristol, by Walter Macfarlane and Co., Saracen Foundry, Glasgow. (cf. Figure 4) (Photo: the author)

4. John Claudius Loudon, *An Encyclopaedia of Gardening* (London: Longman, Hurst, Rees, Orme & Brown, 1822; 2nd edn 1824; 8th edn 1835, etc.).

5. John Hix, *The Glass House* (London: Phaidon, 1974).

6. John Gloag and Derek Bridgewater, *A History of Cast Iron in Architecture* (London: George Allen & Unwin, 1948).

7. W. K. V. Gale, *Iron and Steel* (Telford: Ironbridge Gorge Museum Trust, 1979).

8. T. Jemison, 'Railings', *Landscape Design* (June 1983), 27–30.

9. Sutherland, 'Introduction', in *Structural Iron*, XV–XX.

10. Edward Kemp, *How to Lay Out a Garden* (London: Bradbury & Evans, 1864).

11. Celena Fox, 'The battle of the railings', AA *Files*, no. 29 (1995), 50–60.

12. *The Building Conservation Directory* (Tisbury: Cathedral Communications, 1998).

13. J. Ashurst and N. Ashurst, *Practical Building Conservation*, vol. IV: *Metals*. English Heritage Technical Handbook (Aldershot: Gower Technical, 1998); *Ornamental Ironwork*: *Gates and Railings* (London: English Heritage, 1993); Jemison, 'Railings'; Steven Parissien, *Ironwork*. Guide no. 8 (London: Georgian Group: n.d.); Kitt Wedd, *Care for Victorian Houses*, no. 6: *Cast Iron* (London: Victorian Society, 1994). A particularly helpful, brief and well-illustrated guide to the repair of railings is *Railings in Westminster* (London: Department of the Environment and Planning, Development Division of the City of Westminster, 1997).

14. Nicola Ashurst, 'Heavenly gates', *Traditional Homes* (July 1998), 16–24.

15. The Conservation Section of the Museums and Galleries Commission, 18 Queen Anne's Gate, London SW1H 9AA, holds a register of conserva-

tors. For a small fee they can provide the names, addresses and details of work carried out by local conservators. *The Building Conservation Directory*, published annually, also lists the names of specialist conservation craftsmen and firms.

16. Hix, *The Glass House*; Georg Kohlmaier and Barna von Sartory, *Houses of Glass* (Cambridge, MA: MIT Press, 1986); Stefan Koppelkamm, *Glasshouses and Wintergardens of the 19th Century* (London: Granada, 1981); May Woods and Arete Warren, *Glass Houses* (New York: Rizzoli, and London: Aurum, 1988).

17. Hix, *The Glass House*.

18. *The Building Conservation Directory*, Special Report No. 2: *The Care and Conservation of Historic Garden Landscapes* (London: Cathedral Communications, 1994), 11–12. Brian Morton, 'Iron-framed Conservatories and Greenhouses'.

19. D. Singmaster, 'Wrought iron recycled to restore Turner's splendour', *Architects' Journal* (8 February 1996), 36.

20. Christopher Brereton, *The Repair of Historic Buildings: Advice on Principles and Methods* (London: English Heritage, 1991).

21. The restoration of three important 19th-century glasshouses, the Palm House at Bicton Gardens, Devon, the Conservatory at Syon House, Isleworth, and the great Palm House at the Royal Botanic Gardens, Kew, carried out in the 1980s are helpful case studies: Chris Jones, 'Two glass houses, Syon and Bicton', *Architects' Journal* (29 April 1987), 57–62; J. L. Guthrie, A. Allen and Chris Jones, 'Royal Botanic Gardens, Kew: restoration of Palm House', *Proceedings of the Institution of Civil Engineers*, Part 1, 84 (1988), 1145–91.

22. G. Herbert, *Pioneers of Prefabrication* (Baltimore: Johns Hopkins University Press, 1978).

23. Georg Himmelheber, *Cast-iron Furniture* (London: Philip Wilson, 1996).

Paths

by Brent Elliott

Figure 1: The importance of good drainage is over-evident from this example in the gardens of Schönbrunn, Vienna in 1996. (Photo: Jan Woudstra)

'In the very humid and comparatively sunless climate of England', wrote Henry Bailey, the head gardener at Nuneham Courtenay, in 1850, 'nothing conduces more to the enjoyment of a country residence than a good, firm, and dry walk'.[1]

There is, however, very little information in the published documentation of municipal parks about the way in which paths were laid out. One rarely finds the gardening press saying more (but frequently saying less) than, for example, of Birkenhead Park, a comment on 'the curve for drives and paths (and the effect in the latter is especially excellent)', or criticizing Kennington Park for 'unlevel puddle-holding walks, some of them unsightly and crooked'.[2] Any survey of path-making in 19th century municipal parks must therefore look to the instructions available in the literature aimed at the domestic garden, which inevitably present a wider range of options than were adopted for public gardens. All the major manuals on landscape gardening, from Edward Kemp in the 1850s to Richard Sudell in the 1930s, have sections or chapters on making roads and walks, and these were presumably available to

borough surveyors and park superintendents as well as to independent landscape designers. They have a tendency, however, to spend more time discussing the aesthetics of paths and drives, especially the degree of curvature required or allowed, than on the mechanics of construction; and by the 20th century, if only by way of recognizing the development of new professions, Sudell could refer most of the technical aspects to a consultant engineer, whose services the landscape architect 'will naturally secure'.[3]

There was a thriving literature in the early gardening magazines on the techniques of making garden paths. This contrasts with the comparative silence of the 18th century literature on the subject, when the more extreme landscape gardens restricted paths to the areas away from the principal views, as inconsistent with the image of unaltered nature they were intended to present; John Claudius Loudon criticized Hagley, for instance, where the family 'must cross the open park before they can get to gravel paths of any kind', an especially miserable prospect in winter.[4] Loudon not only encouraged the provision of paths near the house, but also took a functional line on their layout: 'no deviation from a straight line should ever appear, for which a reason is not given in the position of the ground, trees, or other accompanying objects'.[5] In his account of his design for the Derby Arboretum (1840), Loudon elaborated: 'As a terminal object gives meaning to a straight walk leading to it, so it is only by creating artificial obstructions that meaning can be given to a winding walk over a flat surface' — either inequalities in the ground, or trees and shrubs in the line of the walk.[6]

This attitude was a calculated affront to the 18th century tradition of the circuitous approach road, that took the visitor through the scenery by a leisurely route before finally delivering him/her to the house; and the older attitude was slow to die out, as shown by the 'Amateur landscape gardener', otherwise anonymous, who wrote in the *Floricultural Cabinet* in 1842 that 'The refined taste of modern gardening . . . is to reject straight paths. . . .'. It must be acknowledged that this author could take a Loudon-like approach to justifying curvature: 'Walks are not formed by nature, but are the efforts of man or beast, &c., and the difficulties existing in opposing objects render curved lines and circuitous directions to be taken'.[7]

The problems in making garden walks addressed in the early Victorian literature were those of subsidence, damp, weed and worm penetration, and discomfort to the foot in walking.

Foundations

How deep should one dig in laying foundations for a path? The pre-19th century literature is not very helpful; John Rea's instructions for gravelling in the 1660s are to 'lay it something thick, and beat down every course, the worser in the bottom, and fine screened gravel on the top'.[8] Philip Miller, in 1731, offered more detailed instructions: 'the Bottom of them be fill'd with some Lime-rubbish or coarse Gravel, Flint-stones, or other rocky Stuff . . . this Bottom should be laid eight or ten Inches thick, over which the Coat of Gravel should be six or eight'.[9] Such deep foundations continued into the early 19th century. A writer in Loudon's *Gardener's Magazine* recommended using broad-

surfaced stones as a foundation, by analogy with the ancient Roman practice of paving on a bed of masonry.[10]

But a certain suspicion of deeply dug paths gradually transpired through the press. Loudon recommended that woodland walks be made on the surface, without digging, in order to be less conspicuously damaged by underground root action.[11] And then in 1850, Henry Bailey boldly asserted in the *Gardeners' Chronicle* that 4 inches of hard materials were sufficient. A few months later Donald Beaton, head gardener at Shrubland Park, Suffolk, addressed the question in his column in the *Cottage Gardener*, beginning, 'I am he who, some eight years ago, was put to my wits' end about making walks'. Charles Barry was beginning his alterations at Shrubland Park, and, observing his practice, Beaton concluded

> that a road five inches deep, *properly made*, will carry ten tons any day in the year, without in the smallest degree injuring the foundation . . . I have fixed on six inches as the maximum depth of a carriage-road on the worst kind of bottom, and four inches for that of a walk over such bottom, and from two to three inches for the best kitchen-garden walks.[12]

Before long, the landscape gardener Robert Glendinning confirmed Beaton's thoughts in the Horticultural Society's *Journal*:

> Walks for ordinary purposes do not, as some imagine, require a great depth of bottom beneath the fine gravel which constitutes the finish; 9 inches in most cases will be found ample. This foundation has been mistaken by many for drainage, but no such thing is meant, as the surface of the walk when finished ought to carry the rain to the sides; as little as possible should be absorbed by the gravel, because where there is great traffic, in a short time the walks would become a complete puddle.[13]

Bailey, likewise, thought that deeply dug walks acted as reservoirs for drainage water: 'the greatest evil which can happen, by the constant saturation

Figure 2: Different construction techniques, from John Claudius Loudon's *An Encyclopaedia of Gardening* (1834), 641.

of its foundation'. (Bailey's solution was to raise the edges of the walk above the adjoining surface.)

By the 20th century recommended depths for path foundations had increased, but not to their 18th-century level. Madeline Agar, in 1911, was recommending 9 inches, two-thirds to consist of hardcore and the rest of gravel or other surfacing material; W. W. Pettigrew, the influential parks superintendent for Manchester, suggested excavating 8-9 inches for paths intended for foot traffic, and 10-12 inches for carriageways. Clinker and boiler ashes formed his preferred foundation for paths, but stone or brick if vehicular traffic was involved. Richard Sudell recommended a similar treatment for grass paths: a layer of clinker or ash over which the soil would be replaced and rolled.[14]

Loudon had a drainage system laid along the lower sides of the walks in the pioneering public garden he designed at Gravesend, Kent: 'Nothing conduces more to the comfort of a public garden than having the walks at all times fine and dry; and, where these walks are 10 ft. broad . . . such a result cannot be accomplished satisfactorily without a drain along the bottom of each walk, with gratings at the sides of the walk, communicating with the drain at regular distances'.[15] When, three years later, he was laying out the Derby Arboretum (which he boasted contained 'nearly a mile of drains, and . . . 150 cast-iron gratings'), he laid out the drainage line along the centre of the walks, with cross drains feeding into it from path-side gullies.[16]

This system remained standard thereafter, though the materials used for the conduits varied from Loudon's tiles to Doulton's glazed ceramic pipes to brick barrel drains. Pettigrew reverted to Loudon's original practice of placing his land drain pipes alongside the paths rather than directly underneath, so as to reduce disruption if they needed to be dug up for repair.[17] Most discussions of drainage gullies recommended rectilinear subterranean traps with surface gratings and pipes leading to the major drains; 7-inch gratings were recommended for footpaths by both H. E. Milner and Pettigrew, with 9- or 10-inch gratings for carriage drives, and the latter suggested a distance of 30 feet between them.[18] The importance of such gullies is made apparent by the fate of carriage drives in some early cemeteries, which in the 20th century have been narrowed to accommodate additional rows of graves: the original path-side gullies become silted up in the course of adding the new rows, and, deprived of adequate drainage, the narrower drives become quagmires in the winter.

Convexity

Rea, in the 1660s, advised the gardener to 'leave the Walks a little round in the middle'; Miller preferred level paths, and cautioned that too great a degree of convexity hampered walking and made the path seem narrower than it was. In the following century, Bailey advised against convexity: the crown of the path should not be higher than its margins. George Glendinning

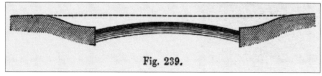

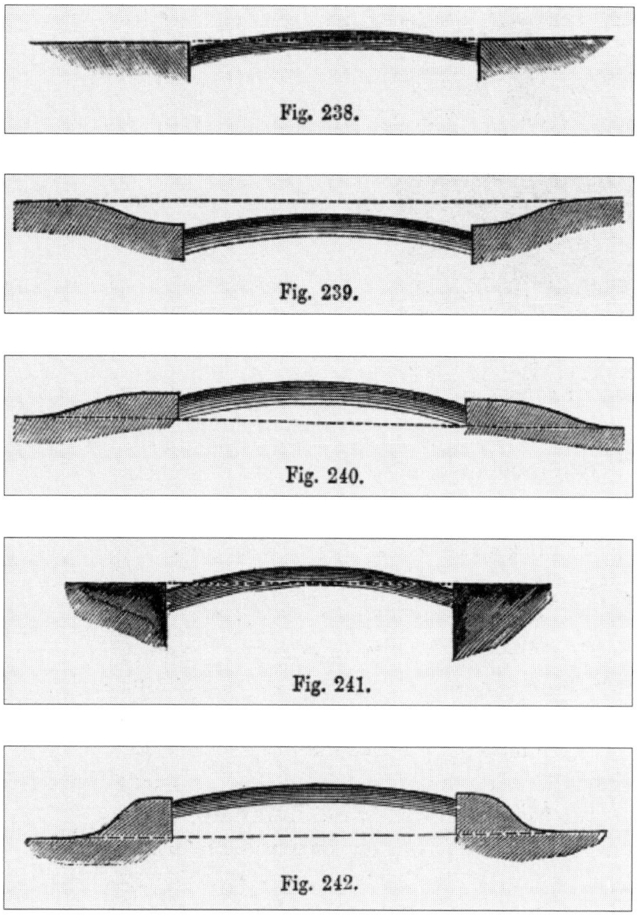

Fig. 238.

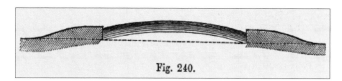

Fig. 239.

Fig. 240.

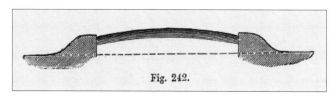

Fig. 241.

Fig. 242.

Figure 3: Illustrations from Kemp's *How to Lay Out a Garden* (London, 1864), advising different path profiles for different purposes: fig. 239, for example, is for serpentine walks; while fig. 242 is for damp ground.

agreed that 'Perfectly level walks, like the floors of a house, are not only more agreeable to walk on, but they are also strictly in conformity with good taste in geometrical gardening . . . the only plea that can justify a deviation from this rule is, that our garden walks are exposed to the atmosphere, while the floors of our houses are protected'. His experience in the Horticultural Society's garden at Chiswick, where he designed a new arboretum, taught him that walks retained water unless they were to some degree convex, a fact 'notoriously exemplified in the Society's Garden on wet exhibition days previous to their being altered'. Thomas Rutger avoided convexity in kitchen-garden walks by recommending that the soil on either side of the path should be kept an inch lower than the path surface.[19]

In 1857, reviewing the new Battersea Park, the *Gardeners' Chronicle* reporter limited himself to faint praise for the walks: 'their convexity is not so great as to render them inconvenient to walk on, and they are tolerably dry and firm under the foot'.[20] Precise degrees of convexity tend not to be cited until the 20th century. During the 1930s, Sudell recommended a 2-inch camber for an 8-foot-wide drive, and Pettigrew a camber of one part in 50 or 60.[21]

Gravel

While Miller discussed the making of grass walks, he suggested no alternatives to gravel as a material for surfacing. 'The best Gravel for *Walks* is such as abounds with smooth Pebbles (as is that dug at *Black-heath*), which being mix'd with a due Proportion of Loam, will bind like a Rock, and is never injur'd by wet or dry Weather . . .'. (Bailey would have been scornful of such optimism: 'the action of the atmosphere, alternate frosts and rain, will in time decompose the surface, in the same manner as it decomposes the hardest rocks'.) Miller recommended that gravel walks be given 'three or four Water-rollings; that is, they must be rolled when it rains so very fast, that the *Walks* swim with Water; this will cause the Gravel to bind . . .'. The importance of avoiding loose gravel remained a constant theme in the literature. Loudon criticized excessive sweeping or raking of

Figure 4 (left): Screened gravel from the New Forest at Chiswick House, London; (right): un-screened, 'raised ballast' Thames gravel at Clissold Park, London. (Photos: Jan Woudstra)

gravel walks: 'The gravel of a walk or road should, if possible, never be disturbed; because doing so not only interferes with its usefulness, that is, its smoothness and dryness as a walk, but [also] conveys the idea of its being lately made, and consequently unsettled'. When raked, the walk should be rolled immediately 'so as to convey the idea of finish, stability, and perfection'.[22]

In 1833, Robert Marnock published an important article, 'On the making and formation of gravel walks', in which he recommended the following procedure for establishing the surface layer of gravel:

> To prevent as much as possible the gravel running down and mixing with the substratum, the first barrow-load being spread, the second is put down on the top of the first, the third on the top of the second, and so on till the whole is finished. In spreading the gravel, it is carefully pushed forward, in a considerable body, with the head of a wooden rake — teeth turned upwards. The gravel being all on, and neatly levelled and raked with a short-toothed wooden rake, to bring the pebbles to the top, the latter ought to be equally distributed over every part of the walk. Two or three boys, when they are well looked after, will do a good deal of this kind of work in a day . . .

Marnock added to the evils of loose gravel 'the horror' that it raised in the minds of those who happen to have 'such things as corns on their feet'.[23] Miller was fortunate in having access to Blackheath gravel; good gravel was not uniformly distributed around the country. 'The want of good gravel in this part of the country is a considerable drawback from the beauty of garden scenery' wrote Marnock from West Yorkshire, where 'every residence having any pretensions to distinction' had to import Kensington gravel; at Bretton Hall, where Marnock was gardener, 'crushed bricks, or the *debris* of brick or tile kilns, are employed as substitutes for gravel in the kitchen-garden'.[24] Coastal areas tended to have ready access to sea gravel, and to shells, which were sometimes recommended as a top-dressing.[25] Some of the older gravels are now obscure in their significance: according to Rea, 'the Cat-brained binding gravel is the best'.

The major walks in the central royal parks in London had been gravelled since the 18th century at least, and gravel remained, through the first decades of municipal park-making, the preferred surface for paths. Loudon preferred brownish yellow as the best colour for gravel; Kemp, a reddish yellow: 'Whitish gravels are usually too conspicuous and cold-looking'; Nathan Cole, in the 1870s, praised the bright yellow gravel of St James's Park.[26] The preference for gravel

81

continued well into the present century; Sudell in the 1930s still thought it the best surface, though he was prepared to spray the completed surface with 'a mixture of tar and pitch' to bind it — in the process allowing for a variety of colour treatments.[27]

Alternatives to gravel

Suggestions for alternatives to gravel as a top-dressing were numerous, cast in both functional and aesthetic terms; but as it is uncertain how many of these alternatives were put into practice in municipal parks, they shall be enumerated here only briefly. Derbyshire spar, broken cockle-shells and gas-lime mixtures were recommended to give a more decorative effect than simple gravel;[28] wood blocks were promoted for road-making from 1832, but were used more in Russia and America than in England;[29] a patent for paving blocks made of India-rubber and charred sawdust was taken out in 1841;[30] and a range of *ad hoc* substitutes for gravel included, by the 1850s, coal-ashes, road sand, saw-dust, pebbles in clay, 'shells, coals, pounded brick-bats, stones, or slates, soapboilers' waste, burned clay, when reduced to powder, etc.'.[31] Brick and flagstones, however long the tradition of using them near the house, met with little enthusiasm during the 19th century, until their revival by the Arts and Crafts Movement.[32]

Asphalt and tarmacadam

Asphalt deposits in France had long been exploited for medicinal purposes before the idea of using it as a surfacing material was conceived. In 1827 the Société Eyquem began using asphalt from the Seyssel deposits for paving; an early English reference describes it as sidewalks 'consist[ing] of a fine gravel, cemented into a solid mass by asphaltum', and appearing 'like an unbroken surface, a pavement without seams'. Seyssel asphalte was introduced into England in 1837 by George Claridge, who used it over the next couple of years for the roofing of catacombs at Norwood and Highgate Cemeteries, and for road surfaces in London and Manchester.[33]

While valuations of its drying capacity varied, it was enthusiastically acclaimed for its weed-suppressing capacity, and gardens like those at Belvoir Castle began to introduce asphalt paths.[34] Various home-made alternatives to imported Seyssel asphalt were suggested, using coal- and gas-tar, which had come into use as a surface dressing for macadamized roads in the 1830s; one useful recipe proposed using dried road sand and finely sifted cinder ashes in a 2:1 mix, stirred into boiling coal-tar.[35]

By 1842 the Horticultural Society had had an asphalt floor installed in a greenhouse range at Chiswick, and in 1852 it conducted a trial of asphalt and Portland cement walks:

> 1. Portland cement 1$^{1/2}$ inch thick, laid on concrete 3 inches thick, very good. 2. Portland cement and smiths' ashes 1$^{1/2}$ inch thick, on concrete 3 inches thick, grey in colour and very satisfactory. 3. Asphalte composed of three parts sand and one part ashes, made quite thick with hot gas-tar, laid on the old walk 3 inches thick, very good. 4. Asphalte composed of hot gas-tar and sand, only 3 inches thick, not quite so good. 5. Asphalte composed of cold gas-tar, sand, and ashes 3 inches thick, not so good as no. 4. 6. Hot gas-tar spread over the old walk, sifted over with sand and well rolled; no weeds have grown on this, but by rights it should have had another dressing the following year. 7. This was done in a similar way, with cold gas-tar, but it is not so good. 8. Road-sand and cinders. The last is very bad and full of moss; but no weeds have grown on any of the others.[36]

After the initial excitement, however, the articles on asphalt walks faded away from the literature; asphalt remained in use, but there seemed to be little more to say about it.

The references to gas-tar in the quotation indicate the emergence of what would become known in the 1880s as tarmacadam (one form of which would be trademarked in 1903 as Tarmac). Experiments with pitch, bitumen and gas-tar as bonding agents for road and path surfaces began in the 1830s; J. H. Cassell took out a patent in 1834 for the use of tar as a surface dressing for paths;

Figure 1: In Boston, Massachusetts, parks have attracted State and Federal funding for regeneration work; here is an aerial view of Boston Common and Public Garden; the initial section of the 'Emerald Necklace', the chain of parks to the Boston town centre (photo: Jan Woudstra)

Figure 2: The quality of greenspace and the use of public parks on the Continent has been an inspiration for the current revival of interest in the UK, such as this example at Jardin du Luxembourg, Paris (photo: Jan Woudstra)

Figure 3: Municipal Gardens, Southport, in 1907. In the 19th and early 20th centuries many parks put on special events that attracted huge numbers (postcard from the collection of Fiona Jamieson

Figure 4: 'We are enjoying the rest and quiet at Felton', Northumberland (1909) (postcard from the collection of Fiona Jamieson

Figure 5: A restoration masterplan for Heaton Park, Manchester (1999), which has been supported with financial assistance by the Heritage Lottery Fund, and which is now underway (photo: Land Use Consultants)

Figure 6: The revival of interest in public parks has been underway for some years now; in many cases this has commenced with providing new functions for existing venues. Existing buildings have been converted to cafés, such as this example at Clissold Park, London (photo: Jan Woudstra)

Figure 7: The Royal Parks, London, have always been in a privileged position in that they have benefited from sustained funding. In the 1960s some excellent tea pavilions were built, such as this beautifully sited one at the end of the Serpentine, Hyde Park, designed by Patrick Gwynne in 1965 (photo: Jan Woudstra)

Figures 8, 9, 10, 11: Some people come and admire the planting specifically, such as these visitors in the rosary of Queen Mary's Garden, Regents Park, London (right). To others the use of a park is about an organized event, such as a game of football (Clissold Park), a marathon (Regent's Park), or riding a horse (Hyde Park). There is always a temptation to claim areas for one specific use only, instead of integrating the different uses in the overall design. No single use, however, should become dominant at the expense of others (photos: Jan Woudstra)

V

VI

Figure 12: Public parks can be the venue for local or regional events, which help to provide a *raison d'être*, such as launching a hot air balloon in Bournemouth Centre Gardens (photo: Alan Barber)

Figures 13 and 14: It is important that park facilities are safe, well maintained and clean, such as these examples of a tennis court in Clissold Park, London (above), or a playground in Pavilion Gardens, Buxton (below). These particular facilities are not however very attractive, but when funding becomes available their design quality can be upgraded. Any improvements like these must be carried out according to an overall masterplan, and not at an *ad hoc* manner (photos: Jan Woudstra)

Figure 15: Small mobile stalls may provide an alternative to tea pavilions and may be brought in for special events, such as this example in St James's Park, London (photo: Jan Woudstra)

Figure 16: In many public parks dog walkers are the most frequent users, which sometimes causes conflicts with other user groups. It may be possible to introduce dog-free zones to accommodate the various interests (Preston Park, Brighton) (photo: Virginia Hinze)

Figure 5: Paving at Iwerne Minster —
possibly a survival of Pulham paving.
(Photo: the author)

the first tarred footpaths were constructed in Cheltenham. Cassell was followed in 1838 by Alexandre Happey, who patented a process for mixing gas-tar with heated gravel as a surface for vehicular roads. (It should not be assumed that there was a close resemblance between these early products and the modern forms of tarmacadam, which were developed from the Edwardian period — especially by John Brodie in Liverpool — to create dustless roads after the advent of the automobile.) Tarring, however, never attracted the publicity that asphalt did in the gardening press.[37]

During the second half of the 19th century asphalt and tarmacadam were increasingly used in municipal parks for carriage drives and smaller paths. By the 1870s the steam-roller had come into use for compacting tarmacadam: 'This sublime leveller adds the weight of years to a macadamized road with once asking'.[38] J. J. Sexby's survey of the London parks at the end of the century reveals asphalt and tarmacadam to be the preferred materials for walks bearing vehicles or heavy foot traffic, while gravel continued to be used for secluded areas such as the walled garden in Brockwell Park.[39] The introduction of Tarmac and its rival forms of tarring to create dustless roads in the early 20th century were not noticed in the gardening press, but they spread wherever the automobile did. Indeed, it is not always possible to

distinguish asphalt from tarmacadam in the published literature. In the interwar years the word 'blacktop' arose in America to cover both processes, and in recent decades this term has started to become used in Britain.

Concrete

'Concreting a path', for the mid-Victorian gardener, meant simply introducing binding materials into gravel to get a firm surface. But concrete as an alternative to gravel was experimented with sporadically in the 19th century. Recommended mixtures at mid-century were beginning to reduce the proportion of lime, by comparison with later Victorian mixtures (possibly reflecting the continued dominance of Roman cement as a model; Portland cement, much experimented with in the first half of the century, was just only becoming widespread). A mixture (for making drainage tiles) cited in the *Gardeners' Chronicle* in 1844 consisted of two parts lime to one part blackened cinders, eight parts sand, and four parts fine gravel.[40]

Pulham and Son, best known for their artificial stone rock gardens, turned their cement mix to other purposes; a visitor to Iwerne Minster, Dorset, reported in 1881 on the walks:

the walks — such walks too! — by

84

Figure 6: 1930s advertisements for Cold Chon (left), a cold-rolled ashphalt treatment, and Colas (right). (From the Royal Horticultural Society, Lindley Library)

Pulham of Broxbourne — made of gravel and Portland cement, with a colouring of brickdust to give them tone. Neither frost, snow, hail or rain makes the slightest impression upon these walks as they are always dry, comfortable, and pleasant to walk upon, and requiring no labour to keep them when once they are made. Other walks . . . were like mud after the severe frost of last winter, while not a stone was deranged upon those made by Messrs. Pulham, so well is their work done, and so good is the material used.[41]

Whether they used the same path material in their public park commissions is not known.

The enthusiasts of the Arts and Crafts Movement frequently saw concrete as a traditional material — simply a variant on cob, impacted earths and other vernacular materials they were investigating. Sudell, in the 1930s, was lukewarm about concrete paths, though objecting specifically only to the colour.[42] In the mid-20th century, in large part as the result of its use by Le Corbusier and others, concrete came to represent an aspiration best expressed in the title of Peter Collins's *Concrete: The Vision of a New Architecture* (London: Faber & Faber, 1959), and attitudes to its use began to change in the landscaping profession; by the last quarter of the century the term 'hard landscaping' had come into existence, in large part as a response to the new emphasis being given to concrete surfaces.

Aggregates and new materials

Pulham & Son was not the only firm dealing in artificial stone, nor the only such firm which turned its attention to path-surfacing materials. As early as 1829, Loudon drew attention to the artificial stone of Messrs Ranger of Birmingham, and in the 1830s Cassell was propagandizing the use of what he called 'lava' as an artificial stone for paving.[43]

The Derbyshire brick-making firm of Butterleys began making concrete blocks for paving in the 1850s, but it was in the wake of the Arts and Crafts Movement, and the revival of cob, chalk and other vernacular building materials that the popularity of concrete paving took off. The En Tout Cas Company, famous for surfacing tennis courts and sports pitches, made a successful use of 'no fines' concrete (cement, shingle and water, excluding sandy aggregates); Solomon Marshall's Halifax-based firm started making hydraulically compressed York stone flags in 1937. In the postwar years, as the cost of natural stone paving increased, resemblance to traditional paving became a selling point for firms like the Atlas Stone Company, whose sand-ballast-and-Portland-cement products were promoted in the 1970s for creating a 'Tudor courtyard appearance'. A wide range of aggregate paving styles became available after the war, among them Bradstone (E. H. Bradley), of oolitic limestone and cement; Charcon's Derbyshire paving, of limestone aggregate; Redland's Kentstone paving, a sand and cement mixture that produced a genuinely non-slip surface; and the BG paving units of Mono Concrete Ltd (who later amalgamated with Marshalls), block paving with a pattern of interstitial apertures for soil and grass.[44] The use, quantity or quality of these materials in urban parks does not appear to have been surveyed.

85

Post-war paving products

Atlas Stone Company — 'Hortex', of washed sand, graded ballast and Portland cement; best cut mechanically

E. H. Bradley Building Products — Bradstone, of oolitic limestone and cement; scratchable

British Dredging Concrete Products — Un-Block

Charcon Products — Derbyshire paving: 'the surface takes on the texture of the linen or paper obviously used in its manufacture' — of Derbyshire limestone aggregate

Ibstock Building Products — bricks of West Midland etruria marl

Marley — Marlstone — 'harsh, unsubtle colours in Colourstone'

S. Marshall & Sons — reconstituted York stone

A. &. J Mucklow — Wenlock range

Mono Concrete — Monolok block paving, tried at Wisley — a long-established firm

Noelite — Vista paving — good for hand cutting, but of a porous texture

Redland Kentstone Garden Products — Kentstone paving: sand and cement mixture with biscuity texture — a genuinely non-slip slab

Sevenoaks Brick Works — coloured pebble aggregates

86

Notes

1. This and all subsequent quotations from Bailey are from *Gardeners' Chronicle* (1850), 148.

2. *Gardeners' Chronicle* (1847), 603 (Birkenhead); (1854), 470 (Kennington).

3. Edward Kemp, *How to Lay Out a Garden*, 3rd edn (London: Bradbury & Evans, 1860), 146–9, 380-6; John Arthur Hughes, *Garden Architecture and Landscape Gardening* (London: Longmans, Green & Co., 1866), 18–26; H. E. Milner, *The Art and Practice of Landscape Gardening* (London: Simpkin, Marshall, 1890), 9–14, 38–9; Thomas Mawson, *The Art and Craft of Garden Making* (London: B. T. Batsford, 1900); Madeline Agar, *Garden Design in Theory and Practice* (London: Sidgwick & Jackson, 1911), 113–31; Viscountess Wolseley, *Gardens: Their Form and Design* (London: Edward Arnold, 1919), 1–11; Richard Sudell, *Landscape Gardening: Planning, Construction, Planting* (London: Ward, Lock & Co., 1933), 101–24; W. W. Pettigrew, *Municipal Parks: Layout, Management and Administration* (London: Journal of Park Administration, 1937), 31–8.

4. John Claudius Loudon, *An Encyclopaedia of Gardening* (London: Longman, Hurst, Rees, Orme and Brown, 1822), 1237–8.

5. John Claudius Loudon, *Gardener's Magazine*, 8 (1832), 86–7, citing *An Encyclopaedia*, 2nd edn, §7243.

6. John Claudius Loudon, *The Derby Arboretum* (London: Longman, Orme, Brown, Green & Longmans, 1840), 73.

7. 'Amateur landscape gardener', 'On forming the directions of pleasure-ground walks, &c.', *Floricultural Cabinet*, 12 (1842), 256–60.

8. John Rea, *Flora, seu de florum cultura* (1665), 5. All subsequent quotations from Rea are from this source.

9. Philip Miller, *The Gardeners' Dictionary* (1731), *s.v.* 'Walks'. All subsequent quotations from Miller are from this source.

10. *Gardener's Magazine*, 5 (1829), 79.

11. Ibid., 7 (1831), 545–6.

12. *Cottage Gardener*, 5 (1850–51), 190–1, 212–13, 225–7. All subsequent quotations from Beaton, unless otherwise specified, are from this source.

13. *Journal of the Horticultural Society*, 7 (1852), 201–5. All subsequent quotations from Glendinning are from this source.

14. Agar, *Garden Design in Theory and Practice*, 122; Pettigrew, *Municipal Parks*, 33, 36; Sudell, *Landscape Gardening*, 112–14.

15. John Claudius Loudon, 'Design for a public garden, made for an English corporate town', *Gardener's Magazine*, 12 (1836), 13–26 (esp. 16).

16. Loudon, *Derby Arboretum*, 74.

17. John Claudius Loudon, *The Suburban Gardener* (London, 1838), 174–6; Pettigrew, *Municipal Parks*, 33–5. Milner, *Art and Practice of Landscape Gardening*, 38–9, also tolerates drainage conduits beside paths, so perhaps experience of path disruption was accumulating by the end of the century. The present author has not seen a good discussion of brick barrel drains, but he has experience of a substantial storm drain of this sort on a steeply sloping site in Highgate Cemetery, London; the barrel and access shafts had been smoothly concreted internally, probably when the drainage system was refurbished in 1920.

18. Milner, *Art and Practice of Landscape Gardening*, 38–9; Pettigrew, *Municipal Parks*, 33–5.

19. *Gardener's Magazine*, 11 (1835), 434–5.

20. *Gardeners' Chronicle* (1857), 805.

21. Sudell, *Landscape Gardening*, 105; Pettigrew, *Municipal parks*, 36.

22. *Gardener's Magazine*, 7 (1831), 545–6.

23. *Gardener's and Forester's Record*, 1 (1833), 193–7; repr. in *Floricultural Cabinet*, 2 (1834), 125–9.

24. *Gardener's Magazine*, 5 (1829), 683.

25. For example, *Gardener's Magazine*, 7 (1831), 21–2.

26. Loudon, *Derby Arboretum*, 74; Kemp, *How to Lay Out a Garden*, 383; Nathan Cole, *The Royal Parks and Gardens of London* (London: Journal of Horticulture, 1877), 25–6, also 8 and 21 for comments on gravel in Kensington Gardens and Hyde Park. *Gardeners' Chronicle* (1874), ii, 456, has extracts from Lord Palmerston's correspondence with Benjamin Hall on the propriety of the public walking on the grass in the royal parks: 'You seem to think [grass] a thing to be looked at by people who are to be confined to the gravel walks. I regard it as a thing to be walked upon freely and without restraint by the people, old and young, for whose enjoyment the parks are maintained . . . As to people making paths across the grass, what does that signify?'

27. Sudell, *Landscape Gardening*, 105–6, 111–12.

28. *Cottage Gardener*, 10 (1853), 444–5; ibid., 15 (1855), 56–7; G. B. N., 'Remarks on the formation, &c., of gravel walks', *Floricultural Cabinet*, 21 (1853), 205–6.

29. *Gardener's Magazine*, 17 (1841), 282; *Gardeners' Chronicle* (1841), 71; (1842), 523–4; (1843), 315, 358, 738; Frank J. Scott, *The Art of Beautifying Suburban Home Grounds* (New York: D. Appleton & Co., 1870), 90.

30. *Gardener's Magazine*, 17 (1841), 638.

31. Ibid., 12 (1836), 181–2; *Floricultural Cabinet*, 27 (1859), 244–5; also *Floricultural Magazine*, 2 (1837), 198-200.

32. *Gardener's Magazine*, 11 (1835), 291–3; also ibid., 15 (1839), 448–9. Brick and flagstone paths were more successful in America during this period; for the revival of brick, see Sudell, *Landscape Gardening*, 115–17.

33. *The Builder*, 4 (1846), 347, etc. *Gardener's Magazine*, 15 (1839), 188–9. The latter cites the date of introduction of 'asphaltic pavement' as 1825, but this is probably a mistake for 1827. The Norwood asphalt surface was destroyed during the Second World War; so the surface of the terrace catacombs at Highgate is now the oldest continuously asphalted surface in this country. For the early history of asphalt, see P. E. Spielmann and A. C. Hughes, *Asphalt Roads* (London: Edward Arnold, 1936).

34. *The Builder*, 4 (1846), 214; *Gardeners' Chronicle* (1847), 308; (1848), 102, 720, 734; (1851), 501, 659.

35. *Gardeners' Chronicle* (1844), 245; (1847), 308 (a reply to a correspondent — later offered, with considerable verbal similarity, by a correspondent in 1848), 102.

36. *Gardeners' Chronicle* (1852), 486–7.

37. For the beginnings of tarmacadam, see A. C. Hughes, *Tar Roads* (London: Edward Arnold, 1938).

38. *Gardeners' Chronicle* (1872), 1420 (on Alexandra Park, Manchester).

39. J. J. Sexby, *The Municipal Parks, Gardens, and Open Spaces of London* (London: Elliot Stock, 1898), 73–5 (Brockwell Park: cf. the gravel path in the old walled garden with the asphalt around the bandstand), 192 (Southwark Park), 265–70 (Victoria Embankment Gardens). Also Pettigrew, *Municipal Parks*, 36; and Agar, *Garden Design in Theory and Practice*, 123–4.

40. *Gardeners' Chronicle* (1844), 14.

41. *Gardeners' Chronicle*, (1881), ii, 471. For material on Pulham & Son, see Brent Elliott, *Victorian Gardens* (London: B. T. Batsford, 1986); A. J. Francis, *The Cement Industry* (1977); and the various articles by Sally Festing in *Garden History*.

42. Sudell, *Landscape Gardening*, 117. For an Arts and Crafts' approach to vernacular materials, see Clough Williams-Ellis, *Cottage Building in Cob, Pisé, Chalk and Clay* (London: Country Life, 1919); and see E. S. Prior's Home Place, Holt, Norfolk, for the same sort of concrete effects praised a half-century later as ultramodern when they were carried out in the Hayward Gallery, London.

43. *Gardener's Magazine*, 5 (1829), 82; ibid., 11 (1835), 435 (notes on J. H. Cassell, *Treatise on Roads and Streets*).

Figure 7: Modern path surfaces with clear polyurethane and epoxy binders provide a good clean finish, and while this may be expensive initially, the limited maintenance requirement enables the initial investment to be recouped. Despite these benefits there are long term mainte-nance implications, which can readily be demonstrated when the material is newly laid — as in this instance, where a contractor has been unable to match two batches (Pavilion Gardens, Buxton). If a specialist contractor is unable to match an earlier batch, it is likely that future patch repairs will be beyond the capabilities of most local authorities. (Photo: Jan Woudstra)

44. Some useful surveys and company histories from *GC&HTJ*: (6 January 1978), 28–29 (En Tout Cas); (23 June 1978), 26–9 (survey of pavers); (4 August 1978), 39–41 (S. Marshall & Sons); (16 March 1979), 29–31 (Bradstone); (24 August 1979), 13–15 (Marshalls), 35–7; (27 March 1981), 19–21 (concrete block paving); (19 February 1982, 43–5 (marketing concrete); (22 August 1986), 6 (Interpave competition); (31 October 1986), 26–7 (Peterborough paving); (23 May 1986 suppl.), 4–12 (survey); (22 May 1987 suppl.), 4–11 (survey); (17 April 1987), 24–29; (24 April 1987), 22–4. For the development of options in paving, cf. Elisabeth Beazley, *Design and Detail of the Space Between Buildings* (London: Architectural Press, 1960); and Adrian Lisney and Ken Fieldhouse, *Landscape Design Guide*, vol. ii: *Hard Landscape* (Aldershot: Gower Technical, 1990), and note the arrival of the term 'hard landscaping' between these two publications.

Shrubbery planting (1830–1900)

by Kim Legate

Figure 1: Lithograph of Baxter Park, Dundee, shortly after its opening in 1863. A rare close up of the 19th-century shrubbery (foreground) provides good indications of line, form and general character within a typically naturalistic planting scheme. As was the custom where there was insufficient space on the lawn, the planting framework of specimen trees and shrubs in this section of the park was being maintained in the beds, amid groups of low-growing shrubs.
(Illustration: Dundee City Council)

The aim of this chapter is to survey the evidence of planting in 19th century public parks with a view to elucidating the design treatment accorded the shrubberies that decorated these formative open spaces. The 'evidence', although somewhat lacking in terms of archival depth or on-site indications — but for the ephemeral nature of the landscape art — is nonetheless substantial. There is, for example, an abundance of data attesting to the wide range of trees and shrubs employed by park designers. Nursery invoices are extant for

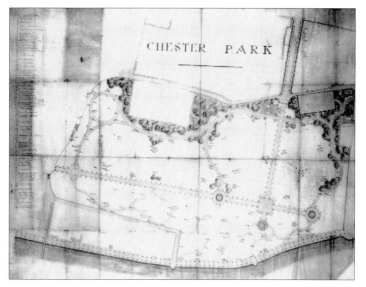

Figure 2: Edward Kemp's planting plan for the lawns of Grosvenor Park, Chester (1867), with its selection of 'choice' ornamental trees and shrubs shows specimen planting in practice: showy flowering shrubs (azalea, barberry, crataegus, rhododendron, arbutus); trees and shrubs of unusual form (rowan, weeping willow, weeping elm, Irish yew); foliage plants (purple beech, bronze-leaved holly, Waterer's dwarf golden holly, variegated narrow-leafed buckthorn); and conifers (Monkey Puzzle, Siberian arbor vitae, Wellingtonia, Deodar cedar, Lawson's cypress). (Illustration: Chester Records Office, Eaton Hall Collection)

various parks; 19th-century nursery catalogues are available from collections at the Lindley Library, London, and the British Library; and plant lists have been located in certain of the guidebooks published for the benefit of early park goers. Among the most exceptional of the last is the 1913 guide book for Aberdare Park, Rhondda Cynon Taff, an account of some 80 plants, arranged during the 1880s and 1890s by nurseryman and park designer William Barron. Two of the more extensive nursery invoices for the period include Grosvenor Park, Chester (Edward Kemp, 1867 — 150 plants) and East Park, Hull (1887 — 120 plants).

The question is how did 19th century park designers use this profusion of plant material to lay out their shrubberies? Illustrated representations (i.e. photographs, engravings, paintings, etc.) as provided by leading 19th century newspapers (*Illustrated London News*) and gardening magazines (*Gardeners' Chronicle*, 1841-; *Gardener's Magazine*, 1826-43; *Cottage Gardener*, 1848-60) seldom allow for precise interpretation, concentrating instead on distant views, park buildings and furnishings, or special events (figure 1). Detailed planting plans are scarce (although one noteworthy example, a Kemp planting plan for Grosvenor Park, pinpoints the precise location of specimen trees and shrubs)

(figure 2). Fortunately, early edition Ordnance Survey maps (from the 1850s) and surviving design plans are available for many parks, providing valuable clues about the original distribution of plants (figure 3). Additionally, there are descriptions of park shrubberies, as provided by the gardening press — usually following park openings — to draw upon. For example, a local newspaper account of the opening of the People's Park, Halifax[1] devoted an entire section to 'The Trees and Shrubs', describing 25 — occasionally with history, country of origin and location in the park — and identifying the supplier of the 'rarer plants' — Messrs Waterer and Godfrey of Bagshot, Surrey. The Halifax Guardian's cross-town rival, the Halifax Courier, provided a detailed description of the Park's boundary belts (figure 4).

But fully to appreciate how the shrubberies of the public park were laid out, it is necessary to consult instructions on the subject, as outlined in the major garden manuals of the day. Several of these were written by designers of public parks. All would likely have been available to the range of professionals involved in building parks during the 19th century (i.e. borough engineers, surveyors, gardeners). An indispensable starting point is the writings of John Claudius Loudon. The first major advocate of municipal parks (Birmingham Botanical

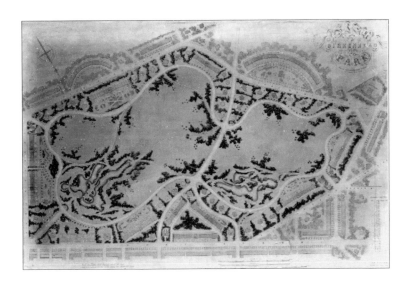

Figure 3: Joseph Paxton's plan of Birkenhead Park, c.1843. (Williamson Art Gallery)

91

Garden, 1831; Terrace Garden, Gravesend, Kent, 1835; the Derby Arboretum, 1840), Loudon kept many of Humphry Repton's ideas on the subject before the 19th century gardening audience in his *An Encyclopaedia of Gardening* (London, 1822) and *Gardener's Magazine*. The latter included Loudon's well-known article of 1835 'Remarks on laying out public gardens and promenades'; the former introduced what would become the most popular method for laying out shrubbery in the 19th century, i.e. the 'select or grouped manner of planting'. Loudon's ideas on park design were eventually reaffirmed in a host of 19th-century garden manuals. The most helpful here are *Theory and Practice of Landscape Gardening* (London, 1852) by the veteran landscape gardener Joshua Major (Philips Park and Queens Park, Manchester; Peel Park, Salford, all 1846); *Parks and Pleasure Grounds* (London, 1852) by Scottish landscape gardener Charles H. J. Smith; *How to Lay Out a Small Garden* (London, 1852) by a onetime pupil of Joseph Paxton, Edward Kemp (Grosvenor Park, Chester, 1867; Hesketh Park, Southport, 1868; Stanley Park, Liverpool, 1872); and *The Art and Practice of Landscape Gardening* (London, 1890) by Henry Ernest Milner, son of another Paxton protégé, Edward Milner (Moor Park, Preston, 1833; Avenham Park, Preston, 1847; Miller Park, Preston, 1864).

Apart from Loudon, the only 19th century writers explicitly to address the subject of public park design in their writings were Major, Smith and Milner. Each wrote a chapter on the subject, advancing the general view that park design must diverge from the design of private gardens on such points as the provision of ground for sports, the need for a more sophisticated circulation system and the requirement for a focal point to compensate for the absence of a mansion house. In the arrangement of trees and shrubs, however, park design was to imitate private gardens. For specific instructions, the reader was referred to sections on the design of same.[2]

Nineteenth-century shrubbery: purpose and organization

In the 1822 edition of *An Encyclopaedia of Gardening*, Loudon provides a good summary of the purposes of shrubbery. Principal among them was the provision of 'an agreeable walk' along a circuit ornamented with plants, whose beauty and interest would induce 'good humour' and 'serenity of mind'. Unlike its 18th-century predecessor the geometric wilderness, which had featured planting on both sides of the walk, the modern shrubbery was seen as having a more open structure, with planting occasionally restricted to one side only, to allow for 'air and ventilation, as well as views and

Figure 4: View of People's Park, Halifax, at the time of its opening, from *Illustrated London News* (22 August 1857), 188. *The Halifax Courier* (15 August 1857) described the park's western embankment (background) as being composed primarily of indigenous trees and 18th-century introductions from eastern North America. Newly developed hybrids, plus a dash of recent arrivals from western North America, Asia and the Continent, enlivened the undergrowth:

> This embankment has been covered with soil 2 to 3 feet deep, in which are planted many large trees, such as Ash, Beech, Elms and Sycamores . . . Among the choicer kinds of trees planted on these banks may be mentioned several plants of the Ailanthus glandulosa, Stag's horn Sumach, and others of the same family, the long divided leaves of which produce, with their warm autumnal tints, a pleasing contrast to those of more sombre hue. Purple Beech, and many varieties of Crataegus will be found here in groups, together with Chestnuts, Maples, Mountain Ash and others. Contrasting with double and single white thorns are masses of Lilacs and Laburnums, while the scarlet-flowering American Currant, Guelder Rose, Syringas and others of the same habit of growth are used as underwood. This embankment is also particularly rich in rhododendrons and Ghent Azaleas. Among the rhododendrons are many choice hybrid varieties of Catawbiense and Caucasicum from Messrs. Waterer and Godfrey's well-known collection, as well as several plants of Campanulatum . . . .

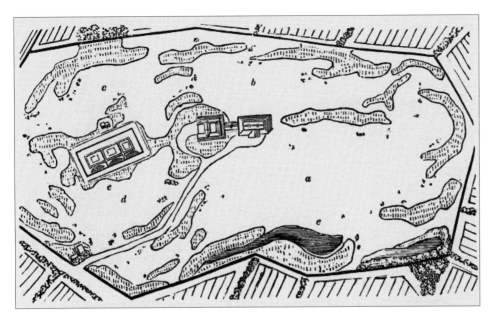

Figure 5: The spatial organization of the 'modern park' according to John Claudius Loudon: a gradation of groups and masses, interspersed with expanses of open spaces and glades of varying form and extent, from *An Encyclopaedia of Gardening* (London, 1834), 1126.

prospects'.[3] Utilitarian considerations were also important. Walter Nicol[4] and Major[5] stressed the need for 'comfort', both in terms of shelter (winter) and shade (summer), a reminder of Repton's insistence on 'convenience' over purely aesthetic concerns. With Loudon, they declared the shrubbery as a link between the house and the lawn (the pleasure ground) and as an essential screening device (i.e. service buildings, the kitchen garden), a function that referred back to the Georgian period, and the open situations of country houses like Woolton Hall, Lancashire, and Garrick's Villa, Hampton, Middlesex.

Loudon also used the occasion to outline the role of tree and shrub plantations in the spatial organization of the 'modern park' (figure 5). He envisaged a 'pasture surface' — his example involved a country residence — divided into discrete open spaces (i.e. 'broad masses which become wholes in their turn') by a framework of groups and masses, connected 'or better, only seemingly so when viewed horizontally' and planted in a gradation of sizes.[6] The largest or 'principal' mass was recommended for screening and channeling views from around the mansion, with progressively smaller plantations to radiate outwards from this to create glades, differing in form, extent — and of particular import to the

public park designer who was being pressured to include everything from archery to arboretums — character and function.[7] Major defined the correct sequence as follows: a mass ('upwards of twenty' trees), then a large group ('from ten to twenty'), then a group ('from two to ten') and finally single trees.[8] He also provided a concrete example of the progression in layouts for the Manchester parks, where the tree and shrub plantations were feathered out from the boundary belts to create a series of broad recesses for sports and games such as cricket, football, quoits and archery.

Smith elaborated on Loudon's hierarchical regime of plantations, specifying 'a few leading positions' for principal masses, namely the house or pleasure grounds, a hill or section of rising ground, and the boundary of the park.[9] (Lakesides were also a popular choice, as evidenced by layouts such as Birkenhead Park, Liverpool, Aberdare Park, and Peel Park, Bradford). With regard to boundary planting, Smith was joined by Kemp and Major in endorsing Loudon's reiteration of the current, but well-established, view that 'regard be had to exclude or admit the view of certain parts of distant scenery',[10] a notion that was later repeated in his *Gardener's Magazine* article.[11] In what became the accepted formula for arranging the structural planting of parks for the

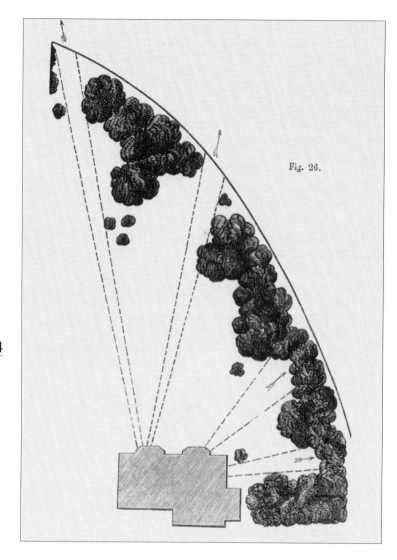

Fig. 26.

Figure 6: Varying the foreground to distant scenery, from Edward Kemp, *How to Lay Out a Garden* (London, 1864), 75. To frame distant views with a suitable amount of variety, Kemp instructed that lines be drawn from the best windows of the house (or, in the case of the public park, from a suitable substitute like a lake or pavilion) in the direction of the boundary. The groups and masses along some of the lines were then to be extended towards the house to create deep irregular bays or recesses (indicated by the arrows between the dotted lines). Suitable plants for the undergrowth of the boundary screen, according to Kemp and his contemporaries, were largely the stock evergreens (rhododendron, laurel, privet, yew, box, holly, etc.) with deciduous plants recommended for variety (dogwood, thorn, Norway maple, snowberries, lilacs, for example).[65] Trees comprised mostly deciduous forest trees of broad round-headed form (sycamore, oak, ash, beech, for example), with a 'sprinkling' of specimen trees, mostly of upright character (poplar, cedar, pine, cypress) also requisite[66] to vary the 'general smoothness of effect' that was, in Kemp's words, the ideal for the upper outline of the boundary screen.[67] (*The Halifax Guardian* compared the aerial line of the western boundary screen in the People's Park to Hogarth's line of beauty.)[68]

remainder of the century, Loudon recommended against placing large masses in the interior of the park, 'for the effect of these is to diminish the apparent space', advising instead that these be placed mainly around the perimeter, 'for the purpose of disguising that boundary or forming foregrounds to the scenery beyond'. This was confirmed by Kemp: 'It will be needful to separate the prospect into two, three, or more divisions . . . by the introduction of very irregular masses of trees and shrubs along or near a property's front boundary (figure 6).[12] Where, however, there were 'no views beyond the boundary, worthy of being taken into consideration'[13] — Loudon's assess-

ment at the Derby Arboretum, and a frequent conclusion later in the century when early 'fringe' parks were being enveloped by urban development — the rule was to plant the entire boundary with trees.

Nineteenth-century planting systems: the mixed and the grouped manners

At the beginning of the 19th century two systems of planting vied for supremacy in the arrangement of the ornamental shrubbery in England: the mixed or mingled manner, a system of alternating single species in parallel rows, and the grouped manner, a system of 'massing' plants. The former was still the most prevalent system — Loudon refers to it as the 'common' method in 1822 — having held sway from the mid-18th century, when writers such as James Meader (*The Planter's Guide*, 1779), Philip Miller (*The Gardeners Dictionary*, 1768) and Joseph Spence (*Observations, Anecdotes, and Characters of Books and Men*, 1820) lauded the merits of alternating species that varied in colour, texture and flowering-time . Its definitive attribute was regularity, imparted by effecting an even distribution of evergreens and deciduous shrubs, and the palette of colours within a quincunx pattern. The contrast between the stiff appearance of the mixed shrubbery and the irregularity of the picturesque variant of the grouped method, as later adopted in public parks, is jarring and would indeed seem strange to the modern observer.[14]

The grouped manner is mentioned as early as 1772 by William Chambers, subsequently drawing comment from Walter Nicol (*The Villa Garden Directory*, 1809) and then Loudon (*An Encyclopaedia of Gardening*, 1822). Loudon provides the best contemporary description of the system (figure 8):

> The Select or Grouped manner of planting a shrubbery is analogous to the select manner of planting a flower-garden. Here one genus, species, or even variety, is planted by itself in considerable numbers, so as to produce a powerful effect. Thus the pine tribe, as trees, may be alone planted in one part of the shrubbery, and holly, in its numerous varieties, as shrubs. After an extent of several yards, or hundred yards, have been occupied with these two genera, a third and fourth, say the evergreen fir tribe and the yew, may succeed, being gradually blended with them, and so on. A similar grouping is observed in the herbaceous plants inserted in the front of the plantation; and the arrangement of the whole, as to height, is the same as in the mingled shrubbery.[15]

By the Regency era the grouped manner was gaining in adherents, praised as a solution to the problem of displaying the increasing number of exotic plant species that were becoming available. Grouping reduced variety, avoiding the danger that the use of too many plants in one area would cause confusion, and, as Sir Henry Steuart expressed it, 'puzzle the spectator'.[16] This concern for reconciling the disproportionate abundance of plant material available with harmony of composition becomes increasingly evident as the century progresses. Repton writes that 'all variety is destroyed by the excess of variety'; John Dennis compares the effect of mixing shrubs to 'the arrangement of the draper's pattern-card;[17] Loudon censures the 'meaningless dotting' of specimen plants in Regent's Park and quotes Nicol on the merits of grouping: 'The method of mixing all kinds of shrubs indiscriminately, prevails too much in modern shrubberies. Much more distinctiveness may be given by judiciously grouping them, than by following the common methods of planting'.[18]

The first record of the use of the grouped manner in public parks is found in the writings of Prince Pückler Muskau (Figure 9). Visiting England in 1826, he documents John Nash's experiments with planting dense masses of shrubs at Regent's Park and St James's Park, but is critical of the lack of massing evident in the 'traditional' shrubberies such as at Chiswick.[19] By the onset of the early phase of the park movement in the 1840s, the grouped manner is being reaffirmed by the gardening press as the leading principle in the development of park scenery: 'Correct grouping is one of the first principles of landscaping' trumpeted Major; 'the key-note of the modern style' stated Charles M'Intosh in *The Book of the Garden* (1853-55); 'of the utmost importance' confirmed Smith.[20]

Picturesque shrubbery
NINETEENTH-CENTURY PLANTING STYLES: THE GARDENESQUE AND THE PICTURESQUE

The picturesque variant of the grouped manner of planting was in the ascendant by the 1820s. The decline of Uvedale Price's idealization of the picturesque aesthetic, as popularized from the

95

Figure 7: Example of the grouped manner of planting by John Claudius Loudon, *An Encyclopaedia of Gardening*, 1834, 1008 (opposite, top). 'To produce a powerful effect' Loudon envisaged a shrubbery composed of masses of evergreen and deciduous trees and shrubs, the whole to be fronted by herbaceous plants: 'Thus the pine tribe, as the trees, may be alone planted in one part of the shrubbery, and the holly, in its numerous varieties, as shrubs. After an extent of several hundred yards, or hundreds of yards, have been occupied with these two genera, a third and forth, say the evergreen fir tribe and the yew, may succeed being gradually blended with them and so on'[70]

Figure 8: A similar grouping is observed in the herbaceous plants inserted in the front of the plantation. The mingled manner, according to Loudon, *An Encyclopaedia of Gardening*, 1834, 1007 (opposite, bottom). The regularity of the system is its defining characteristic:

> To dispose shrubs and trees in a shrubbery plantation in the *mingled* manner proceed as under. The width of the space to be covered with trees, shrubs, and flowers being given, first mark it out in rows lengthways. The first row may be two feet from the margin of the turf or the edge of the walk; the second, three feet from the first; the third, four feet from the second; and so on to the back of the plantation. Suppose the width to admit of ten rows (a to k), then the six rows next the walk will occupy a space of twenty-seven feet, which may be devoted to shrubs, and the remaining three rows will occupy a space of thirty-seven feet, and may be planted with trees. Then the beginning with the first row, which is destined for the lowest class of shrubs, arrange them according to the times of flowering, which will, as in arranging herbaceous plants, be most conveniently done at six times: viz. 1, March; 2, April, Etc. to 6, August; and they will stand as in the flower-border in the order of 1, 6, 3, 5, 2, 4 and with the colours in the same manner.
>
> The second row (b) is to be arranged in the same manner, and as trees, though nearly of the same size when planted, yet attain finally very different degrees of bulk, provision must be made for the plants in each row to expand year after year, till they attain their full growth. This we propose to do by planting two plants of a sort in the second row (b), three in the third, and so on, till in the last or tenth row (k), there will be ten plants of a sort in a line together. It is observed, that a deciduous and an evergreen sort, (marked d, e, in the figure) are to be planted alternatively, in order to ensure an equal mixture in respect to verdure; and that the colors [denoted by r, w, b, y in the figure] are mixed as in a mingled border, to ensure a general display of mixed blossoms. The second or third year such of the plants are to be thinned out as crowd the others, reserving, however, as final plants, one of each sort, (say E for the Evergreens, and D for the deciduous sorts), so placed in respect to the plants in the other rows, as that the whole, when finally thinned out, may stand in quincunx. The largest tree will then occupy about 100 square feet each; and each of the shrubs in the front row about a square yard: there will be the same number of deciduous plants as evergreens; some shrubs of all the four colors in blow throughout the whole season, and a verdant aspect in summer as well as winter . . .
>
> The herbaceous plants only remain to be added. These are to be inserted one row in front of the first row of shrubs (a), and three or more rows (p, q, r, s) in the intervening spaces between the next rows. The plants are to form a quincunx with the shrubs; and the same arrangement as to height, color, and times of flowering, adopted in the mingled border.[71]

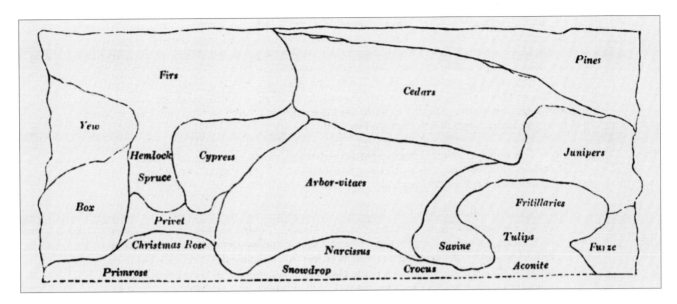

early 1800s in its raw, rugged, unashamedly wild form, was largely responsible for the development, surrendering as it did to the increasingly popular notion that gardens should display a predominantly artistic character. The change of taste was anticipated by the Neoplatonic arguments in Antoine-Chrysostome Quatremère de Quincy's *Essay on the Nature, the End and the Means of Imitation in the Fine Arts*, 1837. Quatremère maintained that gardens laid out in the irregular or picturesque style did not merit being called art because of their close resemblance to wild nature. In his words, 'what pretends to be an image of nature is nothing more nor less than nature herself'.[21]

In *Suburban Gardener and Villa Companion* (1838), Loudon responded to Quatremère's arguments by reaffirming Repton's fundamental principle, that 'Gardens are works of art rather than nature'. In a passage entitled 'The Rules which, in Landscape Gardening, may be derived from the Principle of the Recognition of Art', Loudon envisaged gardens made artistic by introduced plants, arranged according to picturesque principles. Irregularity of form, line and general composition remained fundamental to the aesthetic, but Loudon's 'Nature' eschewed the Pricean costume of moss-covered rocks and stunted trees for the dress and finish of the

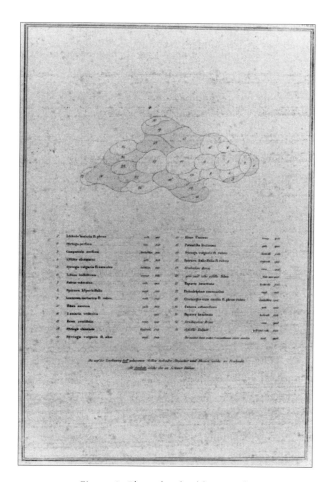

Figure 9: Plan of a shrubbery in the manner of
John Nash by Prince Pückler Muskau, from
Andeutungen über Landschaftsgärtnerei
(Stuttgart, 1826).

98

pleasure ground. For, in Loudon's words, 'polished curvatures and undulations, which shall be, either from the beauty of their form, or from their clothing of herbage, distinguishable at first sight from the natural surface of the ground by which the work of art, that is, the lawn, park, or pleasure ground, is surrounded'.[22]

Loudon had already proposed the concept of the 'gardenesque' as a means of displaying the recent influx of exotics from North America and the East. In the December 1832 issue of *Gardener's Magazine* he had used the term to describe a new style of planting design in which each individual plant was to be allowed to develop its natural form and habit as completely as possible, without the constraints of the 'picturesque' conditions so admired by painters.[23] The misshapen plants often produced in the wild by natural competition for light and space were to be replaced by trees and shrubs 'planted and managed in such a way as that each may arrive at perfection'.[24] Foreign instead of native plants ('exotics') were prescribed so that schemes would be instantly recognizable as art.

Contemporary design plans provide ample evidence of the gardenesque influence with respect to the forerunners of the English public parks, the botanical gardens of the day, for example Loudon's Derby Arboretum and Major's Leeds Botanical Gardens. These were frequently planted according to a third system of planting outlined by Loudon in *An Encyclopaedia of Gardening*: 'the systematic or methodical manner' of planting, essentially a scientific arrangement in which individual trees and shrubs were arranged according to the sequence of botanical orders.

In public parks, the specimen trees and shrubs that typically broke and softened the outline of the shrubbery, either singly or in small groups, as at Birkenhead Park and Grosvenor Park, are the most obvious manifestations of the gardenesque principle (figures 2 and 10). Kemp provided the most comprehensive instructions on their correct disposition in *How to Lay Out A Small Garden*. They included the following rules: wherever possible, place specimens or small groups as outliers of a shrubbery's projections; the more pronounced the projection of a shrubbery, the greater will be the effect of adding them as an adjunct or extension; introduce planting into their recesses, but sparingly so as to avoid the danger of lessening their depth, or overly encumbering the space; and in smaller parks, or where space on the lawn was limited, place specimen trees and large shrubs among groups and masses of lower growing plants for maximum effect.[25]

The paucity of visual and published documentary evidence relating to parks makes it more difficult to interpret how the gardenesque style of planting affected the structure of the shrubbery itself. Kemp, Major and Milner did address the subject in their writing, however.[26] 'They should not be scattered, or dotted, but be planted in uncrowded groups, allowing here and there, some of them to associate with and grow into each other,' wrote Major,[27] who articulated the general view that gardenesque spacing should prevail along the shrubbery's 'ornamental fringe', especially with regard to shrubs of interesting form and foliage or flower colour. Picturesque groups, on the other hand, were the popular choice for the purposes of screening or forming thickets to the rear of the shrubbery, as in under large trees or along the park boundary.[28]

PLAN FORM

The Regency period established the picturesque variant of the grouped manner of planting a shrubbery as a legitimate force in the organization of the garden. Termed 'Sylva florifera' by Henry Phillips in *Sylva florifera: The Shrubbery Historically and Botanically Treated* (London, 1823), his book of instruction on the subject, the 'natural and graceful style' of shrubbery planting drew inspiration from the Revd William Gilpin's analysis of planting in the New Forest (*Remarks on Forest Scenery and Other Woodland Views*, 1791), especially the 'lawndes' which were browsed by deer into a fine turf and 'adorned with islands or peninsulas' of thorns, holly, and gorse.[29] Gilpin's friend, William Mason, may have shown the way forward at Nuneham Park, Oxfordshire, in the 1770s when he enclosed the flower garden from the landscape park with shrubbery and

arranged kidney-shaped beds and other irregular shapes on the lawn. However, irregular beds were being used even before Nuneham, most notably in Robert Greening's 1752 proposal for the shrubberies at Wimpole Hall, Cambridgeshire, and in Thomas Wright's 1760 scheme for Netheravon, Wiltshire.[30] From these transitional schemes came Nash's naturalistic planting campaigns of the 1810s and 1820s at Regent's Park, St James's Park, Buckingham Palace and the Royal Pavilion Grounds, Brighton. His remodelling of St James's Park in 1828 (figure 11) perhaps best exemplified the new formula, supplanting the straight avenues with shrubberies whose ground outlines mirrored the recesses and promontories described by Gilpin for the forest lawn.[31] Paxton's broccoli-shaped beds at Birkenhead Park (1843) demonstrated a similar predisposition towards the forest lawn aesthetic (figure 3), confirming, with the aid of his later works (Crystal Palace Park, 1854; People's Park, Halifax, 1857; Baxter Park, Dundee, 1863) and those of his trainees — Kemp, John Gibson, Milner — the picturesque shrubbery as a leading influence in the formation of the Victorian park.

The theme of irregularity was regularly expressed in Victorian garden literature. 'Deep recesses' and 'prominent projections of bold and pointed forms' corresponded to Major's interpretation of the principle.[32] Kemp's instructions were more detailed. In *How to Lay Out a Small Garden* Kemp agreed with Major, but advised that the irregularity generally prescribed for the ground outlines of individual beds and masses be heightened still further by randomly scattering groups of trees and shrubs along their periphery,[33] a reminder of the 'outliers' that Pückler Muskau had observed as growing out and over the edge lines of Nash's shrubberies in Regent's Park and St James's Park.[34] Kemp stipulated that after the trees and shrubs had advanced in growth — he specified 'some eight or ten years' as the appropriate period — that the resulting series of smaller curves (figure 12) be emphasized by turfing the border over and by planting drifts of showy or early flowering 'British' flowers (i.e. snowdrops, violets, squills, ficaria, primroses, lychnis, wood anemones) along the margins of the shrubbery.[35]

99

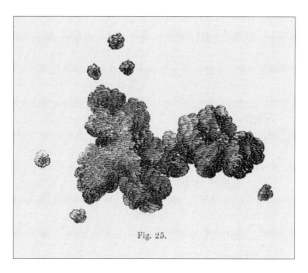

Fig. 25.

Figure 10: The correct positioning of specimen plants and small groups, from Edward Kemp, *How to Lay Out a Garden* (London, 1864), 73.

The second treatment was a traditional wilderness effect, extending back to the 17th century and John Evelyn. The first is reminiscent of Nash's practice of broadcasting grass seed over the bare patches between his shrubs.[36] Not surprisingly, the technique had also been promoted by Loudon, although accompanied by the proviso that a shrubbery so treated could not be expected to perpetuate itself indefinitely: 'This would look remarkably well, both in picturesque and botanical point of view, for another five or six years, when it would become absolutely necessary to root up some of the larger trees, and to prune in, or cut over near the ground, some of the larger shrubs'.[37]

PROFILE

The 'stepped' or 'theatrical' principle of planting had regulated the surface of the shrubbery, from the onset of the Natural Style in the early 18th century, as first outlined by Batty Langley in *New Principles of Gardening* (London, 1728) and Philip Miller in *The Gardeners Dictionary* (London, 1731).[38] In 1829, William Cobbett in *The English Gardener* was still advocating the practice of arranging plants in graduated ranks (shortest in the front, tallest at the back),[39] but the smooth foliage profiles that resulted found little favour among the advocates of the modern shrubbery (figure 13) — 'They are planted too generally in the form of sloping banks, without the least natural beauty whatever' complained M'Intosh in 1838.[40]

'It [theatrical shrubbery] may be likened in form to the sloping roof of a house, wherein only convenience is contemplated' lamented Kemp.[41] Following on Nash's experiments with the natural style at St James's Park and the Royal Pavilion Grounds, Brighton, Kemp proposed added roughness of texture and form to breach the surface of Cobbett's amphitheatres of green (figure 15): 'They [the modern shrubberies] should have a roundness of outline, and yet be in the strongest sense irregular; the tallest plants being brought near the fronts at some of the most prominent parts, and interspersed through the groups at various intervals; being backed up by those of the next size, and the intersperses filled with smaller and middle sized plants'.[42]

'GRADATION'

Loudon's concern with the aesthetic of 'gradation' is also an important theme in 19th-century shrubbery. In these particulars (grouping), he writes, 'the transition should always be gradual' as between the cedar and pines and yew, etc.[43] This desire for subtlety of effects was not new. Eighteenth-century theorists such as Thomas Whately and Philip Miller had regularly pleaded for gradual transitions, whether of height (i.e. the stepped manner), foliage colour or form. Smoothness and gradual variation had been the essence of the 'beautiful'.

Nineteenth-century writers developed specific

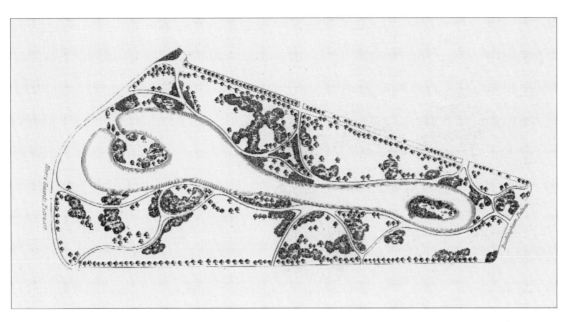

Figure 11. St James's Park, 1835. John Nash's bays and promontories in plan, from John Dennis, *The Landscape Gardener* (London, 1835).

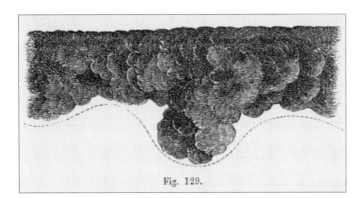

Fig. 129.

Figure 12: The correct treatment of shrubbery margins, from Edward Kemp, *How to Lay Out a Garden* (London, 1864), 161. The dotted line along the front represents the curved outline of the mass, as it was to be marked out on the ground at the time of planting. The broken line immediately behind it corresponds to the more irregular shape the mass would assume, once its 'outliers' had begun to mature.

rules for blending. The most elementary of these was to form groups of plants that shared the same form and mode of growth.[44] Loudon had written of this: 'Thus, among trees, the pines, cedars, firs, and yew, form a regular gradation, and the shrubs that may be planted near them are the arbor-vitae, juniper, whin, &c.'[45] A second possibility was to group trees that shared certain physical characteristics, but which differed sufficiently in others to satisfy the need for variety. In *The Book of the Garden*, M'Intosh provided the best example of the technique, quoting American landscape architect, A. J. Downing on appropriate companion plants for the willow. Downing suggests species that partake of either the form, colour, or foliation of the willow: 'The elm has much larger and darker foliage, while it also has a drooping spray; the weeping birch differs in its leaves, but agrees in the pensile flow of its branches; the common birch has few pendant boughs, but resembles in the airy lightness of its leaves; and the three horned acacia, though its branches are horizontal, has delicate foliage of nearly the same hue and floating lightness as the willow'.[46]

In arranging groups and masses of discordant

forms and foliage colour, the rule was to connect the different species by some third species of an intermediate character. To illustrate, M'Intosh used the problem of how to break and vary into groups the outline of a plantation dominated by broad, light-coloured trees (i.e. maples, birches, etc.). Noting that one might be tempted to use pyramidal evergreen trees, but for the abrupt contrast between their dark masses and the light-coloured foliage of the broad trees he suggested a partial transition from the mellow, pale green of the maples and birches to the darker hues of the oak, ash or beech, and finally to the sombre tint of the evergreens.[47]

The effect of increasing perspective by arranging progressively darker tints of foliage through the visual planes of garden scenery (foreground, middle distance, background) was, of course, a principle that related to the pictorial representation of landscapes, as espoused by 18th century theorists such as Alexander Pope and Uvedale Price. Among the 19th century writers to repeat the principle were Loudon, Phillips, Dennis and Milner.[48] Dennis was the most explicit when it came to the shrubbery, advising that its evergreen framework be planted to a gradation of tints: light tints along the front (laurel, laurustinus, arbutus); darker tints to the rear (holly, black thorn); and intermediate ones in the middle ground (privet, phylirea).[49] This echoed Loudon's advice: 'The depth of recesses may be augmented by darkening the greens as they retire'.[50] Smith went so far as to provide a list of ornamental trees arranged according to the colour of their foliage: 'They are, as it were the colours with which he [the landscape artist] paints'. Smith also mentions 'the tints of the ripening leaf' as requiring consideration in the foliage mix. For autumn colour, he particularizes the yellows of the larch, oak and elm; the reds of the scarlet oak, beech and wild cherry; and the yellow-greens of the ash and the sycamore.[51]

Subtle transitions were also sought with regard to the colours of the flowers of trees and shrubs. Most 19th century experiments with colour in the garden did not begin until the 1830s, and even then such experiments were largely confined to the flower garden rather than the wider landscape.[52]

The bright colours and strong contrasts found among flowers were simply not available in woody plants. But the 'transient elements of colour' present in the flowers of certain trees and shrubs were considered useful for blending. As the following declaration from the *Gardeners' Chronicle* seems to indicate, it was principally in the softer tertiary hues, as well as in the tints and hues, that harmony of colour was sought: 'Quite as appropriate in their sphere are the more sober hues. The remedy we seek is to be found in breadth rather than in intensity of colour'.[53]

Kemp and Mawson recommended creating broad splashes of colour using long drifts and masses of closely spaced flowering shrubs (barberry, daphne, red currant, lilac, for example), particularly in high-profile locations such as the projection of a bed, the swell of a mound or a path junction.[54] 'The effect', enthused Kemp, 'may be more like what one immense specimen would yield'.[55] Major added that those with ordinary habits and general features should be placed behind plants of more interesting form (Dennis recommended concealing them behind low growing evergreens). Major concluded, 'Such must be planted so as to exhibit their tops and blossoms only'.[56] Where two masses of differing colours came into contact, the rule was to blend them by placing a few of each in the adjoining group.[57]

THE PLANT PALETTE

In their choice of plant material, Kemp, Major and their contemporaries benefited from an unprecedented growth in the range and supply of exotics. The core planting of the public park continued, to 'consist, of course, in the greatest number, of those well-known and well-established kinds which have come to be considered "native and to the manner born" in England'.[58] But there was a new accompaniment to the established mix of native plants and 18th century introductions. An influx of new plants from China, western North America and the Southern hemisphere, coupled with the rapid advance of horticultural technology, as epitomized by the invention of the Wardian case, had multiplied the 19th century plant palette beyond all expectations. In 1778, William Malcolm was offering a total of 650 ornamental

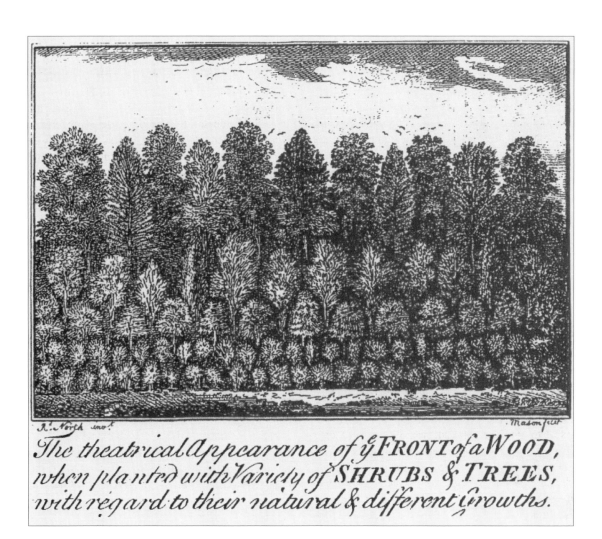

The theatrical Appearance of ỹ FRONT of a WOOD, when planted with Variety of SHRUBS & TREES, with regard to their natural & different Growths.

Figure 13: Frontispiece to Richard North's 1759 catalogue, depicting 'The Theatrical Appearance' of a shrubbery, illustrating planting for regularity of surface. To assist the amateur gardener in laying out his graduated shrubberies, North itemized his inventory of evergreen and deciduous plants 'from the highest to the lowest'.

trees and shrubs in his catalogue. This amount was only marginally exceeded by Conrad Loddiges in 1804, but by 1851 the famous Hackney nursery was advertising over 1300 woody plants.[59]

The shrubbery of the 18th century had been dominated by plants from eastern North America, the fruits of the John Bartram–Peter Collinson partnership, that from the 1730s had successfully imported the seeds and roots of plants such as rhododendron (*Rhododendron maximum* L.), kalmia (*Kalmia latifolia* L.), azalea (*Rhododendron luteum* (L.) Sweet), magnolia (*Magnolia virginiana* L.) and Weymouth pine (*Pinus strobus* L.). Many of these novelties had moved into popular cultivation by the 1770s, appearing in the graduated shrubbery in combination with a supporting cast of Asian and European plants (lilac, syringa, cistus, arbutus, erica, Portugal laurel, for example). From the second half of the 18th century American exotics were often grown in 'American gardens', areas of formal and informal bedding or shrubbery devoted almost exclusively to their distinct cultural

Figure 14: The traditional method of laying out a shrubbery, contrasted with John Nash's new style, from Prince Pückler Muskau, *Andeutungen über Landschaftsgärtnerei* (Stuttgart, 1826). The clean lines of the 18th-century 'theatrical' shrubbery, as shown in sketch (e) with clumps, have given way to the characteristic irregularity of the forest lawn, as shown in sketch (f).

Fig. 23.

Figure 15: Planting for irregularity of surface, from Edward Kemp's *How to Lay Out a Garden* (London, 1864), 72. Kemp's recommended pattern of low-to-high plantings avoided the appearance of the modern shrubbery's 18th-century prototype by the occasional introduction of large shrubs and small trees into the front of the bed. The projecting points of the beds were reserved for the largest of these: 'Ordinarily, the boldest swells in the groups should have the boldest points in them, and the smaller projections be furnished with plants a size or two lower; while the retiring and narrow parts may be made up with low or second-sized shrubs alone'.

requirements (i.e. moist, peaty soil). Increasingly introduced as undergrowths in the margins of wilderness and wood walks, as at Upton, Essex, and Stoke Park, Gloucestershire, the American garden reached its zenith in the early 1800s with the maturation of extensive woodland gardens like Kenwood, London, and Fonthill Abbey, Wiltshire. Ultimately, the experiments of Dr John Fothergill and Thomas Wright would show the way forward to ornamenting the 'wood' of the public park.[60]

As the 19th century progressed, American plants were gradually superseded by a fresh wave of Asian introductions. The 'wave' was initially slow to break on Britannia's shores, however. Perhaps a reflection of their initial cost, or of the time lapse involved in moving from specialist collections into popular cultivation, the new flora of China and Japan appears to have been largely absent from Regency shrubberies. Plant bills from the 1810s and 1820s for the Royal Pavilion at Brighton indicate that William Aiton planted Nash's shrubberies with a fairly standard range of indigenous woody plants, varied primarily by 17th- and 18th-century introductions: tamarisk, box and arbutus, sumach, sea buckthorn, savin, bladder senna and laurustinus, moss roses, striped hollies, laburnum and evergreen oak. *Magnolia liliiflora* Desr., *Kerria japonica* (L.) DC. and *Ligustrum lucidum* Alt.f. are among the few Asian shrubs mentioned. Excepting varieties of the China rose (*Rosa chinensis* Jacq.), dahlia, fuchsia

and tiger lily, the major work of the period on shrubbery planting, Phillips's *Sylva florifera*, makes scant mention of Asian plants.[61] Nursery bills for Grosvenor Park, on the other hand, enumerate 22 trees and shrubs (out of a total of 150) from the Far East including *Chaenomeles japonica* (Thunb.) Spach., *Cryptomeria japonica* D. Don. 'Lobbii', *Leycesteria formosa* Wallich., *Spiraea japonica* L.f., *Forsythia viridissima* Lindl., *Rhododendron japonicum* (A. Gray) Swi. and *Pinus wallichiana* A. B. Jackson. Nurserymen Philip and Richard Discon are known to have adorned the shrubberies of East Park, Hull (1887) with the likes of *Aucuba japonica* Thunb., *Jasminium nudiflorum* Lindl., *Cotoneaster simonsii* Bak., *Parthenocissus tricuspidata* (Sieb. & Zucc.) Planch and *Ligustrum ovalifolium* Hassk. William Baron planted Aberdare Park with *Acer palmatum* Thumb., *Cryptomeria japonica* D. Don., *Forsythia suspensa* (Thunb.) Vahl., *Juniperus chinensis* L. 'Spartan', *Spiraea japonica* L. 'Albiflora' and *Weigela florida* (Bunge) A. DC.

The Grosvenor Park, Aberdare Park and East Park plant lists would also seem to confirm the popularity of specimen conifers in 19th century public parks. The first two feature the broadest selection, including the signature introductions from western North America (*Chamaecyparis lawsoniana* (Murray) Parl., *Cupressus macrocarpa* Hartu ex Gordon, *Calocedrus decurrens* (Torr.) Florin, *Sequoiadendron giganteum* (Lindl.) Buchholz), South America (*Araucaria araucana* (Molina) K. Koch) and the Himalayas (*Pinus cembra* L. and *P. wallichiana* A. B., *Cedrus deodara* (D. Don.) Spach.). Not surprisingly, William Barron, author of *The British Winter Garden: A Practical Treatise on Evergreens* (London, 1852), is slightly richer than Kemp's, his inclusion of trees such as *Chamaecyparis nootkatensis* (D. Don.) Spach., *Chamaecyparis pisifera* (Sieb.) 'Plumosa' and *Cupressus lawsoniana* (Murray) Parl. 'Fraseri' probably as much an indication of his predisposition towards conifers and their use as current fashion. Also striking in the above documents — but not entirely unexpected given the ambitious programs in hybridization being undertaken by the country's nurseries at this time — is the broad range of new cultivars and varieties named. These centre on plants generally considered suitable for specimen planting or for the front ranks of the shrubbery (i.e. of distinctive flower, foliage, form, even branch colour). In addition to such novelties as *Crataegus laevigata* (Poir.) DC 'Paul's Scarlet', *Tilia platyphyllos* Scop. 'Rubra', *Pyracantha coccinea* Roem. 'Lalandei' and *Syringa vulgaris* L. 'Rubra de Marly', East Park, Hull, featured 25 kinds of foliage plants (out of 120 entries), including, for example, *Acer pseudoplatanus* L. 'Atropurpureum', *Sambucus nigra* L. 'Aurea', *Robinia pseudoacacia* L. 'Aurea' and *Buxus sempervirens* L. 'Handsworthensis'. Francis and Arthur Dickson & Sons supplied Kemp with a generous selection of same, but in addition to the likes of *Fagus sylvatica* L. 'Asplenifolia', *Ilex aquifolium* L. 'Watereriana' and *Taxus baccata* L. 'Aurea', they also provided *Ilex aquifolium* L. 'Pendula', *Crataegus laevigata* (Poir.) DC 'Punicea', *Ulmus glabra* Huds. 'Pendula' and *Salix caprea* L. 'Kilmarnock' (figure 2). The most extensive hybridization occurred among roses and rhododendrons,[62] although only 'choice hybrid rhododendrons' are mentioned in the Grosvenor Park bills and the Aberdare Park catalogue. These may have comprised a mix of Himalayan, Turkish and American varieties (*Rhododendron campanulatum* D. Don. [1825], *R. caucasicum* Pall [1803] and *R. catawbiense* Michx. [1809]),[63] as, for instance, employed by Paxton in the People's

Park, Halifax, although Himalayan species (*R. barbatum* G. Don., *cinnabarinum* Hook., *griffithianum* Wright., *falconeri* Hook. and *thomsonii* Hook., for example) became predominant towards the end of the century.[64]

Conclusion

In conclusion, it may be said that the picturesque variant of the grouped manner of planting predominated in the shrubberies of public parks, almost from the beginning of the park movement in the 1840s. It had initially gained adherents in private parks and gardens during the Regency period, eclipsing its main rival, the 'mixed' manner, because of its ability to reconcile the increased richness of the horticultural offerings of the period, with a concern for harmony of composition. The grouped manner subsequently fell under the influence of the 19th century interpretation of the 'Natural' style, as espoused by Repton and Loudon. The picturesque was tamed, exotics were integrated into the shrubbery and the gardenesque mode of planting evolved as a method of displaying the choicest tree and shrub offerings in the land. In form, however, the shrubbery retained its picturesque character. In outline and surface the natural mode of laying out a shrubbery answered the Victorian penchant for variety and intricacy, while blending each plant, each plantation into one striking whole. Change was there too, but it was subtle and easy, controlled and deliberate. Shades mixed, colours fused and edge lines disappeared amid a wistful cloud of green that announced a new urban utopia. This was the style of planting that defined the shrubbery of the Victorian park. At a glance it summoned delight, on closer inspection it engendered reflection, while always behind the evergreen walls, the world outside was forgotten.

Notes

1. *Halifax Guardian* (15 August 1857).

2. Joshua Major, *Theory and Practice of Landscape Gardening* (London: Longman, Brown, Green & Longmans, 1852), 193–6; Charles H. J. Smith, *Parks and Pleasure Grounds* (London: Reeve & Co., 1852), 155–61; Henry Ernest Milner, *The Art and Practice of Landscape Gardening* (London:

106

Norwood; Simpkin, Marshall & Co., 1890), 93–7.

3. John Claudius Loudon, *An Encyclopaedia of Gardening* (London: Longman, Hurst, Rees, Orme & Brown, 1822), 910.

4. Ibid.

5. Major, *Theory and Practice of Landscape Gardening*, 42.

6. Edward Kemp, *How to Lay Out a Small Garden* (London: Bradbury & Evans, 1850), 62; Loudon, *An Encyclopaedia of Gardening* (1822), 912.

7. Loudon, *An Encyclopaedia of Gardening* (1822), 952.

8. Major, *Theory and Practice of Landscape Gardening*, 11.

9. Smith, *Parks and Pleasure Grounds*, 71.

10. Ibid.; Loudon, *An Encyclopaedia of Gardening* (1822), 952; Major, *Theory and Practice of Landscape Gardening*, 152; Kemp, *How to Lay Out a Small Garden*, 62–3.

11. John Claudius Loudon, 'Remarks for laying out public gardens and promenades', *Gardener's Magazine* (1835).

12. Kemp, *How to Lay Out a Small Garden*, 62.

13. John Claudius Loudon, *The Derby Arboretum* (London: Longman, Orme, Brown, Green & Longmans, 1840), 71.

14. Mark Laird, 'An approach to the conservation of ornamental planting in English gardens 1730–1830', MA dissertation, University of York, 1984, 28–31.

15. Loudon, *An Encyclopaedia of Gardening* (1822), 914; (1830), 997.

16. Sir Henry Steuart, *The Planters Guide* (Edinburgh: Ballantyne & Co.; London: T. Cadell, 1828), as quoted in Loudon, *An Encyclopaedia of Gardening* (1830), 997.

17. Humphry Repton, *An Inquiry into the Changes of Taste in Landscape Gardening* (London: J. Taylor, 1806), as quoted in Loudon, *An Encyclopaedia of Gardening* (1830), 956; John Dennis, *The Landscape Gardener* (London: James

Ridgeway & Sons, 1835), 42.

18. Loudon, 'Remarks for laying out public gardens and promenades'; *idem, An Encyclopaedia of Gardening* (1830), 917.

19. Laird, 'Approach to the conservation of ornamental planting', 33.

20. Major, *Theory and Practice of Landscape Gardening*, 157; Charles M'Intosh, *The Book of the Garden*, 2 vols (London: William Blackwood & Sons, 1853–55), vol. 1, 581; Smith, *Parks and Pleasure Grounds*, 75.

21. Antoine-Chrysostome Quatremère de Quincy, *Essay on the Nature, the End and the Means of Imitation in the Fine Arts* (1837).

22. John Claudius Loudon, *Suburban Gardener and Villa Companion* (London: Longman, Hurst, Rees, Orme and Brown, 1838), 164–6.

23. Quatremère de Quincy, *Essay*, 12

24. John Claudius Loudon, 'On laying out and planting the lawn, shrubbery and flower garden', *Gardener's Magazine* (1842), 167.

25. Kemp, *How to Lay Out a Small Garden*, 78.

26. Ibid., 172; Major, *Theory and Practice of Landscape Gardening*, 43; Milner, *Art and Practice of Landscape Gardening*, 48; Henry Phillips, *Sylva florifera: The Shrubbery Historically and Botanically Treated*, 2 vols (London: Longman, Hurst, Rees, Orme and Brown, 1823), 23.

27. Major, *Theory and Practice of Landscape Gardening*, 43–4.

28. Ibid.; Kemp, *How to Lay Out a Small Garden*, 173–4; Milner, *Art and Practice of Landscape Gardening*, 48.

29. Mavis Batey, 'Regency ornamental shrubberies', unpublished paper (August 1991).

30. Mark Laird, *Flowering of the Landscape Garden: English Pleasure Grounds 1720-1800* (Philadelphia: University of Pennsylvania Press, 1999), 358.

31. Laird, 'Approach to the conservation of ornamental planting', 33; Revd William Gilpin,

Remarks on Forest Scenery and Other Woodland Views (London: Blamire, 1791), 307–9.

32. Major, *Theory and Practice of Landscape Gardening*, 150.

33. Kemp, *How to Lay Out a Small Garden*, 164.

34. Laird, 'Approach to the conservation of ornamental planting', 33.

35. Kemp, *How to Lay Out a Small Garden*, 130.

36. Laird, 'Approach to the conservation of ornamental planting', 34.

37. Loudon, *Suburban Gardener and Villa Companion.*

38. Laird, 'Approach to the conservation of ornamental planting', 47.

39. Ibid., 27.

40. Charles M'Intosh, *The Practical Gardener and Modern Horticulturist* (London: W. Witheys of Bridgwater, 1828), 806.

41. Kemp, *How to Lay Out a Small Garden*, 75.

42. Ibid., 75

43. Loudon, *An Encyclopaedia of Gardening* (1822).

44. Thomas Mawson, *Civic Art* (London: B. T. Batsford, 1911), 175; Major, *Theory and Practice of Landscape Gardening*, 166; Kemp, *How to Lay Out a Small Garden*, 168.

45. Loudon, *An Encyclopaedia of Gardening* (1830), 914.

46. M'Intosh, *Book of the Garden*, 583.

47. Ibid.

48. Loudon, *An Encyclopaedia of Gardening* (1822), 1156; Phillips, *Sylva florifera*, 22; Dennis, *Landscape Gardener*, 42; Milner, *Art and Practice of Landscape Gardening*, 46-50.

49. Dennis, *Landscape Gardener*, 72.

50. Loudon, *An Encyclopaedia of Gardening* (1822).

51. Smith, *Parks and Pleasure Grounds*, 84.

52. Brent Elliott, *Victorian Gardens* (London: B. T.

Batsford, 1986), 48–50.

53. *Gardeners' Chronicle* (13 August 1864), 770.

54. Phillips, *Sylva florifera*, 24; Kemp, *How to Lay Out a Small Garden*, 222–3; Mawson, *Civic Art*, 175.

55. Kemp, *How to Lay Out a Small Garden*, 222.

56. Major, *Theory and Practice of Landscape Gardening*, 44.

57. Kemp, *How to Lay Out a Small Garden*, 90; Elliott, *Victorian Gardens*, 92.

58. 'Opening of the People's Park', *Halifax Guardian* (15 August 1857), 4.

59. Laird, *Flowering of the Landscape Garden*, 417.

60. Ibid., 63–98.

61. Virginia Hinze, 'The re-creation of John Nash's Regency gardens at the Royal Pavilion, Brighton', *Garden History*, 24/1 (1996), 45–53.

62. Patrick Goode, Geoffrey Jellicoe, Susan Jellicoe and Michael Lancaster, *The Oxford Companion to Gardens* (Oxford: Oxford University Press, 1986), 562.

63. 'Opening of the People's Park', 4.

64. *Hillier's Manual of Trees and Shrubs*, 4th edn (Winchester: Hillier & Sons, 1977), 264.

65. Kemp, *How to Lay Out a Small Garden*, 174; Major, *Theory and Practice of Landscape Gardening*, 42–44, 196.

66. Kemp, *How to Lay Out a Small Garden*, 175; Smith, *Parks and Pleasure Grounds*, 84–93; Major, *Theory and Practice of Landscape Gardening*, 140–9.

67. Kemp, *How to Lay Out a Small Garden*, 168.

68. *The Halifax Guardian*, 'Opening of the People's Park' (15 August 1857), 4.

69. Laird, *Flowering of the Landscape Garden*, 249–50.

70. Loudon, *An Encyclopaedia of Gardening* (1822), 914.

71. Ibid., 912.

Bedding schemes

by Brent Elliott

Figure 1: Edwardian succulent bedding at Brockwell Park, London. (From the collection of the author)

Beginnings of parks and flowerbeds

'Stern sticklers for the unities in landscape gardening', announced the *Gardeners' Chronicle* in 1866, looking back to the days before bedding schemes had been introduced into the Royal Parks, 'contend that a park is no place for floral prettinesses, but should be sacred to turf and trees . . . When Mr Cowper [William Francis Cowper, later Cowper-Temple] took office, the London parks were large prairies, fairly wooded, and pleasant enough at all seasons of the year. They are pleasant still, but a little artistic landscape gardening has given them a new character without robbing them of one of their old charms'.[1]

This 'little artistic landscape gardening' arrived in the summer of 1859, as a result of an initially controversial decision to introduce flower gardens into the parks. Among those opposed to the idea was Sir Joseph Paxton, who probably feared a fall in attendance at the Crystal Palace if people could see floral displays for free. But, as Samuel Broome, head gardener at the Inner Temple, reported,

> a great improvement had taken place . . . with respect to the introduction of summer-flowering plants into our parks. No fewer than from 30,000 to 40,000 bedding plants have been planted in various parts of them this season, and all have done remarkably well. They appear to have given satisfaction to the public; many have spoken to me on the subject, and have expressed how pleased they were at the great change that has taken place, and how glad they were to find that the working classes could see a display of summer flowers without going to Kew.[2]

How many of the working classes could have been expected to make the journey to Kew to see

Figure 2: The Dell, Hyde Park, in the 1870s: foliage plants were popular at this time to create a 'subtropical' look. (Royal Horticultural Society, Lindley Library)

110

flowers is another question; the important point was that another of the benefits of life, hitherto restricted to the wealthy, was being made available to the wider population at the government's expense.

While bedding — the temporary planting of beds for short-term display — had precedents going back to the 17th century, it developed its modern rationale in the early 19th century as a response to the increasing quantities of exotic plants being introduced into the country. During the 1820s, experiments were being publicized in the summer planting of half-hardy exotics, in Phoenix Park, Dublin, as well as on private estates. The instructions offered on the arrangement of plants in beds were initially brief: John Claudius Loudon and others demanded that plants be grouped in solid masses of one colour, thereby obtaining distinctness and variety, whereas beds planted with indiscriminate mixtures of flowers tended overall to produce monotony.[3]

It was only in 1837–38 that John Caie, head gardener at the Duke of Bedford's garden in Kensington, published the articles that were later regarded as setting the bedding system in motion, with recommendations of planting for high contrast of colour, balance of habit as well as colour, and proportion of bed size to brightness of colour.[4] These early references to solid masses of colour should be seen in the context of a generally accepted tradition of intermingled planting; by modern standards, no early bedding schemes could have presented genuinely solid masses. But once massing had become an aspiration, gardeners and nurserymen turned their attention to producing varieties of half-hardy perennials specifically for bedding purposes, dwarfer in habit than the wild species, with a higher proportion of flower to stem and foliage. The first true bedding plants began to emerge in the 1840s, beginning with pelargoniums, and followed by verbenas, petunias and calceolarias. By about 1860 the variety of colour achieved with these four genera was so great that much of the original range of species used in bedding had been abandoned in their favour.

On private estates the arrangement of bedding plants in the summer parterre became the obsession of the 1840s and 1850s, furnishing the gardening magazines with reams of copy on colour theory and horticultural practice.[5] While some early parks had made provision for flowerbeds, such as Joshua Major's Manchester parks of the 1840s, there are few indications of

Figure 3: Carpet bedding at Hampton Court, 1890s. (Royal Horticultural Society, Lindley Library)

municipal parks devoting significant areas to flower beds until the Crystal Palace Park and then the Royal Parks had set the precedent in the late 1850s; after that, even parks such as Prince's Park, Liverpool, among the closest of municipal parks to the old landscape model, began to experiment with bedding.

Park bedding in the 19th century

Bedding entered the municipal parks just as styles began changing significantly in the wider world. After a quarter-century of emphasis on the contrast of solid masses of colour, the young gardeners of the 1860s turned increasingly to lessened contrast, to the use of foliage instead of flowers, and to the disruption of the solid mass of colour by the addition of distinct edgings or of centrepieces to beds (the centrepieces became known as dot plants). These ideas being very much in the air in the 1860s, and most early descriptions of park beds concentrating more on the fact of their existence than on the details of their planting, it must remain uncertain to what extent the earliest forms of Victorian bedding ever found significant expression in municipal parks.

An interest in foliage plants, growing steadily through the 1850s, emerged in the mid-1860s as a major enthusiasm of the younger generation of gardeners, taking the name 'subtropical gardening' from the Subtropical Garden that John Gibson created at Battersea Park in 1864, the first major public display of the new style. Gibson grouped specimens of large, woody stemmed plants like bananas, wigandias and shrubby solanums with patterned beds of cannas and smaller plants; by the 1870s, rex begonias, philodendrons, dieffenbachias and more or less the entire range of what is now regarded as house plants was being used for summer bedding. The subtropical garden began to decline as a fashion in the private sector from the late 1880s, but remained a staple of the municipal park until the mid-20th century.[6]

Not all the plants that became fashionable during the subtropical years had large leaves: many were quite small — sedums, dwarf succulents, South American creeping plants like alternantheras and iresines. In 1868, the use of such plants to create geometric patterns was named carpet bedding, from the analogy between the thick mass of plants and the compact weave of a Turkish carpet. (There do not appear to be any 19th-century reports of carpet beds imitating the

111

The Carpet Bed, Peckham Rye Park.

Figure 4: An Edwardian carpet bed at Peckham Rye, London. (From the collection of the author)

patterns of Turkish carpets.) By 1870 carpet beds were appearing in public parks; throughout the 1870s they were the foremost horticultural fashion, becoming an international fashion in the 1880s; and while they fell from fashion in the private sector during the later 1880s, they remained a mainstay of public park practice almost to the present day.[7]

In the wake of carpet bedding, there was a return to patterned flower bedding, both in private gardens and in municipal parks, but there was no widespread return to the high colour contrasts of early Victorian practice. Despite the demand by some pundits for gardens and bedding schemes to exhibit primarily tones of one colour, it was more common in practice for bedding schemes to employ a dominant colour with a subordinate amount of contrasting edging or centres to the beds. Another strategy was a return to the pre-Victorian style of mixing colours indiscriminately, so that no colour dominated; this may have been carried out as early as 1875 in Prince's Park, Liverpool.[8] In addition, the planting range was changing: petunias and verbenas were falling from favour, as of variable merit in the English climate, and were replaced by the bedding varieties of tuberous begonia that began to appear in the 1870s.

Spring gardening, the use of spring-flowering bulbs to fill flowerbeds until it was time to install the summer bedding at the end of May, had been pioneered on private estates in the 1850s; its public manifestations began to receive press attention about 1870, when a public commercial garden, the Aston Lower Grounds in Birmingham, showed geometrical patterns of daisies and violas. Its growth in popularity continued gradually, until by the 1880s Battersea Park was famous for its spring displays. The early preference for geometric pattern gave way, by the end of the century, to large sheets of bulbs — again, a style initiated in the 1850s to 1860s, but slow to attract public attention.[9]

Park bedding in the 20th century

The first decade of the new century brought a significant innovation, one that had been pioneered in the late 1880s on a few private estates, but had attracted little attention in the English gardening press until it appeared as a new development abroad. This was sculptural bedding: the creation of a three-dimensional frame, whether of iron or of wire, on which plants were packed. One of the earliest but most popular designs was the joke carpet bed — in the shape of a roll of carpet (about the first design to be reinstated at Blackpool after the Second World War); the year 1911 saw a wave of coronation crowns; and thereafter sculptural bedding became a favourite activity of parks superintendents and staff, peaking in popularity during the 1920s. After c.1913, however, most of its manifestations were ignored by the gardening press, and the evidence for this almost extinct art form is now to be found in postcards, in which one can find floral staircases, musical instruments, suites of furniture and even a floral cenotaph (erected in the Brenchley Gardens, Maidstone, after the First World War — what superintendent today would have the courage to do such a thing, one wonders).[10] The author's feeling is that superintendents regarded sculptural bedding as their answer to topiary: and since it was annually renewable, it offered a chance for experiment that permanent topiary did not.

By far the most widespread and long-lived of sculptural bedding forms was the floral clock. The first floral clock in Britain was set up in the Prince's Street Gardens in Edinburgh in 1903, by John M'Hattie, the Parks Superintendent for the city, and former head gardener to the Duke of Wellington.[11] Again, the interwar years formed the peak period for these, some of which, as at Weston-super-Mare, were created outside municipal parks, on traffic islands and the like. In his *Municipal Parks* (1937), W. W. Pettigrew attacked 'the growing craze for installing floral clocks in public parks', attributing their proliferation to the taste of town committees rather than to that of parks officers.[12] Nonetheless, they were a form of gardening that was functional as well as ornamental: the clock in the Bromley Library grounds (extant until the 1960s) indicated closing time. In the second half of the century, the number of floral clocks has diminished as a result of vandalism, cost cutting and taste. (If one finds a bed in a municipal park that has been built up to present an angled face, without it being required by any feature of the terrain, there might well be the mechanism of a clock still buried under its surface.)

Figure 5: 'Carpet' bedding at Grove Park, Weston-super-Mare, c.1913. (From the collection of the author)

Figure 6: A floral crown at West Park, Wolverhampton: 1911 saw a wave of coronation crowns. (From the collection of the author)

Figure 7: Floral cenotaph, Brenchley Gardens, Maidstone, 1920. (From the collection of the author)

113

Figure 8: Bromley Library's floral clock — shown here in the 1930s but extant until the 1960s — was functional as well as ornamental, indicating closing time. (From the collection of the author)

114

During the interwar years, subtropical and carpet bedding continued to be staples of park practice, and spring gardening experienced another return to fashion in the 1920s, with tulips undergoing one of their periodic surges into fashion.[13] Successional bedding, in which there was no fallow season of empty beds, but a continuing display throughout the year, had first been remarked in Regent's Park in 1898, and had become a recognized trend by the end of the Edwardian period: 'Under the newer system the "bedding" never can be said to have terminated. It is bedding all the while'.[14] The First World War forced a hiatus in this frantic schedule; after the War it was revived, but usually only in the most central and prestigious of display parks — Hyde Park, Piccadilly in Manchester, Prince's Street Gardens in Edinburgh.

There were attempts to expand the range of bedding plants, though how widespread they were may be doubted. Thomas Hay used his displays in the Central Royal Parks to promote new introductions, and to influence the public taste in favour of novel exotics.[15] In 1936, for example, one can find listed among the flowers used in summer bedding schemes in seaside resort displays, lavateras, godetias, clarkias, lupins, candytuft, cornflowers, violas, phlox and poppies.[16] South African annuals such as nemesias and dimorphothecas were vigorously promoted in the late 1930s.[17] But the only serious challenges to the ascendancy of pelargoniums and begonias came with the new varieties of salvias, antirrhinums and tagetes that emerged from breeders during the first half of the century — to be followed by impatiens, and a new concentration on fibrous-rooted instead of tuberous begonias, in the second.

The literature on bedding declined in quantity during the 20th century, the only significant textbook being J. R. B. Evison's *Gardening for Display* (1958); and the impression conveyed in that book is that bedding design had changed little since the development of tiered bedding in the Edwardian period. Nonetheless, the arguments about colour combination continued, so there was obviously room for experiment in practice. Although much early 20th-century bedding had either continued the late Victorian tendency to return to mixture instead of massing, the Loudonian emphasis on contrasting blocks resurfaced in the 1930s, possibly as a result of the Edwardian emphasis on the massing of bulbs in lawns: a writer in 1934 said that 'It is impossible to emphasise too forcefully the vivid impression

Figure 9: Floral organ at Wibsey Park, Bradford, 1928. (From the collection of the author)

created by large masses of one kind of flower or shrubs compared with a combination of several kinds'.[18]

As the century progressed, more and more gardening pundits expressed a distaste for bedding as something vulgar and *infra dig*. Parks' officers defended the practice by invoking the preferences of the public ('the colour craving of those who have to live in dismal streets').[19] But bedding served an important purpose, especially in the inner cities, as a way of ornamenting parks whose levels of air pollution militated against much experiment with hardy plants. Pettigrew, then Superintendent of Parks for Manchester, gave some statistics on the effects of air pollution in Philips Park in that city:

> Among trees, the Ash, Poplar, Willow, Thorn and Elm are the only kinds worth one's while attempting to grow. As for shrubs, the Rhododendron, Privet, Elder and . . . Lonicera Ledebouri, are about the very limit of one's choice. Beyond the Lupin, Funkia and the German Iris, few other herbaceous perennials are likely to live out-of-doors during the winter at Philip's Park . . .
>
> Generally speaking, Rhododendrons live

115

Figure 10: Floral staircase at Bridlington, 1920s. (From the collection of the author)

Figures 11,12: Philips Park, Manchester: (top) an Edwardian postcard entitled 'The Big Trees', and (bottom), a 1913 photograph of bedding. By 1928 the effects of air pollution meant that not only the bedding, but also many trees and shrubs had to be re-planted annually. (From the collection of the author)

only for three years in this park. The first summer after they are planted, a fairly large percentage of them bloom, for the flower buds are already formed on them when they are brought in from the nursery in the country. Afterwards, hardly one per cent of them bear bloom . . . by the end of the third year the majority of them have to be thrown away . . . . With Poplars, their period of life is somewhat longer, but, nevertheless, the mortality among even the hardiest species is exceedingly heavy . . . .

Philip's Park is about thirty acres in extent, and in order to maintain it in a presentable condition, so far as furnishing the borders with trees and shrubs is concerned, it has to be planted up each year with 2,500 Rhododendron bushes, 2,500 Poplar trees, 1,000 Willows, 750 Elders and about 300 different kinds of flowering shrubs.[20]

In heavily polluted districts, in other words, even trees and shrubs required to be treated as a sort of larger and slightly longer-lived bedding plants. It is little wonder that, until the Clean Air Act came into effect, seasonal bedding remained the park superintendent's most trustworthy method of beautifying the park.

Bedding in decline

The Second World War brought with it the erection of shelters and anti-aircraft guns in municipal parks, with attendant tree-felling; the establishment of allotments and vegetable gardens in available areas; and restrictions of funds. Initially, the continuity of the flowerbeds was not greatly affected. W. H. Christian, Park Superintendent for Barrow, wrote in October 1939 that 'Flowers are as necessary to the well-being of a community in wartime as are fresh fruits, vegetables and salads. They are, perhaps, more necessary in war-time than in any other, giving as they do, brightness, cheerfulness and a sense of hope and faith in brighter days to come'. As late as March 1941 the *Gardeners' Chronicle* was asking:

(1) Having regard to . . . the psychologi-

cally tonic value of flowers, especially in the spring, what is the smallest possible area that should be devoted to them?

(2) Will it be possible to maintain even small stocks of bedding plants if displays are drastically curtailed?[21]

By that time, park superintendents were having to wrestle with a previously little-experienced phenomenon: vandalism. The first wave took place in 1940, when the locking of park gates was discontinued to allow access in case of air raids, until the scale of overnight damage moved authorities to return to locking and provide extra keys for air-raid wardens. But in 1943 came the wholesale removal of park railings, allegedly for use in making munitions. The consequent wave of destruction — of flowerbeds, trees, park furniture and buildings, swans — provoked fears for the future of horticulture in the parks. Pompey (the pseudonym of the superintendent of Victoria Park Portsmouth) wrote: 'I sometimes wonder if the death-knell has not been rung on ornamental gardening in public parks . . . unless there is a great improvement in the behaviour of those who visit the parks, and for whom they are provided, it will not be possible to regain the high standard of floral displays to which we were accustomed . . .'. A *Chronicle* leader sympathized with 'the park superintendents who have seen their life's work defaced and defeated'.

When, after the war, several voices were raised in favour of unfenced parks, a *Chronicle* correspondent remarked, 'The argument . . . is that the railings make the parks look ugly and forbidding from the outside; but at least in the old days there was something worth looking at inside . . .'. Beginning in 1948, railings were re-erected around some parks, and park patrols stepped up, but vandalism, if not on the wartime scale, now remained as a fact of life. '[T]o practice horticulture as we knew it in pre-war days in fenceless parks', wrote a superintendent in that year, 'is not only heart-breaking but [also] a waste of time, money and labour'.[22] Confidence gradually returned during the 1950s, but subsided again in the 1960s, as vandalism became more respectable.[23]

117

The passage of the Clean Air Act removed, during the 1960s, a principal functional justification for bedding, but the tradition was already under attack. The late 19th century had seen two lines of criticism: William Robinson's, against geometric patterning of colour,[24] and Forbes Watson's, against seasonal display (when plants, as living things, ought to be appreciated from seedling stage to death).[25] During the 20th century these attitudes were increasingly adopted by large sectors of the gardening press (as distinguished from the gardening public), and bedding, in large part because of its association with municipal parks, came to be regarded as vulgar, fit only for the masses. The modernist aesthetic in landscape came to reject colour patterning in favour of the uniform and unbroken swathe; in 1963 one writer wondered whether 'a better solution would not be to turf over beds in lawns completely and lose them in a bold, exhilarating sweep of grass'.[26] A couple of generations of active lobbying in favour of sports was not matched by lobbying in favour of passive recreation, even though analyses of use showed that more people visited parks to look at the flowers than to use sports facilities.[27] Defences of bedding became progressively more apologetic in the second half of the century.[28]

Above all, there came to be financial restrictions. In 1974, as a result of the Bains Report, Parks Departments were incorporated into Departments of Leisure and Amenity Services, and park superintendents were no longer able to submit their budgets directly to the local authority; parks had to compete with swimming pools and libraries at a lower level of the hierarchy, with a consequent winnowing of funds for bedding. The Institute of Parks and Recreation Administration underwent a similar evolution when it was incorporated into the Institute of Leisure and Amenity Management in 1983; since then, the attention shown to horticulture in its journal has largely switched to fitness equipment and leisure centres. Against this steady trend on the part of the relevant authorities, such initiatives as the Britain in Bloom competition, initiated in 1963, and Evison's demonstration of the effect of horticulture on visitor figures by staging a flower show in the Brighton parks,[29] had little effect. The grassing-over of lawn beds, and the conversion of beds to permanent planting, have been major trends of the second half of the century. For many parks, the final nail in the coffin of bedding was the introduction of compulsory competitive tendering in 1986, though bedding schemes have in many places been included in compulsory competitive tendering maintenance contracts.

Nonetheless, the practice of bedding has continued, and sales of bedding plants seem to be continuously on the increase. The concentration on F1 hybrids, and the mechanisation of plug production, has greatly increased the profitability of bedding plants for commercial growers; Springfields, in Spalding, now acts as a showcase for bedding, and the British Bedding Plant Association attempts to act as a general promoter. A good rhetorical ploy, the promotion of 'craftsman gardening', began to be used during the 1980s, particularly in relation to carpet bedding, while the first experiments have recently been made in the use of computerized design for bedding schemes. The International Garden Festival at Liverpool in 1984 provoked publicity for its innovative designs for bedding schemes, but the examples offered then appear to have had little effect in the wider world of municipal parks.

Notes

1. *Gardeners' Chronicle* (1866), 879–80.

2. *Gardeners' Chronicle* (1859), 726. For Paxton's speech against flowers in parks, see *The Times* (25 November 1859), 5.

3. *Gardener's Magazine*, 1 (1825), 12–13; 2 (1827), 309–10; 3 (1827), 257–9; 5 (1829), 564–7.

4. John Caie, 'On a proper arrangement of plants . . .', *Gardener's Magazine*, 13 (1837), 301–4; 'Descriptive notice of Bedford Lodge', ibid., 14 (1838), 401–11.

5. For the history of bedding theory generally, see Brent Elliott, *Victorian Gardens* (London: B. T. Batsford, 1986), 87–90, 123–38, 148–52.

6. For Gibson, see *Gardeners' Chronicle* (1863), 915, 963–4, 986–7; and Nathan Cole, *The Royal*

Figures 13,14: South Park, Darlington: (top) an
Edwardian postcard view, (bottom) early 1990s view of
the same site. (From the collection of the author)

Parks and Gardens of London (London: Journal of Horticulture, 1872), 31-4. Also, for subtropical bedding, see Elliott, *Victorian Gardens*, 152–4.

7. For carpet bedding, see Elliott, *Victorian Gardens*, 154–8.

8. Ibid., 203–5. For Prince's Park, see Shirley Hibberd, *The Amateur's Flower Garden* (London: Groombridge & Sons, 1875), 30–1.

9. Elliott, *Victorian Gardens*, 136–8. For Aston, see *Gardeners' Chronicle* (1870), 1284–6.

10. For a brief account of sculptural bedding and references to early discussions in the press, see Elliott, *Victorian Gardens*, 209–11; and, for some illustrations, 'The vagaries of carpet bedding', *The Garden*, 118 (1993), 62–3.

11. *Gardeners' Magazine*, 46 (1903), 456.

12. W. W. Pettigrew, *Municipal Parks* (London: Journal of Park Administration, 1937), 172–3; also *Gardeners' Chronicle* (1939), i, 27.

13. For the range of early 20th-century bedding, see Sydney Ashmore, *Flower Beds and Bedding Plants* (London: W. H. & L. Collingridge, n.d. [192–]), to see the continuity into the second half of the century. For spring bedding, see *Gardeners' Chronicle* (1925), ii, 281 and pl. (Falinge Park, Rochford), 321–2 and pl. (Alexandra Park, Oldham); (1927), ii, 498 and pl. (The Dingle, Shrewsbury); (1930), i, 379 (St James' Park), 399 and pl. (Alexandra Park again).

14. *Gardeners' Chronicle* (1898), ii, 156–7; (1938), ii, 87; *Journal of Horticulture*, 60, n.s. (1910), 459–60.

15. Thomas Hay, 'Gardening in London', *Journal of the Royal Horticultural Society*, 56 (1931), 207–16; also idem, *Plants for the Connoisseur* (London: Putnam, 1938).

16. *Gardeners' Chronicle* (1936), ii, 273–4; (1938), i, 132–3.

17. Ibid. (1938), ii, 87.

18. Ibid. (1934), i, 202.

19. For example, ibid. (1938), i, 31, 360; (1949), i, 114–15.

20. Ibid. (1928), ii, 308.

21. Ibid. (1939), ii, 238, 'The garden in war-time'; (1941), i, 91–2, 'Our parks in wartime'.

22. For wartime vandalism, see ibid. (the ones quoted in the text are italicized): 'The rape of the parks': (1939), ii, 297; (1940), i, 233; (1943), ii, *98-9*; (1943), i, 116–17, *223*; 'Railings in post-war parks': (1945), i, *243*; 'Fenceless parks': (1948), i, *38*; 'Return of park fencing': (1948), ii, 105.

23. For a few examples, see ibid., 'Vandalism in municipal parks': (1960), ii, 481; 'Vandalism': (1964), i, 472; 'Patrolling our parks', *Parks and Sports Grounds* (February 1977), 18–22; 'Public order in public places', ibid. (May 1978), 34–7.

24. For the real inception of the debate, see *The Garden* (1872), 265–6, 287–8, 333–4, 384, 406–10, 503–5.

25. Forbes Watson, *Flowers and Gardens* (London: Strahan & Co., 1872), esp. 121–2, 149–50, 178–80.

26. Howard Venison, 'A plea for lawns', *Gardeners' Chronicle* (1963), ii, 414; also F. A. Boddy, ibid. (1953), ii, 82–3. For the perspective of experience, see Michael Branch, 'Activity in urban parks', *Leisure Manager* (July 1991), 16–18: 'Large areas of mown grass may be functional in so far as they provide opportunities for sunbathing, football and kickabout areas, but the dull form of the surrounding shrub borders and space forming elements results in grassy spaces which are visually dull and unattractive'.

27. Brent Elliott, 'From people's parks to green deserts', *Landscape Design*, no. 171 (February 1988), 13–15, passim. A survey in 1968 showed that 32 per cent of park visitors went for the trees and flowerbeds, and only 16 per cent for games and sports; *Gardeners' Chronicle* (23 August 1968), 2–3.

28. For example, J. Craig Wallace, 'The parkie's piece', *Parks and Recreation* (January 1982), 33–4.

29. J. R. B. Evison, 'Brighton floralis?', *Parks and Recreation* (December 1971), 12–13; also David Welch, 'Horticulture as recreation', *Leisure Manager* (October 1986), 12: 'Horticulture is a major British recreation'.

Late 20th century bedding practice

by Frazer Chapman

Figure 1: Extensive bedding displays signified the skills of the superintendent and the park's garden staff, as seen here in Southampton. (Photo: Jan Woudstra)

Bright, colourful spring and summer bedding displays, plus complex carpet bedding schemes, are today often seen to be the 'naughty schoolboys' of the horticultural world, paying little heed to modern taste or horticultural discipline. Spring and summer bedding schemes disturb and torment the aesthetic values of the landscape architect by their often garish and impudent displays, while unsettling the cultured elegance of the garden designer and knowledgeable plantsman. Derision for bedding is also drawn from the evangelists eulogizing the current vogue for sustainable and ecologically sound planting. Despite the barrage of criticism, more bedding plants are grown and sold than ever before, suggesting that people want colour in their domestic gardens, while continuing to respect and admire their local park's bedding displays. The recent resurgence of interest into the current condition of council parks accompanied by concern for their future has sparked discussion on the components that form a 'public park'. Two of the main elements for comment have been horticultural content and horticultural skills.

Before 1974 and the publication of the Bains Report (which advised the integration of municipal Parks Departments into Leisure Services), a park's character was often defined by the colour and flair shown in the execution of the spring and summer bedding displays. Park superintendents could promote their horticultural prowess, plus the appeal of the park that they governed, by the volume of bedding, accompanied by the variety and quality of plants that made up the displays. Extensive bedding displays signified the skills of the superintendent and the park's garden staff (figure 1), publicized an authority's commitment to horticultural excellence and defined the — unspoken — expression of Civic Pride.

Figure 2: Carpet bedding on the city walls in York, 1986. Maintenance and creation of intricate geometrical patterns is a skilled task and labour intensive. (Photo: Jan Woudstra)

The years that followed the recommendations of the Bains Report witnessed the transformation of the parks superintendent from horticultural journeyman into business manager, and financial accountability rather than horticultural flair and innovation became the order of the day. Over the 15 years before the introduction of compulsory competitive tendering in 1989 (so often portrayed as the villain in the decline of the park), the municipal park's nursery, flower beds, 'shield beds' and planters had become an easy target for cost-cutting exercises within the Leisure Department or Directorate. As a consequence, many beds in parks have been 'turfed over' to lessen the continual need for plant material and to reduce bedding maintenance costs, thus creating the green desert that has become the blight of the suburban (and urban) landscape in the latter part of the 20th century. The demise of interest in bedding is best illustrated by the data in the main standard work, *The New Royal Horticultural Society Dictionary of Gardening* (1992),[1] which provides just four pages of bedding material compared with eight pages of detailed information in F. J. Chittenden's 1956 edition of this work.[2]

Cost is the principal factor that determines how many beds will be planted and which plants will be used to create both spring and summer bedding displays. A secondary factor is the level of horticultural skill that a contractor can deploy to plant, establish and maintain bedding displays. Despite diminishing resources, accompanied by a dwindling skill base (for planting and maintenance), substantial spring and summer bedding schemes continue to feature in towns and cities where parks, gardens and open spaces are an important component of a council's economy.

An element of floral display that has achieved an unexpected renaissance in recent years is the carpet bed. The mid-19th century's innovation that led to the widespread use of foliage material (such as alternantheras, echeverias and sedums) to create intricate geometric patterns for bedding display (figure 2) has re-emerged as a late 20th century promotion tool.

For instance, Haringey Borough Council (north London) governs a large multicultural area and suffers from many of the problems associated with inner-city areas: poor housing, unemployment and insufficient resources adequately to support services. Carpet bedding has been used as a visual medium to promote and communicate the council's commitment to employment training and fighting racism. In 1997 Haringey allocated funding that allowed two carpet beds to be planted using the logos of the following organizations: Investors in People and European Year Against Racism. It actively promoted the carpet designs in the local press and their own corporate publications and newsletters — the carpet designs were used to get the message across and thus justified the commitment of scant resources.

Plymouth City Council has planted their shield bed with the message 'Welcome to Plymouth' in recent years. The National Trust, too, at Waddesdon Manor, Buckinghamshire, has resurrected carpet bedding designs. Waddesdon received the award 'Museum of the Year' and 'Best National Trust Property' in 1997 and they have combined this statement (Museum of the Year) with the Rothschilds' family emblem to create one of two large rectangular carpet beds that dominate the formal garden.

Tourism and bedding

Tourism and bold prestigious bedding schemes are inextricably linked in both coastal resorts and historic towns where visitors consider being able to admire the park's floral displays an essential part of their 'day trip' or holiday. For example, Eastbourne, Bournemouth, Worthing and Skegness are coastal towns where colourful and extensive bedding schemes are recognized as being an integral part of the resort's attraction to visitors. As a consequence the value of parks and gardens is acknowledged by council members approving forthcoming annual budgets for Leisure Departments, thus financial restrictions are not so severe as in other non-tourist areas.

However, the attraction of the coastal resort for holidays and tourism has not been the only factor in securing the survival and continuation of spring and summer bedding displays. Cities that (until recently) have not been readily associated with tourism, as for example Glasgow, Colchester and Rochester, have skilfully promoted their heritage and cultural assets to attract visitors and generate (much needed) revenue. This in turn has encouraged well-maintained spring and summer bedding displays, carpet beds and extensive use of floral hanging baskets throughout their urban configurations. Participation in the 'Britain in Bloom' competition by a local authority is a good indication that quality bedding schemes will feature in a city town or village and are thus worth visiting.

Britain in Bloom is Britain's largest horticultural competition. It is promoted by the Tidy Britain Group[3] and attracts about 1,400 entrants: success in any of the event's ten categories helps in raising a town's profile with regard to tourism. Fierce competition and rivalry between councils, parishes, towns and villages has encouraged the practice of bedding to continue, ensuring the survival of many flower beds and generating sales within the commercial growing market. Taking part in the competition demands commitment from councillors, council officers, contractors and the business community. Unfortunately, the financial burden placed on an authority that enters Britain in Bloom is often unacceptable and unless the expenditure can be justified (by attracting revenue) the authority is forced to withdraw. The guidelines for judging Britain in Bloom have changed in recent years, and while the competition continues to be associated with immaculately maintained bedding schemes, accompanied by 'Victorian style lamp-posts' sporting floral baskets, recent competition briefs focus on sustainability, conservation and community issues. However, receiving an award in Britain in Bloom continues to evoke civic pride in local authorities and the East Devon town of Sidmouth has placed a series of photographs of its award-winning bedding schemes on the Internet for the entire world to see.[4]

The trade journal *Horticulture Week* provides valuable information with regard to the 'politics of bedding'. These are, for example, reports on which councils are either expanding or cutting the size of their displays and bedding schemes, what plants are being promoted or have become unpopular, plus articles covering a variety of design and maintenance issues.

Funding issues

Tourism, the beach and a well-marketed heritage do not guarantee provision of sufficient budgets capable of sustaining the creation and maintenance of elaborate planting schemes. To seek a — partial — solution to the ceaseless problem of budgets, council parks and horticultural officers have sought funding through partnerships with the business sector.

The development of partnership between an authority and the private sector has often been successful in supporting bedding schemes through commercial sponsorship in coastal resorts and towns where heritage is the selling point. Funding for planting and maintaining summer bedding or carpet bedding may be provided by local businesses sponsoring the schemes in return for the authority advertising the companies' involvement on signs displayed at the planting site.

An example of commercial sponsorship that supports the planting and maintenance of sculptural bedding (in the shape of a telephone) may be found in Devonshire Park, Eastbourne, East Sussex. During the Ladies Tennis Championships, held in Devonshire Park each summer, a three-dimensional floral telephone is created using red and green alternanthera planted on to a hollow metal frame. The floral telephone depicts the logo of Direct Line Insurance and advertises the company's financial support for the event. Direct Line's logo is easily recognized by the public and extensive televised coverage of the event ensures a successful and lasting partnership

between Eastbourne Council and the insurance company (figure 3).

The limitations of this partnership are that it is only for the creation and upkeep of the sponsor's own schemes, but other partnerships with more traditional beds and discreet signs are a possibility. For example, almost all the shops and business premises on Guildford High Street, Surrey, lease hanging baskets from the council to decorate their shop fronts during the summer months. The authority's Direct Services Divison plants, hangs and maintains the baskets on behalf of the businesses at virtually no cost to the council. The payoff from this partnership is a high street that is ablaze with colour during the summer months, helping attract revenue from visitors — as well as giving excellent prospects in the Britain in Bloom competition.

Councils that have been unsuccessful in raising sponsorship or have had to suffer severe financial restraint reflect their position in the number of beds planted and the choice of bedding material used in their displays, or indeed in the removal and 'turfing over' of redundant beds.

Plants for use in contemporary bedding schemes

The loss of the large municipal nursery over the past 25 years, accompanied by the expansion and success of the major commercial seed and bedding producers, has produced a restrained palette from which plants for bedding schemes may be chosen. The position was different in the early part of this century when a broad range of plants was planted and maintained throughout Britain's parks and gardens. During the 1920s an extensive range of bedding plants was raised within a park's nursery. For example, the gardens at Hampton Court Palace used the (now) old-fashioned pelargoniums 'Paul Crampell', 'Madame Crousse' and 'Monsieur Hammelin' in their summer displays.[5] Plants for each successive years' displays were produced in the palace's nursery by means of vegetative propagation, thus securing and sustaining the variety of pelargonium stock.[6]

Over the past 20 years there has been a general

Figure 3: The floral telephone depicts the logo of Direct Line Insurance and advertises the company's financial support for the event. Direct Line's logo is easily recognized by the public and extensive televised coverage of the event ensures a successful and lasting partnership between Eastbourne Council and the insurance company, 1997. (Photo: the author)

acceptance of F1-hybrids. These have replaced the old varieties, which have been relegated to the collector's and enthusiast's greenhouse and have completely vanished from the contemporary parks officer's planting palette. An F1-hybrid is the first generation derived from crossing two distinct plants, usually when the parents are purebred lines and the offspring are vigorous. This discovery made it commercially viable to grow uniform geraniums cheaply and quickly from seed. Examples of well-known contemporary F1-hybrid geraniums are *Pelargonium* 'Multibloom' and *P.* 'Century', which exhibit a uniform growth habit and consistent colour compared with the old cultivars. Large quantities of the F1-hybrid geranium, bought in ready for planting in summer bedding schemes may be too expensive for impoverished councils. Local authorities that have written the supply of bedding material into their grounds maintenance or plant propagation contracts are often bound by the contractor's (often inflated) price. For example (at 1999 prices) a geranium bought in ready for planting may vary between £0.45 per unit from a commercial grower and £2.75 per unit within a plant propagation contract.

Unfortunately, the majority of local authority bedding is determined by financial constraints. Thus, those authorities with a small budget for purchasing plants, or trapped in an expensive propagation or maintenance contract, will resort to specifying cheaper plant material. As a result it is common to find examples of summer bedding schemes that are planted using just one of the cheaper species, either as a single colour block or using a colour mixture from the same variety. For example, impatiens or petunias and spring flowers such as wallflowers are frequently planted *en masse*, while coleus, geraniums, polyanthus and bellis are more expensive and remain an indulgence. The effect of this mass planting is that displays are often without character and lack visual impact. Dot plants such as kochia, ricinus or cordyline would alleviate some of the negative effects of mass planting but their use has declined due to their high unit cost (often more than £8.00 per plant). Dot plants form an attractive target for both theft and vandalism and these factors also influence their use in bedding schemes. It is easier for a local authority to replace a display of cheap petunias that have been stolen or vandalized than repairing a bed of geraniums and dot plants.

Recently there has been a resurgence of interest in using annuals to create summer displays[7] and this in turn has led the University of Sheffield's Landscape Department to run and evaluate trials on sowing annual flowering meadows.[8] The meadows re-interpret the medieval concept of the 'flowery mead' by using a mixture of annual, exotic and native plants. The annual border may look spectacular, but it is labour intensive and often difficult to establish, whereas a large tract of

125

ground sown as an 'annual flowering meadow' is visually impressive, ecologically sound, sustainable and requires minimal maintenance.

The loss of the municipal nursery, rising propagation and maintenance costs, plus contract issues have all played a part in the demise of the dahlia border, the canna bed and the tuberous begonia display. Despite the hurdles, bedding survives; in some areas it thrives and continues to thrill people with often bold and garish displays of colour. For those given the task of designing spring and summer bedding schemes, the trade journal *Horticulture Week* and the catalogues of the large commercial growers are the main sources of information on plant material. Unlike former times when council nurseries raised a rich variety of plant material, the only way to make a bedding scheme cost-effective today is by purchasing from the commercial nursery.

Financial considerations make the exact reconstruction of historic (Victorian) planting schemes prohibitive. Yet, in exceptional instances this option may well be worth pursuing, as indeed has been done at Hampton Court Palace for many years. One of the prerequisites, however, is greenhouse space where historic varieties can be propagated and grown on. The 1951 edition of *The Royal Horticultural Society Dictionary of Gardening* continues to be a useful source of information on traditional bedding plants, their growth habit, colour and propagation.

Investigating sources of historic material is most easily carried out with *The Plant Finder Reference Library* CD-ROM or *RHS Plant Finder*, in book form. These are updated annually and are excellent sources for searching plant material, which is difficult to locate elsewhere in the catalogues of the modern bedding plant firms.

Bedding design

Nursery catalogues and The *RHS Dictionary* are not only useful with regard to information on plant material, but also they contain useful sections on design. The *RHS Dictionary* provides a practical section that classifies bedding according to seasonal interest: spring, summer and winter

bedding. The latter, containing evergreen shrubs and small conifers, has not been practised for many years. A more up-to-date source is D. G. Hessayon's *The New Bedding Plant Expert* (1996). It offers a concise account of techniques, schemes and plant information, which provides an uncomplicated introduction to bedding practice for the inexperienced designer. It also offers a useful, if slightly unusual, classification of bedding styles: formal bedding (the standard garden bedding scheme and the standard park bedding scheme); informal bedding; subtropical bedding; raised bedding (planters); carpet bedding; picture bedding (a variation on the carpet bed); vertical bedding (the three-dimensional bedding sculpture); and blanket bedding.[9]

Sadly, present-day bedding schemes are frequently directed by the commercial nurseries, which, between the principal growers, determine the range of plants available, and their catalogues often include suggestions on plant combinations and schemes. The displays at their headquarters are open to the public and business sectors on a select number of days throughout the year. These 'open days' are used to full effect to show and promote what will be available for purchase for the coming year's schemes and they demonstrate realistic combinations of how new varieties may be used.

The traditional methods for bedding designs have centred on creating displays that use blocks of plants in regular geometric shapes such as diamonds, circles or squares. However, there are other possibilities. The introduction of 'Best Value' policies within the municipal context has generated awareness of the importance and value of involving the community in local government at a variety of levels, and the design of bedding schemes is no exception. Art and design colleges, junior and senior schools have all contributed towards designing bedding schemes in partnership with local councils. In the Medway area, Kent College of Art and Design provided a series of abstract paintings that was used as the plan for planting summer bedding schemes in a series of rectangular beds located on the A2's grass verges between Gillingham and Twydall in 1998. The

126

planting mirrored the abstract designs in colour and form, and the paintings were printed onto a series of weatherproof canvasses which were displayed individually next to the relevant scheme.

Community involvement in bedding design engenders 'ownership' of the display and may reduce vandalism, plus providing new and innovative ideas into an authority's bedding repertoire. The introduction of the 'annual flowering meadow' (the flowery mead) into parks may help span the council/community divide by providing colour (a long flowering season) an educational resource (a rich variety of native plants and insect life) and yet not create another unacceptable financial burden. However, this type of planting is not suitable in a traditional setting in small (historic) beds.

The location of flower beds

In recent years beds have been located not only within parks and open spaces, but also on highway verges, roundabouts and shopping precincts. The ideal position for flowerbeds is within level, well-maintained lawn areas away from visual distractions. This enables the lawn to display the flowerbeds to their greatest advantage. In public parks flowerbeds were normally in separate areas enclosed by shrubberies or defined by formal hedges. In cases where the flowerbeds have been grassed over, the former flowerbeds can normally be traced from the depressions in the ground, and can easily be re-instated with some archaeological assistance. An accurate survey of the area including field archaeological evidence at an appropriate scale, before any works, is an invaluable tool. It is important that the geometry is restored and that the outlines of the beds are clear and crisp. If there is no finance to re-instate all the historic flowerbeds, it may be possible to restore alternate beds, or perhaps one section where it adjoins the path. However, it is no use being too dogmatic and changes to surrounding vegetation, as for example a spreading canopy of a nearby tree, will have to be accommodated.

Historically the size and shape of beds would have related to their surroundings and changes to the shape of beds may affect the re-instatement. A series of small flowerbeds on the verge of a road originally designed as a walk to be seen by pedestrians will not create any impact to the passing motorist. A simple and clear concept is generally most effective. Eastbourne's carpet gardens provide an example whereby a series of large rectangular beds is used to display the geometrically patterned carpet beds during the summer months. Long linear borders planted with uncomplicated formal displays frame the carpet beds. These complement the carpet schemes without detracting from the garden's main visual subjects (figures 4 and 5).

Bedding techniques

The resurgence of carpet bedding in recent years has drawn attention to the decline in the horticultural skill-base for the design, planting and maintenance of carpet beds. The plotting of a logo or emblem onto a large sheet of graph paper followed by the transference of the design onto the planting site, using silver sand and string, before days of labour-intensive planting constitutes a series of complex and painstaking tasks. This may deter some authorities and their officers from creating carpet-bedding displays. Various experiments have been undertaken in an attempt to economize on labour, maintenance and material costs. In one instance, East Lindsey District Council in the coastal resort of Skegness has sprayed vegetable dyes onto several block plantings of sedums to create eight carpet bedding designs adjacent to the sea front. The seeds of this idea were sown by the council's need to reduce bedding costs; however, it produced a rather tatty effect as the dye faded and necessitated several re-sprays to preserve the design.[10]

The problems of reducing costs and addressing insufficient skill issues with regard to carpet bedding have been resolved in a more sophisticated manner by Kernock Park Plants, a major supplier of carpet bedding plants to local authorities for many years, by developing the 'InstaPlant' system. This innovation has been created to simplify the design and planting process by offering a package that allows carpet beds to be created immediately on-site by, what is in essence,

127

a system of planting by numbers.[11]

The design chosen for the carpet bed is sent to Kernock's nursery where the image is scanned into a computer. The scanned image is divided into sections, which are numbered and colour-coded, and each part of the design is allocated carpet bedding plants pertinent to the design, alternantheras, echeverias, kleinias, etc. The planting plan for the design is created by using numbered horticultural trays, which are planted with appropriate carpet bedding material. The planted trays are allowed to 'grow on' and receive regular feeding and clipping to encourage the foliage to 'bush out' and thicken, thus forming the design. In mid-June the trays are dispatched, arranged in situ by number and planted according to the computer-generated planting plan, thus creating an 'instant' carpet bed that is immediately recognizable and easy to establish. This planting system has been adopted by many authorities (including Plymouth City Council and the National Trust at Waddesdon Manor) who consider the innovative service a solution to the traditional lengthy planting process (figure 6 and 7).

These modern innovations in carpet bedding have not crossed over into the area of traditional bedding schemes, and flower beds for spring and summer displays continue to be prepared and planted following time-honoured modus operandi.

For autumn preparation a flowerbed should ideally be turned over by hand, using a garden spade and incorporating mild organic matter into the soil, plus a slow-release fertilizer scattered to secure the healthy flowering of spring bulbs. In past years mild organic matter has often been purchased in the form of spent hops or depleted mushroom compost, while a slow-release fertilizer such as sterile bonemeal would have been incorporated during ground cultivation. After flowering, the spring display's bulbs should be removed and the bed forked over, incorporating a quick-release fertilizer, before planting summer bedding. Summer bedding should be slightly starved of nutrients to encourage flowering and discourage lush vegetative growth. All operations should be carried out when beds are not wet to prevent

unnecessary soil flocculation and unwelcome production of clay.

Unfortunately, the contemporary contractor will not cultivate flowerbeds by hand unless it is expressly written into the contract's specification document. The authority that specifies manual cultivation in its grounds' maintenance contract documents will also have to accept a hefty price for the privilege of a contractor performing this operation. A contractor will use a mechanical rotavator wherever possible for cultivation; however, continual use of a rotavator may cause drainage problems by panning the soil at a depth of 150–200 millimetres. Consequently, a rolling programme of manual cultivation is recommended to offset problems arising from excessive mechanical cultivation.

Maintenance of bedding schemes

Regular skilled maintenance by direct labour or contractor's employees is the key factor in achieving success with spring, summer and carpet displays. The visual pleasure that may be achieved by a well-designed scheme may be undermined in various ways. Rogue tulips that have not been removed from a previous year may affect the colour harmony of tulip displays. Marigolds choked by weeds and damaged carpet bedding swiftly become eyesores. All too often the maintenance of bedding schemes falls under the umbrella of general grounds maintenance specifications and, consequently, displays may suffer neglect and disrepair.

Maintenance of bedding displays planted throughout a series of parks and urban sites is often difficult to monitor and the ambiguous use of language within a contract specification may lead to conflict. For example, instructing a contractor to irrigate bedding when 'plants exhibit stress' is difficult to quantify. Stress to the contractor may be understood as plants toppling and dying in drought conditions while a client officer may view a number of dry days as sufficient to cause stress to bedding.

Unfortunately, frequent maintenance visits are

Figures 4 and 5: The same view of Eastbourne, *c.*1928 and present day. A series of large rectangular beds is used to display the geometrically patterned carpet beds during the summer months. Long linear borders planted with uncomplicated formal displays frame the carpet beds. These complement the carpet schemes without detracting from the garden's main visual subjects. (Photo: the author)

Figures 6 and 7: A computer-generated planting system has been adopted by the National Trust at Waddesdon Manor. (opposite) The bedding design is plotted on a computer, which enables the sowing of the individual varieties in their exact position in large square plastic trays. The seeds are germinated and the plants grown on in a greenhouse. Once the plants are fully developed the trays are buried in the beds. (above) The finished design *in situ*. (Photo: the author)

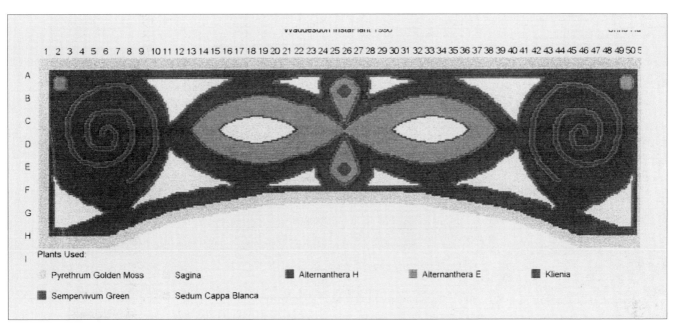

Plants Used:

Pyrethrum Golden Moss   Sagina   ▪ Alternanthera H   ▪ Alternanthera E   ▪ Klienia

▪ Sempervivum Green   Sedum Cappa Blanca

131

expensive, often not necessary and with today's financial restrictions difficult to justify. While concise and exact descriptions of horticultural operations are essential to grounds' maintenance contracts, a key issue with regard to successful maintenance is understanding what level of service is required by the client and what level of service the contractor is prepared to provide for the contract price. Consensus about bedding maintenance (and, indeed, other maintenance operations) between client and contractor can reduce conflict (defaults, etc.) within a grounds maintenance contract. Adequate irrigation, weeding and dead heading, plus swift replacement of diseased or vandalized plants, are all essential tasks necessary to secure the success of a bedding scheme and this may only happen when council officers and contractors work together.

Community involvement in maintenance issues may become viable in the future facilitated by volunteer programmes, for example 'adopt a bed' and 'Friends of . . .' community schemes. However, the rigid terms and conditions that apply to the large quantitative maintenance contracts that are so commonplace and which contain vast amounts of minute maintenance detail hinder

community and volunteer maintenance schemes. Until the prohibitive aspects of grounds maintenance contracts are addressed, the problems that surround flowerbed maintenance and indeed many horticultural operations will continue.

The future for bedding

The production of seasonal bedding material contravenes many of the ideals found in the Local Agenda 21 documents of local authorities. For example, bedding uses the earth's valuable resources (peat and oil) and by its very nature, being a seasonal product, is not sustainable. Bedding is expensive to produce, plant and maintain and often places an unacceptable and unwelcome burden on the restricted budgets of local authorities. The preceding points make bedding displays hard to justify. The general public, however, cannot get enough of bedding plants (over the Easter and the Spring Bank Holiday nurseries and garden centres are stripped of bedding produce) while demand for tickets to garden festivals and flower shows often far exceeds supply. The future for the commercial bedding plant market appears sound but competitive, sustained by the large growers vying with each other for the lion's share of the market by introducing plants that flower prolifically and require minimal maintenance. The prognosis for municipal bedding is that poorly maintained, low-profile bedding sites will continue to disappear and be turfed over, while securing sponsorship to support the displays of the prestigious tourist centres will be increasingly commonplace and necessary. Bedding forms an element of the public park and indeed the future of the public park is under threat. The 'golden age' of the public park has long gone and only innovative management involving community adoption and business partnership will secure the future of the public park and its bedding displays.

Notes

1. A. Huxley (ed.), *The New Royal Horticultural Society Dictionary of Gardening* (London: Macmillan, 1992), 315–18.

2. F. J. Chittenden (ed.), *R.H.S. Dictionary of Gardening*, 2nd edn, vol. iii (Oxford: Clarendon, 1956), 246–53.

3. Tidy Britain Group, Chandos House, 26 North Street, Brighton, West Sussex BN1 1EB; tel: 01273 722723.

4. www.eastdevon.net/sidmouth/bloom/index.htm

5. Ernest Law, *The Flower-lover's Guide to the Gardens of Hampton Court* (London: George Bell & Sons, 1923).

6. The nursery at Hampton Court Palace continues to propagate and raise a wide variety of 'traditional' geraniums for bedding purposes.

7. Graham Rice, 'Pride or prejudice?', *The Garden*, 124/3 (1999), 164–7.

8. Nigel Dunnett, 'Annuals on the loose', *The Garden*, 124/3 (1999), 168–9.

9. D. G. Hessayon, *The New Bedding Plant Expert* (London: Transworld, 1996), 101–8.

10. Frazer Chapman, 'Carpet bedding — tapestries of delight', unpublished dissertation, Architectural Association, London, 1998, 100–3.

11. Kernock Park Plants, Pillaton, Saltash, Cornwall PL12 6RY; tel: 01579 350561; e-mail: Kernock.Park@virgin.net

Lakes and water features

by Hilary Taylor

Figure 1: The fountain at Ropner Park, Stockton-on-Tees, no longer works. Often, the only time when the significance of a body of water is really acknowledged is when it is absent. (Photo: Peter Vickers)

It would be difficult to identify an historic public park that does not feature water in some form. There are certainly other kinds of open space, recreation grounds or public walks, for example, that are devoid of water; but scarcely a single public park. Given the difficulty that is sometimes associated with creating a body of water in the landscape — the expense, the engineering, the sheer physical effort — it is clear that water must carry with it such a weight of meaning that no individual or committee, scrutinizing the costs of a new public park, could think of suggesting that the water could go.

One consequence is that it is all too easy to overlook the role played by water in a given design. Often, the only time when the significance of a body of water is really acknowledged is when it is absent; when a lake is degraded or has been filled in, or when a fountain is dry. For example, at Ropner Park, Stockton-on-Tees, the lavish form of

the fountain is belied by the fact that it no longer provides any water (figure 1), while at Stanley Park, Liverpool, the boat house stands high and dry.[1] The element that reveals the personality, captures and conveys light, shade and reflection through all the seasons is gone. The opportunity to hear the music of water running, cascading or falling from a fountain, has disappeared.[2] To the character of a landscape and its impact on the viewer this is a catastrophe.

It is important, then, to examine a variety of bodies of water in public parks and to identify something of their structure and meaning.

The first point to make is that water, perhaps more than any other element, symbolizes life itself. Indeed, the history of civilization could be charted as the history of the capture, containment and movement of water. This would have been very evident to those who had only recently given up the attempt to scratch a living from the land,

and had flocked to the rapidly growing towns. Once in the towns, the difficulty of obtaining a satisfactory water supply was a major cause for consideration. As early as 1827 there was the first of several Royal Commissions concerned with these issues, this one 'to inquire into the State of the Supply of Water to the Metropolis', some time before there was either the political will or the planning machinery to effect any significant improvement. Thus, for the new urban communities — largely for whose benefit the public parks were laid out — to find that they not only had access to, but also a possessive interest in, a significant or showy body of water would not have been empty of meaning.[3]

Water was presented in lakes, cascades, streams, formal basins and fountains, sometimes ostentatious, occasionally quite modest. In the early years, in particular, far more important than any recreational activity — boating or swimming — was the desire to create a work of art, a composition to delight the spectator, for 'if there was one thing which more than another would assist in promoting both the mental and physical welfare of the community it was to bring the masses of the people into contact with such beauties of nature'.[4]

From the beginning, public parks included water features. Derby Arboretum, for example, one of the first in the country when it was opened in 1840, was but 4.5 hectares. Financed by the local industrialist, Joseph Strutt, it was laid out by John Claudius Loudon. The only water included was as a fountain placed at the junction of the principal paths in the park — the tall and elegant structure was clearly designed to attract attention.

Sometimes the water embraced within a park was already on-site and its presence was the main reason for the selection of that site. The first public park in Birmingham, Calthorpe Park, was opened in 1857, the land having been made available on a short-term lease from Lord Calthorpe who was developing the neighbouring area of Edgbaston. The local authority, uncertain of the future of the site, invested little money in the design, but despite this the park was enormously popular from

the start and its attractions were greatly enhanced by the River Rea which defined the eastern boundary, its picturesque variety enlarged by the fact that it had earlier functioned as a mill race.[5]

More often a water-body was created artificially, a beautiful signifier of ambition, optimism and civic pride. This is certainly true in one of the first important urban parks at Birkenhead, where, in 1842, the town's Improvement Commissioners were the first to apply to Parliament for permission to use public funds for the establishment of a park.[6] It was no accident that this historic development took place in Birkenhead. The town's commissioners had determined that this was to be the first new city of the modern world, with all necessary attributes. Hence, Joseph Paxton, head gardener at Chatsworth, was selected to undertake the important commission. Hence, also, the young Frederick Law Olmsted, visiting Birkenhead in 1850, returned to his native America and, with Calvert Vaux before the end of the decade launched Central Park in New York. There can be little doubt that the substantial bodies of water included in Birkenhead Park were not only just a convenient answer to the problem of dealing with marshy ground,[7] but also an essential part of a design that proclaimed the values of the new society.

Water, then, in some form or another, was an intrinsic part of a public park layout. As a consequence there are very few parks today where neglect or removal of a water feature is not one of the most visible signals of a failure to recognize and protect the value of these landscapes.

There is no escaping the fact that repairing, restoring and maintaining bodies of water is complex and sometimes challenging, especially if that body is a lake of any size. Success is absolutely dependent on thorough research into every aspect of the feature.

Where to build a water feature

Many 19th-century commentators devoted a good deal of attention to identifying 'rules' that should govern the placement of water. Henry Ernest Milner's influential *The Art and Practice of*

Landscape Gardening (1890) passed on some of the wisdom Milner had acquired from his father, Edward. He wrote, 'we should imitate the spirit of beauty in Nature's operations, but not distort her effects'.[8] Milner Sr had been a close associate of Paxton and, from the late 1840s, was responsible for the design of numerous fine parks including Miller and Avenham Parks in Preston, Lincoln Arboretum and Buxton Pavilion Gardens. Perhaps even more significantly he had been given the task of supervising Paxton's Crystal Palace Park at Sydenham, London, where he had also been an important teacher, passing on his wisdom to his successors.

At the end of the century Thomas H. Mawson — whose successful career was launched in the 1890s with the layout of Hanley and Burslem Parks in the Potteries — was offering similar advice. He insisted that the designer must always follow Nature's model and 'never belittle' her by 'feeble imitation'. Mawson castigated alike the 'absurd engineering feats of Capability Brown' and the 'ridiculous miniature lakes squeezed into suburban gardens'. Instead, 'it is from observing the flow of natural water courses, that lessons are stored for incorporation in our plans'.[9]

Having identified a suitable place for a lake or a stream, the next problem was to build it.

Construction techniques and materials

One very useful source of information about the construction of early public park lakes is Edward Kemp, introduced as Superintendent of Birkenhead Park by Paxton and responsible for much of the detail of the layout. Kemp spent most of his career at Birkenhead, but he also designed several private grounds and, in the 1860s and 1870s, was responsible too for Hesketh Park, Southport, Stanley Park, Liverpool and Saltwell Park, Gateshead, all of which included substantial lakes.

Kemp's *How to Lay Out a Small Garden* first appeared in 1850 and went into several editions. He wrote that if there were a watercourse, then a dam could be thrown across a stream at an appropriate place and a 'lake may probably be formed in a very inartificial manner'.[10] Needless to say, however, that is not all there was to it:

The first requisite in making a dam is to place it at a point where the valley narrows, and the adjoining banks are tolerably steep and high. A trench of at least four or five feet wide should then be taken out across the hollow, and be cut down till solid ground is reached. If this be clay, it will be so much the more satisfactory. The trench should then be filled up with puddled clay, and this latter be added as much as possible in a sloping bank on the side toward the intended lake, a good broad embankment being carried up simultaneously on the outside.

Probably more frequently the ground for park lakes had to be excavated. There must then be 'thorough puddling for the bottom and sides' to render them watertight. Puddling involved working a mixture of wet clay usually with sand so that it became malleable and impervious and so could be used to line the base and sides of a lake; only if the clay mixture dries out will it crack and be breached.

Milner, characteristically, provided more detailed instructions than Kemp. For puddling, clay could be cut and cross-cut, mixed with water and worked 'in a mortar-mill, or by treading, till it is plastic'.[11] The puddle should then be laid on the excavated ground, 'not less than 1 ft. thick on the bottom and 18 in. on the sides. As it is laid, it must be well trodden and rammed till the formation is complete and as homogeneous as possible'.

To combat erosion of the banks — exacerbated by scour, groundwater outflows, undercutting or vermin — Milner recommended that the sides of a fairly shallow lake be covered with gravel. In larger lakes, both Milner and Kemp employed 'some kind of pitching near the surface', the application of a particularly resistant material round the lip of the pool. For Kemp this was sometimes created by means of a series of stones set into the sides of the lake. He illustrated this technique (figure 2), and early photographs of Birkenhead reveal its use (figure 3).

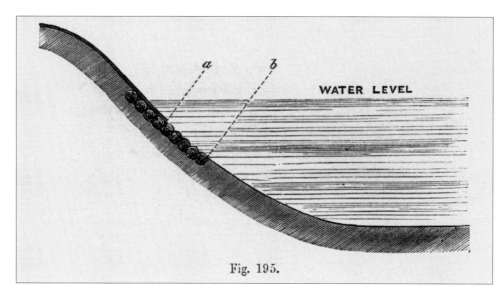

WATER LEVEL

Fig. 195.

Figure 2: Illustration from Kemp's *How to Lay Out a Garden*, 1864 edition, showing pitching the banks of a lake with stone.

Mawson, in turn, presented a useful illustration in *The Art and Craft of Garden Making*, and noted that the 'breadth of the band of pitching will depend on whether any variation in the water level can be efficiently prevented'. He also advised that if lining a long, narrow stretch of water, such as a canal, 'the breadth of pitching will need to be much greater at the ends than at the sides, as ripples crossing the canal will not have the force of the lengthwise ones'.

In 1898 Mawson won a competition for East Park, Wolverhampton, 'an area of fifty acres, consisting entirely of cinder heaps, excepting for a flooded depression which gave an opportunity for a lake large enough for boating'. He tackled the job of creating the lake on this inauspicious site by uniting the 'various . . . hollows' by cutting through the intervening 'old spoil banks or pit mounds'. The additional presence of old pit shafts 'necessitated that the whole area to be covered with water should be treated with a layer of puddled clay, which in this instance was dug from the site and put through a brick-makers' pugging machine'.[12]

Puddling was a venerable technique and could be used to create lakes both small and large. In the latter case it was sometimes necessary to do the work in sections to prevent the clay from drying and cracking. Today it is still possible to puddle a lake and, in many circumstances, this can be the most long-lasting and effective lining method. Even in the 19th century, however, it was not the only technique employed.

In suitable areas where stone was plentiful this was sometimes used to create the sides of a lake. For example, Milner's Buxton Pavilion Gardens were laid out during the early 1870s. The principal water features were the swiftly running River Wye and associated pools and cascades. During the following decade a new lake was completed. The walls were built from substantial, rock-faced local gritstone, only the bed being puddled. If these handsome walls were a statement of local pride, then so was the engineering of the underground boathouse, also of stone and large enough to accommodate several boats.

By the late 19th century different materials and techniques were becoming more widely used. There was a growing interest in the history and properties of cement and concrete. Loudon's *The Architectural Magazine* frequently included articles about concrete mixed from different materials and for a variety of purposes. For example, in June 1834 Felix Austin was insisting on the durable properties of his 'artificial stone', which he made at his works on New Road, Regent's Park, London.

Figure 3: Early postcard showing stones protecting the banks at the lip of the water in Birkenhead Park. (From the collection of the author)

I beg most confidently to assert, that I consider [my material] more durable, and considerably superior to Portland stone; having for several years made fountains and reservoirs of large dimensions that have withstood the severest winters, and having had basins in my own yard, where the water contained in them has been frozen into solid bodies of ice, which have not sustained the least injury.[13]

Certainly, when creating a body of water where the subsoil was particularly porous, cement and concrete could seem easier materials to work with than a clay puddle. Milner noted:

If the soil be sandy or gravelly, and no clay is available, and above all, if a solid foundation can be found, then concrete may be used. It should be deposited not less than 12 in. thick on the bottom and 18 in. at the sides, and should be composed by mixture of 1 part hydraulic lime with 4 parts of broken stone and sand, or 1 part of Portland cement with 6 parts of broken stone and sand. This is to be floated with a layer 1 in. in thickness of cement. Before the concrete is laid, the natural bottom must be worked solid and firm.[14]

F. W. Meyer also offered useful advice. A landscape designer working with the nurseryman Robert Veitch from the 1880s, Meyer specialized in rock and water gardens, mainly in the south of England. He was responsible for the layout of several public parks, including that at Truro, built in 1894 on land reclaimed from the River Fal. More ambitious still were his 1898 Northernhay Public Gardens, Exeter, and The Pageant Gardens, Sherborne, from 1905. Both included rockeries, cascades, pools and lakes, demonstrating the extent of his expertise.[15] In 1910, after his death, his published articles were collected and edited by E. T. Cook in an influential volume entitled *Rock and Water Gardens*. Herein, Meyer warned of some of the problems associated with using cement to line a lake. If a pool or lake were excavated in very soft or fill-up ground, this could often 'settle down considerably if any heavy weight were put on it' and the 'cement concrete would sink into it before it had time to harden, with the result that a series of troublesome cracks would appear'.

Meyer's answer to this problem was to incorporate a form of reinforcement. For a relatively small pool 'a network of strong fencing wire across the bottom before the concrete is put on . . . helps considerably in holding the concrete together'.[16]

By the 1920s reinforcement was more sophisticated. The thickness of concrete was adjusted according to the size of the lake: about 6 inches in most cases, or up to 8 or 9 inches thick for a larger lake. The surface of the concrete was scratched before setting to take a final render of a strong mixture of sand and cement. In 1934 Percy Cane advised that for larger lakes in particular the 'beds should be reinforced with steel rods or expanded metal. The thickness of the rods, which should be laid crossing each other so that they form a pattern of squares, will vary according to the bearing quality of the soil and the size of the pools'.[17]

Throughout the period it is certainly clear that the creation of a body of water of any size necessitated detailed understanding both of the requirements of design and the demands of engineering. Once the bed was constructed, however, securing the provision of water could be equally demanding.

Provision and management of water

If a lake were created from an existing stream, this would certainly be the best means of obtaining an adequate through-put of clean water. Milner was thorough in his analysis, noting the average rainfall in London and 'approximately ascertaining the quantity of water available from a flowing stream'. To prevent erosion there should be a 4- or 6-foot wide apron of paving laid down the slope below an inlet. Milner, ever efficient, also noted that when forming such an inlet, the designer should 'bear in mind the practicability of introducing either a hydraulic ram or a turbine, where the useful work it can do may be needed. For example, a stream that fills a 3-in. pipe with a fall of 6 ft. will force the delivery of 2,000 gallons of water daily to a point 100 ft. above the water-level'.[18] At the outlet there must be a grating to prevent 'the escape of fish or leaves and rubbish', and, of course, this must be frequently cleaned. Kemp advised that the outlet should also be equipped with 'a strong sluice' so that the movement of the water could be controlled.

Perhaps more often, park lakes were created in low-lying, sometimes boggy ground, and were fed principally by surface water, as at Birkenhead Park. This was true, too, of Central Park, New York. In the late 1850s this was being developed and, under the guidance of the young engineer, George Waring, 'the drainage gangs had laid twenty miles of drain tiles in the southern portion of the park'.

> Waring's team of four hundred laborers . . . excavated trenches three to four feet deep at forty foot intervals across the entire park, and laid one foot sections of joined clay pipes or tiles. Placed at a proper slope, the well-fitted pipes would draw surface water downward to collecting drains, which then would channel it through brick sewers to the lakes.[19]

Then as now, lakes thus supplied with surface water drainage were more likely to suffer from a range of problems than those created from a fast-flowing stream. Flooding is a possibility that necessitates a storm overflow. Kemp advised that the overflow chamber and drain should be constructed of cement, the water being carried in a barrel drain and emerging, if possible, 'where the slope of the bank would naturally give it exit'. If the water were of sufficient volume a feature could be made of this outflow 'with or without the accompaniment of rocks to break it up into falls'.[20]

The more obvious problem, however, was likely to be a lack of water. Milner warned that the 'average evaporation from a water surface amounts to . . . about 30 in. in the year'.[21] Moreover, even in the 19th century it was sometimes the case that the water table dropped in response to the ever-increasing call on the resource. Today, this can be a severe problem, where groundwater and surface water levels are dramatically reduced by abstraction upstream, for potable, agricultural or industrial purposes. Important, too, is the fact that in urban parks since the turn of the century there has been an enormous increase in hard surfaces: heavily compacted ground or expanses of asphalt and concrete greatly reduce the amount of water percolating naturally into the watertable. On the other hand, in storm conditions, the volume of water running off these hard surfaces can be such that the storm overflow cannot cope. In these circumstances it is not

138

unusual for a lake to be contaminated, either with excessive soil run-off from compacted banks or from the foul water system. Thus, the delivery of water to a lake was the subject of extensive investigation — and is, today, of continuing concern.

In all the texts, however, it is quite clear that the greatest emphasis was placed not on any of the constructional issues, but on discussing how the lake should be shaped and planted.

The disposition and planting of a lake

Kemp's instructions were detailed for the disposition and planting of a lake. There must be a 'varied outline for water' but — unless broken by rockwork — a smoothness in the junction between water and bank was essential. No line of earth should be visible between water and planting; several inches of turf should be taken down the side of a lake, covering the hard pitching and obscuring the soil. It was also essential that 'every trace of cement is . . . masked in such a way that no-one can possibly suspect its presence'. Meyer's device for thus masking the cement margins was to build in a shelf or shoulder towards the top of the lake. This formed a firm resting place for stones, turf or other vegetation below the water-line.

Kemp also required that the promontories should be mounded, leaving the bays or recesses smooth and unplanted, 'except . . . here and there a single specimen, or a small cluster of shrubs'. On promontories and islands Kemp's style of planting was generally lush, exploiting the reflective capacity of water and the effects of light and shade. Groups of alders, willows, swamp cypress and liquidambar 'will be highly effective', enhanced, by contrast, with elegant, weeping trees such as willows and birch, 'overhanging and dipping their branches into the water'.[22] Thickets of thorn, holly, furze and 'masses of flowering shrubs', including rhododendrons, tamarisk and lilacs, should be added. There might not be much evidence of this kind of planting now either at Birkenhead or at Kemp's other parks, but early photographs show the rich and colourful effect for

which he aimed.

Milner's approach — as articulated by the son and practised by the father — was even more subtle and sophisticated. Variety conveyed by bays, creeks and promontories was, of course, important. No 'vast sheet of water', out of proportion with the landscape, should offend. The bays must not be semicircular, for this is unnatural; instead, the prevailing line must be concave. In forming the bay, the ground inland should also be hollowed out, and views from selected points directed along these bays and across the water.

By the 1880s many gardening journals were including regular advice on the planting of ornamental lakes. Typical was an article in *Gardening Illustrated* (October 1885), admiring the 'graceful appearance of . . . Lombardy and other Poplars, and the Weeping Willow' in association with water. In fact, by this date the widespread use of colourful shrubs seems to have declined somewhat, replaced by a preference for unassertive, 'natural' vegetation.

Mawson at the end of the century was certainly more interested in employing native plants, including flags, reeds and ferns, moss and lichens. This taste for native plants finds a particularly sympathetic echo today. But he was not exclusive in his enthusiasms, being also impressed by the very varied planting of Battersea Park lake.

Battersea Park was laid out for the people south of the River Thames in the 1850s and 1860s. Sir James Pennethorne, architect of the Office of Works, first created the structural underpinning of the site, raising much of it so that it was no longer a 'dismal marsh'. It was John Gibson, however, yet another pupil of Paxton's, who was the real visionary. He developed the design, including the planting and the extensive lake.[23] This large stretch of water — 6.16 hectares — complete with islands and bridge, has a very varied profile. Contemporary illustrations reveal that the treatment was sometimes broad and sweeping, with grass running down to the water's edge. Scattered across the turf were individual specimen shrubs, or a bank of ornamental plants. On the busy, irregular promontories, trees and flowering

139

Figure 4: The Rockery at Battersea Park. (From the collection of Stewart Harding)

140

shrubs, often evergreens, reached the water's edge, their form and colour reflected in the water. Kemp's model was clearly very influential here.

Elsewhere, the effects were elaborated. By the early 1870s — just before Gibson left for Hyde Park — a greater range of incident and experience was offered to the thousands of visitors who thronged the park. In places, the lake was densely framed by native sedges and flowers; 'grasses are planted in and at the edge of the water, fringing the projecting parts with graceful drooping leaves and erect and noble inflorescence.'[24]

Here the beauties of feral nature were evoked. Erupting through some of these grassy margins were the occasional native flowering shrubs or evergreens, including Irish yews, 'in all the beauty of native wildness'. Along the northern banks of the lake the evocative poetry of 'native wildness' concluded with a dramatic highlight. On a promontory, water cascaded over Pulhamite rockwork, once richly planted with 'Vines, Virginia Creepers, Clematises . . . and occasionally a nook or protuberance shows some alpine plant — a Pink, an Iberis, a Sedum — precisely at home'. This was no small show, but a bravura performance (figure 4). 'The rocks represent a mountain side, as if it had been rent asunder by some volcanic eruption, and the water meanders between the rugged walls into the lake below.'[25]

But nothing prepared the uninitiated visitor for the next in the sequence of theatrical displays. The planting took on an appearance of lavish abundance: the lake was full of water lilies, the banks luxuriant with leaves. Thus was announced the most remarkable ornamental feature in Battersea Park, the Sub-tropical Garden, the first such spectacle in London. Gibson was the imaginative creator of this lush and exotic region, inspired by his 1835 'botanical mission to India, which . . . well fitted him for the task'.[26]

By the 1870s and 1880s the influence of such luxuriant lake-side planting was widespread, encouraged by the sudden arrival of a magnificent range of new waterlily varieties, bred principally by M. Latour Marliac in France, and introduced to Britain in the closing years of the century. Until this date only the native yellow and white waterlilies had been employed. By the early years of the 20th century there was available a 'race which for beauty of colour and variety merits the highest praise we can bestow'.[27] They were grown at Leopold de Rothschild's gardens at Gunnersbury — now a public park — and at William Robinson's Gravetye Manor. They were so hardy and accommodating that they also graced the lakes of numerous well-tended public parks throughout the land.

Sporting demands

By the end of the century there were many demands on public park lakes that inevitably had an influence on their appearance, planting and management. Most particularly, from *c.*1870, lakes in public parks were often used as a site of energetic sporting activity; swimming, perhaps, or boating and skating. The lake in Buxton Pavilion Gardens offers a good example. Buxton, as a spa town, depended on the influx of visitors who came to find comfort in the waters, the baths and the bracing air. It was essential that it should make the most of its attractions at all seasons and one advantage was that it was the highest town in England, where a big winter freeze could be guaranteed. Its park lake was, therefore, ideally suited for skating. To facilitate this a 6-inch deep square-section channel was built round the side of the lake, from inlet to outlet. By opening this, the water could be swiftly drained to an exact depth. Even more ingenious was the design of the Central Park Lake where a gravel path with stone edges was situated two and a half feet below the summer water level. In winter, when the water was lowered, skaters could walk along the gravel and sit on the stone curb.

Probably still more popular than skating was bathing, which did occur in some of the early park lakes, but was frowned upon. In Victoria Park, London, opened as early as 1845, visitors bathed from the first, but specific provision for this use came later. In the design of 1879 for Stamford Park, Altrincham, prepared by the John Shaws, father and son, there was a bathing pool planned within one of a series of circular and elliptical areas defined by paths and planting. And, by the end of the century, while numerous new parks were designed to include swimming lakes, a good number of older sites had to make shift to accommodate the demands for swimming.

Broomfield Park, Enfield, for example, was developed from a private estate acquired by the local authority in 1896. There was already a series of formal pools designed as part of an ambitious water garden in the early 18th century.[28] From the start the focus was on developing the sporting facilities of the park — and swimming in one of the lakes figured largely. As early as 1904 a high diving stage was permitted.[29] In the winter there was permission to bathe before 9.00 a.m. — presumably when there was not the requisite 5 inches of ice on the lake, at which time it was available for skating. By 1911 swimming was one of the major activities in the park, but it was beginning to cause the council problems. It had had to reinforce the hard edges of the pool and concrete the floor, reducing the maximum depth to no more than 7 feet. The council had introduced a settling pond in an attempt to cleanse the water. Nevertheless, there was anxiety about the quality of the water which, when it was tested, was found to be 'badly contaminated with animal matter and human excretions . . . little better than the average sewage effluent'.

There were numerous other activities that changed the ways bodies of water were designed and managed. Water splashes — mini-roller coasters, crashing through the water — proved a great attraction for a while and their remains can still be seen in East Park, Hull, or Lister Park, Bradford. Spectacular ornamental cascades, such as that which tumbles from a Chinese pagoda into the lake at Peasholm Park, Scarborough, were added to some parks, especially if they were in holiday resorts. Very popular for much of the 20th century were children's paddling pools and shallow, concrete ponds for sailing model yachts (figure 5), such as that built in Broomfield Park in *c.*1911. While the former tend to have fallen foul of modern Health and Safety requirements, the latter are often still very popular, not only with children but also among men of all ages, proud

141

Figure 5: Boating lake in Torquay, 1905. (From the collection of Nigel Temple)

142

owners of magnificent model boats.

Undoubtedly, however, almost since the first public parks were opened, the most popular activity on lakes of almost any size was boating. Many of the enchanting images of parks that have come down to us from the years before the Second World War feature boats — evocatively named 'Sandpiper' or 'Lupin' — picturesque boating pavilions and the colourful accessories of a day on the water or the romantic delights of boating in an urban park as dusk draws the day to a close.

Modern problems and some answers

BANKS AND MARGINS

Given the popularity and intensity of use of lakes in public parks it is not surprising that many are now suffering from serious problems. Among the most visible of these is often the erosion and/or compaction of the bank. Sometimes the miscellaneous and *ad hoc* remedies taken over the years — including the application of concrete, paving slabs or timber campshedding — are even more unsightly than the original failures.

Steps to deal with these problems may include improving the soil, removing earlier patching and regrading the bank. But care must be taken to retain the character of the edge and not to smooth out the designed irregularities of a plan, or to apply a hard treatment where a natural finish was intended (figure 6).

The only way of securing the banks naturally is, of course, by establishing vegetation, so that roots and rhizomes reinforce the soil (figure 7). At a practical level it is necessary to identify mean water levels so that appropriate plant material can be employed; most grasses can only be used above normal summer water level because the roots do not survive prolonged submersion. Immersed foliage, on the other hand, is useful to absorb and dissipate flow momentum and to reduce scour. Biodegradable geotextiles, sometimes pre-seeded, can be used to stabilize a bank until vegetation is established.

The selection of aquatic or semi-aquatic plants also requires discretion in relation both to the character of the body of water and to the habit of the plant. In a formal lake it is unlikely that that extensive 'natural' planting is appropriate at all. On the other hand, in the right setting, native plants might be compositionally desirable — but, if ill-chosen, practically disastrous. Reed mace (*Typha latifolia* L.) or common reed (*Phragmites australis* (Cav.) Trin. ex Stend.) are substantial and very invasive, and would quickly transform the whole quality of a lake, obscuring the margins and causing new management problems.[30] Yellow flag (*Iris pseudacorus* L.), too, though very attractive, spreads rapidly. More appropriate might be a few plants that root at the bottom and produce floating leaves, and other, slightly taller plants, such as the flowering rush (*Butomus umbellatus* L.) or the water plantain (*Alisma plantago-aquatica* L.). Also critical is the quality of the water, particularly pH and nutrient levels. For example, while there might be a spot for the marsh marigold (*Caltha palustris* L. sensu lato), it would be unlikely to thrive in nutrient-enriched waters.

In some places willow and alder can be used to protect a bank. These plants can tolerate regular inundations in the root zone and can be implanted near the mean summer water level.[31] Rarely should they be allowed to grow unchecked; rather, they should be treated as shrub-wood and regularly coppiced. This will secure both the banks of the lake and the important views and vistas.

LAKE USE AND MANAGEMENT

None of this repair and planting can be successful without a detailed examination of how the lakes are being used, and the consequent development of a plan to manage that use. Angling has a very significant impact on a lake. The anglers themselves can cause erosion and frequently introduce a miscellaneous selection of materials to create their fishing platforms. Similarly, water-fowl — especially the ubiquitous Canada goose — can be devastating.

Railings can keep out people and even, to some extent, animals. It is much less simple to deal with water birds. Many strategies have been tried. In recent years at Battersea Park some very determined efforts have been made to protect new marginal plantings. In the hope that, once established, the material will be able to withstand some depredation, temporary metal fencing was erected round the banks, within the lake, excluding the birds from the important areas. The short-term effects are impressive. In the long run, of even greater significance are the programmes to control the populations of water-fowl, especially

143

Figure 6: Edge restoration in progress at Clissold Park, London, 1998 and 1999. (Photos: Jan Woudstra)

Figure 7: Vegetation reinforcing a bank, from Franz Sales Meyer, Friedrich Ries and Carl Scholtz, *Die Gartenkunst in Wort und Bild* (Leipzig, 1904).

the geese. Advice was received from the WWT Wetlands Advisory Service. A detailed examination of the numbers and behaviour patterns of the birds on the site was undertaken. This proved essential in initiating the development of an integrated management strategy, which has already seen some positive results.

WATER QUALITY

It is not only the edges of lakes that can suffer. Often, the water in an urban lake is hypereutrophic, that is, in a highly nutrient-rich condition, normally characterized by high organic silt levels and a lack of higher aquatic plant species. This can undermine ecological health and lead to the development of algal blooms and low oxygen levels resulting in summer fish kills.

There are many reasons for this situation, not least a failure to clear autumn leaf litter. The quality of the inflowing water is often doubtful. The amount of bird faeces and the quantities of bread thrown for the water-fowl can be very significant. The sometimes excessive biomass of fish, especially carp or bream introduced by anglers, can also have a profound effect on bodies of water, resulting in murky water and low numbers of plants and invertebrate species.

At Battersea Park the management of the water-fowl was part of a much larger project undertaken by Wandsworth Borough Council, which took over responsibility for the Park after the demise of the Greater London Council. As so often, the council first 'became aware of problems with its lakes when algal blooms coloured the water bright green and fish started to die'.[32] Recognizing the urgent need to remedy the situation — and knowing, too, that these problems were multiplied across the country — the council initiated the London Lakes Project 'to demonstrate restoration and management techniques for urban lakes'. In 1997 Wandsworth hosted the international 'London Lakes Conference' where some of the developments that had been examined over the past few years were outlined. It was emphasized that the first step in tackling any problem must be basic research.

One source of poor quality water was the

Thames itself, long used to supplement the Lake. To provide access to a source of water other than the Thames the advice of an hydrological engineer was sought and a bore hole sunk in March 1994. From that date the bore hole has been a source of replenishment. The great success of this strategy has excited much interest. But there are no universal panaceas. Wandsworth Council sank another bore hole at King George's Park lake but found that the supply was significantly less abundant. To be effective in reducing the phosphorus concentrations in nutrient-enriched lakes, it is necessary to replace a 20 per cent volume of lake water per day and, of course, the inflowing water itself has to be of an appropriate quality. This is certainly not easy to guarantee.

Another operation that is often resorted to as the main — even the only — answer to poor water quality is desilting. It is true that many urban lakes have not been desilted for years, and a serious build-up of sediment can be very detrimental. At Battersea, however, dredging had been undertaken in the early 1980s — and, clearly, this had not been an adequate remedy.[33] It is interesting to read the view of an ecologist. 'If a pond is one hundred years old and the silt is one metre deep in a two metre deep pond, then the pond probably has another one hundred years of open water left, and there is no urgent need to dredge.'[34]

If appropriate controls are put in place then this advice is sometimes very apposite. These controls will include an efficient silt trap, the management of water-fowl and fish, and the regular removal of leaf litter. If the silt is of a high organic nature then the use of a suitably designed aeration system in conjunction with applications of powdered chalk causes consolidation of the silt.

Another route to cleansing lake water that arouses much interest is the introduction of a reed bed. As Peter Worrall announced in 1992, 'since the mid 1980s, there has been a gathering interest in the use of constructed wetlands for the treatment of' polluted water.[35] There is no doubt that this can be successful. The early experiments were conducted in Germany and there has been extensive research into the methods by which

144

Figure 8: Lining the lake at Buxton Pavilion Gardens, 1998. (Photo: the author)

'organic wastes, nutrients and a variety of chemical compounds can be broken down and stabilised'. For the technique to work, however, the reed bed must be properly designed and large enough, and there also has to be an adequate throughput of water. Thus, many urban lakes are ruled out. Moreover, given that the character of a lake, as defined by its marginal treatment and planting, is often so central to the particular expressive power of an historic park, it is essential to confine the technique only to appropriate environments.

LEAKS

The retention of the historic finish can sometimes be a problem, however. The large lake in Buxton Pavilion Gardens, constructed with stone walls and puddled bed, had long been beset with many problems. The gardens were sometimes inundated; on other occasions, the water birds were surviving in a tiny pool. There was water penetration behind the structural masonry, the consequent dilapidation of bridge and walls, collapsed control systems and a threat to the whole environment. Various attempts had been made to effect repairs to the system, but only the award of a substantial Heritage Lottery Fund grant allowed the problem to be tackled in a more fundamental manner.

Investigations were extensive. Eventually it was the geological survey that pointed to the root of the difficulties.[36] When originally constructed, the lake has been laid over an area of springs. Furthermore, a stratum of local sandstone ran through the site, surrounded by limestone: the bed of the lake lay across the junction between the two. It was this discovery that led to the decision to replace the original clay with a new, artificial liner and completely reconstructed masonry walls (figure 8).

Conclusions

One of the principal aims of this chapter is to emphasize that whatever the cause of the many problems now associated with lakes and bodies of water in urban parks, the first and absolute requirement is that there must be detailed research into the history, construction, character, use and management of that feature. Only then can there be any serious attempt to find an answer. It may be appropriate to employ traditional or modern techniques to effect improvement. What must be respected is the formal design and poetic meaning of the composition. And, while this chapter has focused on lakes, the same should be said of rivers,

145

Figure 9: Many of the enchanting images of parks that have come down to us from the years before the Second World War feature boats — evocatively named 'Sandpiper' or 'Lupin'. (Photo: Peter Vickers)

cascades and fountains, basins, rills and splashes, all of which are associated with their own particular range of problems and opportunities.

There can be little doubt that many of the most beautiful, significant, entertaining and pleasurable features of a public park are — or were — associated with its bodies of water. It is now often the case that these bodies are both the most important and the most neglected and misunderstood of the features of a park. If they are lost, then much of the value of the park landscape will also evaporate.

Notes

1. The design for Ropner Park was put out to competition and the initial construction works were directed by J. A. Mann of Crystal Palace Gardens.

2. The author is not aware if the musical possibilities of water were specifically pursued in public parks, but this was certainly a characteristic of some 17th- and 18th-century water features, and not only in Italy. The steps in the cascade at Chatsworth, Derbyshire, for example, have individual profiles and the water flows over them with a variety of musical pitch.

3. In this context it is worth referring to the extraordinary architecture of some early pumping stations. Papplewick Pumping Station, near Nottingham, is ornamented as if it were a miniature cathedral, so glorious was the achievement of bringing an adequate supply of clean water to the city in 1884 after several decades of struggling with a dropping watertable.

4. Newcastle City Council, *Minutes* (July 1880), on the opening of Armstrong Park, Newcastle-upon-Tyne.

5. The incorporation of features that had formerly performed an industrial function was also found elsewhere, as, for example, at Armstrong Park, partially laid out on land donated by William Armstrong, the arms manufacturer, and opened in 1880.

6. This followed the recommendation of the Select Committee of Public Walks in 1833 that freely accessible parks should be financed from public funds.

7. The site was available for the park because it was not suitable for building development, being predominantly boggy. Edwin Chadwick referred to Paxton's victory in transforming 'a mere marsh over which thick mists hung at nightfall' into an environment of 'comfort and salubrity'; General Board of Health, *Minutes of Information Collected in Respect to the Drainage of the Land forming the Sites of*

Towns, to Road Drainage, and to the Facilitation of the Drainage of Suburban Lands (January 1852).

8. Henry Ernest Milner, *The Art and Practice of Landscape Gardening* (London: Simpkin, Marshall, Hamilton, 1890), 61.

9. Thomas Mawson, *The Art and Craft of Garden Making* (London: Batsford, 1900, 1926 edn), 199.

10. Edward Kemp, *How to Lay Out a Small Garden* (London: Bradbury & Evans, 1850; New York: John Wiley, 1872 edn), 298. The following quotations are taken from the same source.

11. Milner, *Art and Practice of Landscape Gardening*, 65. The following quotations are taken from the same source.

12. It should be noted that this technique was not foolproof. At Burslem, where the lake is similarly laid out over pit shafts, the water has been known to disappear.

13. Felix Austin, 'Durability of Austin's artificial stone', *The Architectural Magazine* (July 1834), 216.

14. Milner, *Art and Practice of Landscape Gardening*, 65.

15. Harriet Jordan, 'Public parks, 1885–1914', *Garden History*, 22/1 (1994), 85–113 (107).

16. F. W. Meyer, *Rock and Water Gardens* (London: Country Life, 1910), 92.

17. Percy Cane, *Garden Design of Today* (London: Methuen, 1934), 110.

18. Milner, *Art and Practice of Landscape Gardening*, 67.

19. R. Rosenzweig and E. Blackmar, *The Park and the People* (Ithaca: Cornell University Press, 1992), 164. For full information about the drainage of Central Park, see the Board of the Commissioners of Central Park, Annual Report (1888), 79–82.

20. Kemp, *How to Lay Out a Small Garden*, 300.

21. Milner, *Art and Practice of Landscape Gardening*, 67.

22. Kemp, *How to Lay Out a Small Garden*, 296.

23. Gibson started the planting in the winter of

Figure 10: A sculpture provides a focal point for the lake at Wimbledon Park, south west London. (Photo: Jane Porter)

147

Figure 11: Edge treatment of ponds dedicated to fishing has often degenerated to such an extent that this conflicts with nature conservation interests; but it is frequently possible to devise a compromise which is both attractive and robust. This example shows the lake in Hillsborough Park, Sheffield, in 1997. (Photo: Jan Woudstra)

1856-57. There is little evidence of much planting on the site before this.

24. Nathan Cole, *The Royal Parks and Gardens of London* (London: Journal of Horticulture Office, 1877), 32.

25. Ibid., 33. In letters, Pulham makes it clear that this display was intended as a *pièce de résistance*, an advertisment to London of all he could achieve.

26. The Hon. Mrs Evelyn Cecil, *London Parks and Gardens* (London: Constable, 1907), 158.

27. Meyer, *Rock and Water Gardens*, 189.

28. This supposition was confirmed by archaeological investigation, which traced a series of bodies of water, of a geometric formality, not all of which are visible today.

29. These and subsequent references are taken from the Minutes of the Parks and Open Spaces Committee.

30. It is worth recounting that even the removal of the most invasive weeds can be a sensitive issue. In Boston, MA, in 1994, when *Phragmites* was being removed from the Emerald Necklace river system, local protesters laid armfuls of the plant on a makeshift altar and held a religious service to mourn its loss.

31. Where appropriate, these plants can be introduced by means of wattle hurdles, which then grow into a living barrier.

32. *London Lakes Project* (London: Wandsworth Borough Council, 1997), 2. The borough's Lakes Project has been both ambitious and influential, culminating in a major European conference at Battersea. The project team, comprising Mike Wilkinson, Robert Wells and Janice McCaskie, was inspired by Jacqueline McCabe, 'whose vision and vitality made the London Lakes Project possible'.

33. There are, of course, various ways of cleaning a lake of silt and when there is a clay lining care has to be taken not to damage it and thus cause leakage.

34. Anne Sanson and Ros Walmsley, *Ponds and Conservation* (London: National Rivers Authority, 1993), 5.

35. Peter Worrall, 'The reed bed revolution', *Landscape Design* (March 1992), 16.

36. The British Geological Survey's headquarters are at Nicker Hill, Kingsley Dunham Centre, Keyworth, Nottingham NG12 5GG. Geological Surveys are available for the whole of the UK.

Play and sport

by Brent Elliott
and Ken Fieldhouse

Figure 1: Play provision is a major factor in measuring the success or failure of a park. (Drawing by Erik Glemme for play provision in Årsta, near Stockholm, 1949, from the collection of Jan Woudstra)

Play and sport are two essential reasons why urban spaces are needed and why we continue to visit parks. Unlike more obviously passive uses, play and sport require both structural space and also less defined provision — demands that frequently put such activities into conflict with other users.

The story of play and sport provision does not really go back as far as the origins of public urban parks in this country. Initially those providing the patronage associated with health and public good perceived sporting activities as often antisocial and an unfortunate pastime of the working classes. Recreational pursuits of the ruling classes required little public provision except as an arena to see and be seen!

Yet in the ensuing century of development of urban parks, play and sports provision became increasingly synonymous with both the public perception of what was expected and also a major reason for visiting the parks. Play provision remains a desirable aspiration for most parks and is a major factor in measuring their success or failure. Sport, especially team games, has an almost insatiable demand for land, yet it often condemns large areas of urban park to a bleak, uninhabited grass sward, unpopulated except for an occasional intense afternoon of activity.

Active recreation

The 1833 Select Committee on Public Walks envisaged recreation primarily as walking, with no emphasis on games or sports. It listed 'low and demeaning pleasures' such as 'drinking houses, dog fights and boxing matches' among pursuits to which working classes were attracted for lack of other opportunities. Emphasis on what is today called 'active recreation' only came later.

Queen's Park, Manchester, designed by Joshua

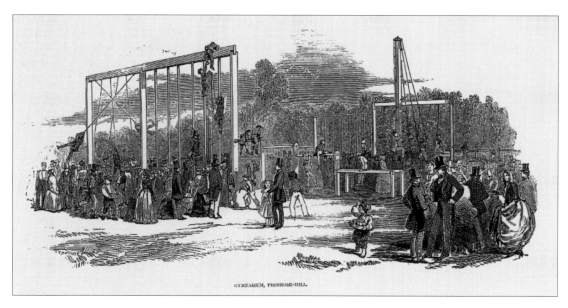

GYMNASIUM, PRIMROSE-HILL.

Figure 2: The picturesque and concerns for health and privileged access began to give way to the perceived demands of the wider public. The gymnasium in Primrose Hill was established in 1847. (*Illustrated London News*, 29 April 1848)

Major, was opened in 1846 and was one of three parks designed by him in Manchester and Salford that were the first public parks not to charge an entry fee; they included facilities for 'innocent athletic games'.[1] The *Gardeners' Chronicle* at the time criticized Major for poor design, including the use of right angles and straight lines in laying out the games area. Major's defence was revealing: 'Imagine a number of impetuous youths fresh let loose from their different employments, and excited by some athletic game, carefully attending to the preservation of curves and sweeps. We had adaptability to study, as well as landscape beauty'. To this argument, John Lindley, the *Chronicle*'s Editor, replied: 'Will they kindly furnish us with a list of the games which can adapt themselves to these peculiar shapes, and none besides?'[2]

The picturesque and concerns for health and privileged access began to give way to the perceived demands of the wider public. Hyde Park in London permitted boating; cricket and archery facilities were established in Birkenhead Park, and Primrose Hill, also in London, saw a gymnasium

established, all in 1847.[3]

The year 1871 saw Alexandra Park, Manchester, boast the first bowling green in a Manchester park (others appeared soon), followed by tennis in 1886. Soon after, Battersea Park, London, had cricket and football grounds, a gymnasium and lawn tennis facilities, adding a quoit-ground and bowling green during the 1890s.

Boating facilities made an appearance in Ward End Park, Birmingham, in 1910 and from 1920 the city allowed games on Sundays. The spread of Sunday games throughout the country in the 1920s met with opposition, particularly from the church. In 1922 a churchman thundered, 'a Sunday for games, devoted to games, is a sorrier waste than a defaced sovereign'.[4]

The legal status of the provision of recreation grounds evolved slowly. The Town Improvements Act of 1847 allowed local authorities to provide places that could be used for 'resort or recreation'; it was not until the Recreation Grounds Act of 1859 that provision for active recreation could be said to have received separate legal acknowledge-

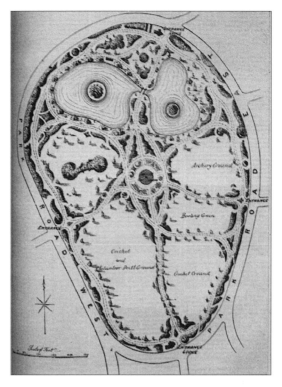

Figure 3 (right): West Park, Wolverhampton, from the *Gardeners' Chronicle*. This park, opened in 1880, included segregated areas for archery, bowling and cricket. (*Gardeners' Chronicle*, 1880, sourced from RHS Lindley Library)

Figure 4 (below): Stamford Park, Altrincham, opened in 1881 and included separate playgrounds for boys and girls. (*Gardeners' Chronicle*, 1881, sourced from RHS Lindley Library)

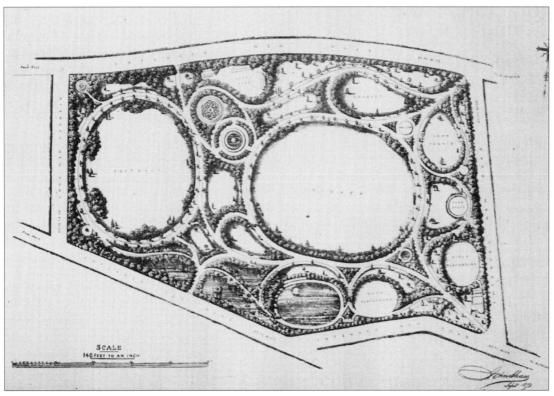

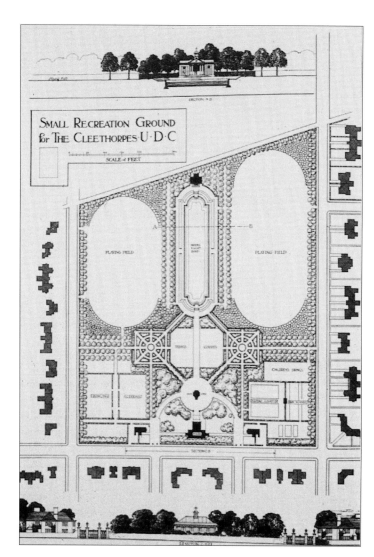

152

Figure 5: The landscape architect Thomas H. Mawson designed some rigorously formal recreation grounds, for example at Cleethorpes. (Illustration from Mawson, *Civic Art, op. cit.,* sourced from RHS Lindley Library)

ment. Most enactments that dealt with municipal parks treated active recreation as one among many possible uses of public open space. It was not until the establishment of the Olympic Games that the central government began to notice sports as something worthy of specific encouragement,[5] and not until the 1937 Physical Training and Recreation Act, with its provision for the creation of a National College of Physical Training, that local authorities were given their greatest extension of power to acquire land for the specific purpose of laying out playing fields.

While sporting activities began to be tolerated or catered for, their popularity fluctuated, making provision a challenge for authorities and parks superintendents. Football, which at the beginning of the 19th century was widely disapproved of for its violence, seemed to be on the way out until the public schools revived it.[6] Roller skating (1890–1914), cycling in the 1890s and 1990s, miniature golf (interwar years), and recently skateboarding and rollerblading are examples of these changing fashions and fortunes within the urban park, a process which has clearly not finished.

Development of the sports park

Bit by bit, facilities for sports and games began to be incorporated into municipal parks, but it was not until *c*.1880 that the idea emerged of making sports provision the organizing principle of a park. At that time two parks opened, in Wolverhampton and Altrincham, introducing the concept of the sports park.

West Park, Wolverhampton (figure 2), opened in 1880, was designed by the Birmingham nurseryman and landscape gardener Richard Vertegans in an axial layout including segregated areas for archery, bowling, cricket (and a drill ground).

Stamford Park, Altrincham (figure 3), opened in 1881, was designed by John Shaw, the only English follower of Edouard André, who had introduced French curvilinear style into England a decade earlier with Sefton Park, Liverpool; Shaw adopted André's use of circles and ovals to organize the landscape, segregating areas for cricket, croquet, lawn tennis, football, and separate playgrounds for boys and girls.[7]

Col. J. J. Sexby, London County Council's first Superintendent of Parks, designed Ruskin Park, Lambeth, in 1907. Three adjacent villa gardens were knocked into one, the result being a concentration of ornamental garden at the east end of the park, while playing fields stretched out to the west (later extended in size).[8]

The model that Sexby developed became the norm for 20th-century parks in London. As late as the 1960s one finds Queensbury Park in Harrow showing the same division of grounds, only with the horticultural portion considerably shrunken in comparison with the great spread of playing fields; it contained 'hockey and football pitches, children's playground, cricket table, putting green, tennis courts, car parks and drinking fountain and a landscape setting of trees and shrubs', most of this 'landscape setting' sited almost centrally in the vicinity of the pavilion. The pavilion in particular was treated to a glowing write-up in *Parks and Sports Grounds*, with some of the measured drawings published: it offered accommodation for four teams in separate rooms.[9] Today, Queensbury Park is almost a prototype of the 'green desert': marginalized by the arrival of the motorcar, on no one's route from one place to another, it is empty most of the time, the pavilion covered with graffiti.

By the turn of the century smaller recreation grounds were beginning to appear, designed specifically to include facilities for games without the horticultural content that characterized the larger parks. The landscape architect Thomas H. Mawson designed some rigorously formal recreation grounds, for example at Cleethorpes, the plan of which (figure 4) was reproduced in his *Civic Art: Studies in Town Planning, Parks, Boulevards and Open Spaces* (1911).[10] A. E. Sandys-Winsch, stylistically a follower of Mawson, consolidated the development of the recreation ground in Norwich in the 1920s and 1930s, notably with the attractive Mile Cross Gardens, which are now sadly derelict.

Early sports facilities, like tennis courts and bowling greens, were small in scale and frequently required screening for seclusion. They could thus be incorporated into parks with minimal interference with the horticultural character emphasized. There still exist enough examples of such courts and greens surrounded by pergolas or rockery borders to prove the point. But football in particular is greedy of space, and requires grass expanses on such a scale as to preclude enclosure. Already by the late 1930s it was becoming commonplace that the fencing traditional in ornamental parks as a means of protecting flower beds and shrubberies did not fit the new facilities for active recreation: 'whether the park is maintained chiefly for ornamental or for recreational purposes . . . adequate fencing is more essential for the former than for the latter'.[11]

Increasing lobbying throughout the 20th century for sports facilities from the various organizations founded to promote particular sports, including the more general National Playing Fields Association (founded 1925) and later the Sports Council, has applied unremitting pressure on urban parks. W. W. Pettigrew, in his

153

manual of *Municipal Parks: Layout, Management and Administration* in 1937, encouraged park superintendents to accept the new emphasis on sports, and to abandon what seemed to him a retrograde desire to make decorative horticulture the park's main priority:

> One such deputation, when paying a visit to a large town in the West of England, was, after laying its aims before the council, taken to inspect the parks and open spaces belonging to the town. Instead, however, of being taken to see the provision that was made for the playing of games, the deputation's time was mostly taken up by visiting the largest and most beautiful parks and pleasure grounds and the members were called upon to admire the fine floral displays for which the parks were justly noted. Knowing as he did wherein the main interest of the deputation naturally lay, these arrangements certainly showed a want of tact on the part of the chief superintendent. But an equal lack of tact was indicated on the part of the leader of the deputation, who, when paying a similar visit immediately afterwards to an adjoining town, narrated in sarcastic terms in an after-dinner speech the deputation's recent experiences and told how the parks superintendent had appeared to think more of how the display of dahlias would impress the members of the National Playing Fields Association than would the facilities provided for the enjoyment of games.[12]

Pettigrew's distress can be measured in the way his grammar falls apart in that last sentence. Nonetheless, when one contemplates the decline in park horticulture over the past half-century, one can sympathize with the superintendent, and see him not as a misguided fool but as the last of the old guard protecting what he saw as a precious heritage.

The Bains Report and the 1972 Local Government Act resulted in the Parks Departments being absorbed into Departments of Leisure and Amenity Services from April 1974, thus consolidating the bias in favour of active as opposed to passive recreation.[13]

Significantly, the Institute of Parks and Recreation Administration was incorporated into the Institute of Leisure and Amenity Management in 1983; horticulture, once a prominent feature of *Parks and Recreation*, quickly became a rarity in the new journal *The Leisure Manager* and this has remained the same ever since.

What is not certain, however, is whether this trend is a map of expediency and cost-cutting commitment by hard-pressed public authorities, or actually reflects the aspirations of most users of most urban parks. There is a growing belief that the position is far more complex: 'It is not so much the public interest in sports that has increased, as the effectiveness of the sporting lobby'.[14] With the energy being applied under the Urban Parks Programme, there are many friends' groups and public authorities attempting to find a more conducive balance between the competing demands of the sports park and other uses.

Gymnasia and children's play equipment

'In quite a number of instances in many large towns children's playgrounds are merely small plots of ground shaled over and marked off by tubular iron posts and rails, the whole place being accessible during both day and night', wrote Pettigrew in the 1930s; he also referred to sand gardens and paddling pools as frequently provided, and cited Bermondsey as the first local authority to provide a play area covered by netting so that children could play ball games without the risk of breaking nearby windows.[15] Information on children's play equipment in 19th-century parks has so far proven elusive, so this statement will have to suffice for the moment as an indication of the background for the development of the most important firm in the manufacture of play equipment in British history: Charles Wicksteed & Co. of Kettering.

Wicksteed (1847–1931) began as an agricultural engineer, then turned to the making of bicycles and their gears, and to munitions during the First World War, but the final stage in his entrepreneurial development stemmed from his desire to form a municipal park for Kettering. He began purchasing the land for the future Wicksteed Park in 1914. He wrote:

> For the last seven years I have been forming a Public Park in Kettering. When it was first opened I was disappointed that so few people made use of it, in spite of the beautiful situation. I had always intended to make a Play Ground but did not consider this an essential part of the Park. However, one day there was a large School Treat, and temporary swings, made of scaffolding poles, were put up. These were so much enjoyed that I decided to put some up permanently, of a similar nature — which I did . . . .
>
> In the meantime I was very much bothered by boys taking forms [seats] that I had about the Park, and piling them up upon a raised piece of land under a tree, using them as slides, and ultimately breaking them. This made me think I would make a slide that would not break . . .
>
> Giant Strides were then added, also Horizontal Bars etc., and the things became so popular that I determined to lay a whole hockey pitch out as a Play Ground. On this Play Ground at present there are:

14 See-saws.	4 Giant Strides.
2 Plank Swings.	8 Slides.
50 Swings.	2 Horizontal Bars.

1 Sand Pit.

And thus Wicksteed's firm was started on the way to becoming England's, and probably Europe's, largest manufacturer of play equipment.

The characteristic qualities of Wicksteed equipment were stability and resistance to damage. 'I used to be told', he wrote in the Introduction to his 1924 Playground Equipment catalogue, 'how boys abused everything, and what a disgraceful thing it was for two men to swing together on the same swing. So I made up my mind it would be far easier for me, as an engineer, to make the play things so strong that they could not be broken, rather than try to reform the users'. The reference to 'two men' indicates that there was no expectation that the use of the equipment would be confined to children: 'My Play Ground is not confined to boys or girls, or old or young, it is open to all. I have seen a dozen women of forty on the Jazz [plank swing] together, and enjoying it as much as the children. I have also seen old ladies of eighty go on the slides'.[16]

The desire for specialized play equipment was making itself felt generally by the 1930s; Pettigrew recommended 'light swings, giant strides, joy-wheels, coaster slides and ocean wave slides, with rocking horses, paddling pools and sand gardens, for children under school age'.[17] Some of the elements on this list would strike terror into the hearts of playground officials today; by the 1980s there was much relief being expressed over the final disappearance of ocean wave slides and plank swings from playgrounds, as having been chronically unsafe. The Department of the Environment did not issue any official instructions to local authorities on safety in playgrounds until 1990, but by that time a campaign for improved safety had long been underway, particularly associated with the play equipment firm of SMP. Much attention, of course, focused on the surfaces used for playgrounds: the earlier hard surfaces were, by the 1980s, being replaced by rubber tiles, such as those promoted by Recticel Sutcliffe, and shredded bark, not to mention SMP's Playscreed surface.[18]

Most play equipment, then and now, has been based on the principle of separate pieces of equipment for different physical functions (climbing, sliding, etc.) Possibly the first significant equipment for unstructured play, in which the nature of the child's interaction with the structure was left for the child to determine, was the short-lived movement on behalf of play sculpture in the late 1950s and early 1960s, in which pieces of more or less abstract sculpture were placed in the playground to be explored or used imaginatively.[19] During the 1980s the PlayCube Modular System, marketed by Webster & Associates under the

155

brand name Playcare, was installed in thousands of playgrounds. In 1982 the Playground Equipment Association was formed, the founders being Wicksteed Leisure, SMP, Recticel Sutcliffe, Game and Playtime, and Record.[20]

Playgrounds with children in mind

Some of the earliest instances of playgrounds and recreation grounds for children are found in the 1877 Burbury Street Recreation Ground, Birmingham (but no records of what it looked like are known to the authors) and the Children's Happy Evenings Association, founded in 1888, that had nearly 100 centres in London by the outbreak of the First World War. In Manchester in 1911, playgrounds were opened by voluntary groups and adopted shortly afterwards by the Municipal Parks Department. But it was in the 1920s that a public park was first dedicated specifically to children, with the proviso that adults would only be allowed to enter if accompanying them: Coram's Fields in London opened in 1929 on the site of a former foundling hospital; Lord Rothermere had raised £500,000 to purchase part of the site to prevent it from being built upon.

The history of the child-centred movement in education and play provision has yet to be written, despite the great quantities of polemic it has generated. Wherever it has flourished it has reacted against formal games and the regimentation of play by educational organizations. It began in Britain in the closing years of the 19th century, with the growing interest in children's games as an object of nostalgia and cultural continuity.[21] In America in the 1950s its leading text was Robert Paul Smith's *'Where did you go?' 'Out' 'What did you do?' 'Nothing'* (New York, W. W. Norton, 1957) (a complaint that the informal games he had played as a child were unknown to modern children who had been coerced into formal team sports like Little League baseball), followed three years later by Jane Jacobs, who criticized the segregation of children's games into parks and praised informal play in the streets, one function of which was 'assimilating children'.[22]

As early as the 1920s the Danish landscape architect C. Th. Sørensen observed that playgrounds he had designed remained underused while adjacent building sites proved very popular with children. In 1931 he suggested the establishment of so-called 'skrammellegepladser' (waste material playgrounds) where children could play with old cars, boxes and timber,[23] and he put these plans into practice in the 1940s. This approach clearly challenged the more orthodox and deterministic design being practised by most park managers. In England, Marjorie Allen (Lady Allen of Hurtwood) became the chief promoter, with the Under Fourteens Council, the first adventure playground was set up in Camberwell, London, in 1948 (and lasted for three years). She campaigned long and hard to create a more flexible, tolerant climate that defied the notion that easy-to-manage resources should be planned at the expense of challenging and adventurous play.

The phrase 'adventure playground' became popular for a playground with a certain type of equipment, marketed widely by the Swedish firm Kompan; but the original concept corresponded more truly to the phrase 'junk playground' — described by Lady Allen as

> the most revolutionary experiment we know for absorbing the interest and releasing the energies of young people from two to eighteen years of age. Their deep urge to experiment with earth, fire, water and timber, to work with real tools without fear of criticism or censure, and their love of freedom to take calculated risks are recognised in these playgrounds and are met under tolerant and sympathetic guidance.[24]

As in Britain, the USA found shifting patterns of attitude and use threatened established management which did not readily adapt to the implications of a revolution in play and sport provision within urban parks. For example, in the 1960s New York City's Park Department responded to Mayor Lindsay's call for fresh thinking in park provision and the 'campaign initiated the first municipal promotion of the European adventure playground idea. . . . But municipal parks never accepted the idea that the children themselves

Figure 6:
Gymnasium in a
Manchester park,
from W. W.
Pettigrew's
*Handbook of the
City Parks* (1929),
showing heavy
swings of the sort
Pettigrew was
replacing for safety
reasons in the
1920s.

Figure 7:
Stoneydown
Recreation Ground,
Walthamstow; when
it opened in 1955, it
boasted gateway,
seats, and
ornamental gardens
as well as the
catwalk and
crawling tunnel
shown here.
(Illustration: *Parks
and Sports Grounds*,
November 1955)

Figure 8:
Stoneydown 30
years later: catwalk
and crawling tunnel
still survived, but
the gateway, seats
and gardens had
vanished. (Photo:
Brent Elliott)

Figure 9: A 1980s playground at Victoria Park, London, showing ground modelling and imitation rockwork. (Photo: Brent Elliott)

158

should build play equipment. . . . Moreover, popular understanding and use of the new model quickly became conventional. The physical forms of adventure playgrounds became similar'.[25]

The provision of public play facilities in British parks continues down an uneasy path as budgetary constraints, health, safety and technical demands all make the necessary commitment harder to achieve. As early as 1966 the Council for Children's Welfare called for an overhaul of planning standards so that they meet 'the needs of our children rather than our parents'. A follow up report by Anthea Holme and Peter Massie called for comprehensive play service provision. A 1999 survey by the National Society for the Prevention of Cruelty to Children (NSPCC) has found overwhelming evidence that parents consider most parks unsafe due to lack of supervision. This perception consequently feeds the downward spiral of use and enthusiasm for park provision.

However, as new life is beginning to be breathed into the body of public parks, advances in specification for equipment and surfaces, along with a realisation that supervision and management are essential, playgrounds are due for a revival in the same way that outdoor cafés are increasingly part of our everyday living — themselves something of a rarity 20 years ago.

This is a hugely exciting subject that challenges authorities, designers and parks managers faced with finite resources. It is also a dynamic process in which fashion, technological advances and targeting of funding exert distinct and often conflicting pressures. It has an important international dimension enabling experience and achievement to be shared; in Britain we are increasingly reliant on continental European and North American examples to validate our own approaches. The call for a more holistic approach to parks is being heard increasingly vehemently; in

159

Figure 10: Much of post-war inspiration for play came from abroad. Denmark contributed the adventure playground, and Sweden the use of natural material, such as stones and logs, in the creation of play facilities; this 1958 photograph shows a playground in Stockholm. (Photo: John Evans)

turn this must test our resolve in understanding the demands of play and sport.[26] No revival of urban parks can ignore the significant part given to children's play and sport provision.

Notes

1. Joshua Major, *Theory and Practice of Landscape Gardening* (London: Longman, Brown Green & Longmans, 1852), 196.

2. *Gardeners' Chronicle* (1847), 236–7; for Lindley's reply, see ibid., 267, 817. See also Brent Elliott, 'The Manchester/Salford parks: two additional notes', *Journal of Garden History*, 6 (1986), 141–5.

3. For Primrose Hill, see A. D. Webster, *The Regent's Park and Primrose Hill* (London: Greening & Co., 1911), 85.

4. For Manchester, see W. W. Pettigrew, *Handbook of the Manchester Parks and Recreation Grounds* (Manchester, 1929). For Battersea, see J. J. Sexby, *The Municipal Parks, Gardens and Open Spaces of London* (London: Elliot Stock, 1898), 15–17. For Sunday games, see *South London Press* (11 August 1922). Pettigrew confirmed that as late as 1937, Wednesday and Saturday afternoons were the principal days for games in parks; W. W. Pettigrew, *Municipal Parks: Layout, Management and Administration* (London: Journal of Park Administration, 1937), 94.

5. For a splendid cartoon on the proposals for a Ministry of Sport, see *Punch* (17 July 1912).

6. H. E. Meller, *Leisure and the Changing City* (London: Routledge & Kegan Paul, 1976), 225–36. In the past decade, the social history of sports has become a major academic growth area. Useful background is in Tony Money, *Manly and Muscular Diversions: Public Schools and the Nineteenth-Century Sporting Revival* (London, Duckworth, 1997); Derek Birley, *Sport and the*

160

Figure 11: A playground created in St James's Park in 1995 by Colvin and Moggridge is both visually attractive and challenging. The use of natural materials helps to integrate this playground with its surroundings. (Photo: Hal Moggridge)

Making of Britain (Manchester: Manchester University Press, 1993); and idem, *Land of Sport and Glory: Sport and British Society 1889-1910* (Manchester: Manchester University Press, 1995). So far, however, attention has been focussed on school grounds rather than on municipal parks and playgrounds.

7. 'A park for Wolverhampton', *Gardeners' Chronicle* (1880), i, 586–7, 593 (plan); 'The Stamford Park, Altrincham', *Gardeners' Chronicle* (1881), i, 44–5. For these two parks and their significance, see Brent Elliott, *Victorian Gardens* (London: B. T. Batsford, 1986), 211–14; and Hazel Conway, 'Sports and playgrounds and the problem of park design in the nineteenth century', *Journal of Garden History*, 8 (1988), 31–41.

8. *Gardeners' Magazine* (1907), 93; Mrs Evelyn Cecil, *London Parks and Gardens* (London: Archibald Constable, 1907), 168–70; Marie Draper, *Lambeth's Open Spaces* (London: Borough of Lambeth, 1979), 51–2, 88.

9. 'Development of Queensbury Park, Harrow', *Parks and Sports Grounds* (July 1963), 732–4.

10. Thomas Mawson, *Civic Art: Studies in Town Planning, Parks, Boulevards and Open Spaces* (London: B. T. Batsford, 1911), 341–2.

11. *Gardeners' Chronicle* (1939), ii, 84.

12. Pettigrew, *Municipal Parks*, 22.

13. For the impact of the Local Government Act, see *Gardeners' Chronicle* (19 October 1973), 26–31; and 'Municipal parks — after reorganisation', *Parks and Sports Grounds* (November 1976), 16–21, passim.

14. Brent Elliott, 'From people's parks to green deserts', *Landscape Design*, no. 171 (February 1988), 13–15.

Figure 12: Standard play equipment is available from catalogues of different firms, and can be extended or customised to individual requirements. While perhaps not always aesthetically the most pleasing it is relatively cheap to erect and easy to maintain. This example is at St George Park, Bristol. (Photo: Alan Barber)

Figure 13: Children's playgrounds can be distinctive and enjoyable; this example in Finsbury Park, London was designed through a competition involving local schools and created a unique play environment. However it was removed in 1999 as a result of illegal night-time activities, due to its siting near the main street in a dark shady corner of the park, without natural surveillance. It shows that play and sport cannot be considered as separate issues and should be part of the overall vision for each park. (Photo: Jan Woudstra)

15. Pettigrew, *Municipal Parks*, 14–15.

16. Charles Wicksteed & Co., *Play Things as Used in The Wicksteed Park, Kettering* (trade catalogue, 1921). Biographical information on Wicksteed is from Hilda Wicksteed, *Charles Wicksteed* (London, J. M. Dent, 1933). Acknowledgement is made to Mr R. J. Wicksteed for kindly providing materials on the history of the Wicksteed Co.

17. Pettigrew, *Municipal Parks*, 14–15, 92–9.

18. For surveys of safety conscious surfaces, see *GC&HTJ* (6 April 1984), 32; and ibid. (5 April 1985), 'Play Equipment' special issue, 26–7.

19. See *Journal of the Institute of Landscape Architects*, 53 (February 1960), 10, for a statement about play sculpture by John Bridgeman; and ibid., 8–9, for a description of Hawkesley Moat Children's Play Area, which used one of Bridgeman's pieces.

20. *GC&HTJ* (5 April 1985), 30–9, passim. For the announcement of the Play Equipment Association, see ibid. (12 November 1982), 5.

21. See Alice B. Gomme, *The National Games of England, Scotland and Ireland* (London: David Nutt, 1894–98); Norman Douglas' less well-circulated and therefore less influential *London Street Games* (London: St Catherine's Press, 1916); and the culminating work of Iona Opie and Peter Opie: *The Lore and Language of Schoolchildren* (Oxford: Oxford University Press, 1959) and *Children's Games in Street and Playground* (Oxford: Clarendon, 1969). Note the hierarchy in that last title: street as more important than playground.

22. Jane Jacobs, *The Death and Life of Great American Cities* (New York: Random House, 1961), chs 4, 5.

23. C. Th. Sørensen, *Parkpolitik i Sogn og Købstad* (Park politics in parish and town) (Copenhagen: Nordisk, 1931).

24. Housing Centre Trust Pamphlet, *New Playgrounds* (1964). For an early British notice of adventure playgrounds, see *Parks and Sports Grounds* (June 1954), 550; also M. Paul Friedberg, *Do-it-Yourself Playgrounds* (London: Architectural Press, 1975). For the history of the adventure playground movement, see Anthea Holme and Peter Massie, *Children's Play* (London: Michael Joseph, 1972), 45–8. This work was the result of a report commissioned in 1966 by the Council for Children's Welfare that called for the overhaul of planning standards so that they met 'the needs of our children rather than our parents', and for comprehensive play service provision. For various sociological studies of play and resulting design recommendations, see, for example, Arvid Bengtsson, *Environmental Planning for Children's Play* (London: Crosby Lockwood, 1970); Joseph Levy, *Play Behaviour* (New York: John Wiley, 1978); and Mitsuru Senda, *Design of Children's Play Environments* (New York: McGraw-Hill, 1992).

25. Galen Cranz, *The Politics of Park Design: A History of Urban Parks in America* (London: MIT Press, 1982), 147.

26. Noranne Scott and Eddy Fox in Reports, *Landscape Design*, no. 286 (December 1999), 16–17.

Select bibliography

General historical works

Bucht, Eivor, *Public Parks in Sweden 1860–1960: The Planning and Design Discourse* (Alnarp: Swedish University of Agricultural Sciences, 1997)

Cecil, The Hon. Mrs Evelyn, *London Parks and Gardens* (London: Constable, 1907)

Chadwick, George F., *The Park and the Town* (London: Architectural Press, 1966)

Conway, Hazel, *People's Parks* (Cambridge: Cambridge University Press, 1991)

—, *Public Parks* (Princes Risborough: Shire, 1996)

—, 'Sports and playgrounds and the problem of park design in the nineteenth century', *Journal of Garden History*, 8 (1988), 31–41

Cranz, Galen, *The Politics of Park Design: A History of Urban Parks in America* (London: MIT Press, 1982)

Elliott, Brent, *Victorian Gardens* (London: B. T. Batsford, 1986)

Gloag, John and Derek Bridgewater, *A History of Cast Iron in Architecture* (London: George Allen & Unwin, 1948)

Hennebo, Dieter, *Geschichte des Stadtgrüns*, vol. I: *Von der Antike bis zur Zeit des Absolutismus* (Berlin: Patzer, 1970)

— and Erika Schmidt, *Geschichte des Stadtgrüns*, vol. III: *Entwicklung des Stadtgrüns in England* (Berlin: Patzer, 1975)

Himmelheber, Georg, *Cast-iron Furniture* (London: Philip Wilson, 1996)

Hix, John, *The Glass House* (London: Phaidon, 1974)

Jellicoe, Geoffrey, Susan Jellicoe, Patrick Goode and Michael Lancaster, *The Oxford Companion to Gardens* (Oxford: Oxford University Press, 1986)

Jordan, Harriet, 'Public parks, 1885–1914', *Garden History*, 22/1 (1994), 85–113

Kohlmaier, Georg and Barna von Sartory, *Houses of Glass* (Cambridge, MA: MIT Press, 1986)

Koppelkamm, Stefan, *Glasshouses and Wintergardens of the Nineteenth Century* (London: Granada, 1981)

Lasdun, Susan, *The English Park: Royal, Private and Public* (London: André Deutsch, 1991)

Pettigrew, W. W. *Handbook of the Manchester Parks and Recreation Grounds* (Manchester, 1929)

Rosenzweig, R. and E. Blackmar, *The Park and the People* (Ithaca: Cornell University Press, 1992)

Sexby, J. J., *The Municipal Parks, Gardens, and Open Spaces of London* (London: Elliot Stock, 1898)

Wiegand, Heinz, *Geschichte des Stadtgrüns*, vol. II: Entwicklung des Stadtgrüns in Deutschland zwischen 1890 und 1925 am Beispiel der Arbeiten Fritz Enckes (Berlin: Patzer, 1975)

Woods, May and Arete Warren, *Glass Houses* (New York: Rizzoli, and London: Aurum, 1988)

Design manuals and issues

Agar, Madeline, *Garden Design in Theory and Practice* (London: Sidgwick & Jackson, 1911)

Ashmore, Sydney, *Flower Beds and Bedding Plants* (London: Collingridge, n.d.)

Beazley, Elisabeth, *Design and Detail of the Space between Buildings* (London: Architectural Press, 1960)

Bengtsson, Arvid, *Environmental Planning for Children's Play* (London: Crosby Lockwood, 1970)

Cane, Percy, *Garden Design of Today* (London: Methuen, 1934)

Chittenden, F. J. (ed.), RHS *Dictionary of Gardening*, 2nd edn (Oxford: Clarendon, 1956)

Cole, Nathan, *The Royal Parks and Gardens of London* (London: Journal of Horticulture Office, 1877)

Dennis, John, *The Landscape Gardener* (London, 1835)

Douglas, Norman, *London Street Games* (London, St Catherine's Press, 1916)

Evison, J. R. B., *Gardening for Display* (London: W. H. & L. Collingridge, 1958)

Friedberg, M. Paul, *Do-it-Yourself Playgrounds* (London: Architectural Press, 1975)

Gilpin, Revd William, *Remarks on Forest Scenery and Other Woodland Views* (London: Blamire, 1791)

Gomme, Alice B. *The National Games of England, Scotland and Ireland* (London: David Nutt, 1894–98)

Hay, Thomas, 'Gardening in London', *Journal of the Royal Horticultural Society*, 56 (1931), 207–16

Hessayon, D. G., *The New Bedding Plant Expert* (London: Transworld, 1996)

Hibberd, James Shirley, *The Amateur's Flower Garden* (London: Groombridge, 1875)

Holme, Anthea and Massie, Peter, *Children's Play* (London: Michael Joseph, 1972)

Housing Centre Trust Pamphlet, *New Playgrounds* (1964)

Hughes, John Arthur, *Garden Architecture and Landscape Gardening* (London: Longmans, Green & Co., 1866)

Huxley, Anthony (ed.), *The New RHS Dictionary of Gardening* (London: Macmillan, 1992)

Jacobs, Jane, *The Death and Life of Great American Cities* (New York: Random House, 1961)

Kemp, Edward, *How to Lay Out a Garden* (London: Bradbury & Evans, 1864)

Kemp, Edward, *How to Lay Out a Small Garden* (London: Bradbury & Evans, 1850)

Levy, Joseph, *Play Behaviour* (New York: John Wiley, 1978)

Lisney, Adrian and Ken Fieldhouse, *Landscape Design Guide*, vol. II: Hard Landscape (Aldershot: Gower Technical, 1990)

Loudon, John Claudius, *An Encyclopaedia of Gardening* (London: Longman, Hurst, Rees, Orme & Brown, 1822; 2nd edn 1824; 8th edn 1835, etc.)

—, *Suburban Gardener and Villa Companion* (London: Longman, Hurst, Rees, Orme and Brown, 1838)

—, *The Derby Arboretum* (London: Longman, Orme, Brown, Green & Longmans, 1840)

Meller, Linda, *Leisure and the Changing City* (London: Routledge & Kegan Paul, 1976)

M'Intosh, Charles, *The Book of the Garden*, 2 vols (Edinburgh: William Blackwood, 1853–55)

—, *The Practical Gardener and Modern Horticulturist* (London, 1838)

Major, Joshua, *Theory and Practice of Landscape Gardening* (London: Longman, Brown Green & Longmans, 1852)

Mawson, Thomas, *Civic Art: Studies in Town Planning, Parks, Boulevards and Open Spaces* (London: B. T. Batsford, 1911)

—, *The Art and Craft of Garden Making* (London: B. T. Batsford, 1900)

McCullough, Jamie, *Meanwhile Gardens* (London: Calouste Gulbenkian Foundation, 1978)

Meyer, F. W., *Rock and Water Gardens* (London: Country Life, 1910)

Milner, Henry Ernest, *The Art and Practice of Landscape Gardening* (London: Simpkin,

Marshall, Hamilton, Kent, 1890)

Opie, Iona and Opie, Peter, *The Lore and Language of Schoolchildren* (Oxford: Oxford University Press, 1959)

Opie, Iona and Opie, Peter, *Children's Games in Street and Playground* (Oxford: Clarendon, 1969)

Pettigrew, W. W., *Municipal Parks: Layout, Management and Administration* (London: Journal of Park Administration, 1937)

Phillips, Henry, *Sylva florifera: The Shrubbery Historically and Botanically Treated*, 2 vols (London: Longman, Hurst, Rees, Orme and Brown, 1823)

Repton, Humphry, *An Inquiry into the Changes of Taste in Landscape Gardening* (London, 1806)

—, *Observations on the Theory and Practice of Landscape Gardening* (London, 1803)

Scott, Frank J., *The Art of Beautifying Suburban Home Grounds* (New York: D. Appleton & Co., 1870)

Senda, Mitsuru, *Design of Children's Play Environments* (New York: McGraw-Hill, 1992)

Smith, Charles H. J., *Parks and Pleasure Grounds* (London: Reeve & Co., 1852)

Smith, Robert Paul *'Where did you go?' 'Out' 'What did you do?' 'Nothing'* (New York: W. W. Norton, 1957)

Sørensen, C. Th. *Parkpolitik i Sogn og Købstad* (Park politics in parish and town) (Copenhagen: Nordisk, 1931)

Steuart, Sir Henry, *The Planters Guide* (Edinburgh and London: William Blackwood, 1828)

Sudell, Richard, *Landscape Gardening: Planning, Construction, Planting* (London: Ward, Lock & Co., 1933)

Thomas Mawson, *The Art and Craft of Garden Making* (London: B. T. Batsford, 1900, another edn 1926)

Tunnard, Christopher, *Gardens and the Modern Landscape* (London: Architectural Press, 1938)

Wicksteed, Charles & Co., *Play Things as Used in The Wicksteed Park, Kettering* (1921)

Wicksteed, Hilda, *Charles Wicksteed* (London: J. M. Dent, 1933)

Wolseley, Viscountess, *Gardens: Their Form and Design* (London: Edward Arnold, 1919)

Magazines and journals

Cottage Gardener (1850–1855)

Floricultural Cabinet (1834–1859)

Gardener's and Forester's Record (1833)

Gardener's Magazine (1825–1841)

Gardeners' Chronicle (1844–1968)

Gardeners' Magazine (1903)

GC&HTJ

Horticulture Week

Journal of Horticulture (1910)

Journal of Park Administration (1937)

Journal of the Horticultural Society (1852)

Journal of the Institute of Landscape Architects (1960)

Landscape Design

Leisure Manager (1986)

Parks and Recreation (1982)

Parks and Sports Grounds (1954, 1963, 1976–78)

The Architectural Magazine (1834)

The Builder (1846)

The Garden (1872–1999)

Works dealing with regeneration and conservation issues

A New Vision, A New Future (Glasgow: Glasgow City Council, 1996)

Agenda 21: Programme of Action for Sustainable Development. Proceedings of the 'United Nations Conference on Environment and Development',

165

Rio de Janeiro, Brazil, 1992; this resulted in Secretaries of State of the Environment *et al.*, *Sustainable Development: the UK Strategy* (London: HMSO, 1994)

Application Pack (London: Heritage Lottery Fund, 1998)

Ashurst, John and Nicola Ashurst, *Practical Building Conservation,* vol. IV: *Metals.* English Heritage Technical Handbook (Aldershot: Gower Technical, 1998)

Ashurst, Nicola, 'Heavenly gates', *Traditional Homes* (July 1998), 16–24

Bains Committee, *The New Local Authorities: Management and Structures* (London: HMSO, 1972)

Birnbaum, Charles A., *Guidelines for the Treatment of Historic Landscapes* (Washington, DC: US National Park Service, 1997)

Birnbaum, Charles A., 'A reality check for our nation's parks', *CRM Bulletin*, 16/4 (1993), 1–4

Branch, Michael, 'Activity in urban parks', *Leisure Manager* (July 1991), 16–18

Brereton, Christopher, *The Repair of Historic Buildings: Advice on Principles and Methods* (London: English Heritage, 1991)

Burgess, Jacqueline *et al.*, 'People, parks and the urban green: a study of popular meanings and values for open spaces in the city', *Urban Studies*, 25 (1988), 455–73

Catalytic Conversion: Revive Historic Buildings to Regenerate Communities (London: SAVE Britain's Heritage, 1998)

Clarke, Richard and David Mount, *Site Management Planning: A Guide.* Publication no. 527 (Cheltenham: Countryside Commission, 1998)

Conservation Plans for Historic Places (London: Heritage Lottery Fund, 1998)

Conservation-led Regeneration (London: English Heritage, 1998)

Conway, Hazel and David Lambert, *Public*

Prospects: Historic Urban Parks under Threat (London: Garden History Society and Victorian Society, 1993)

Costonis, J. J., *Icons and Aliens: Law, Aesthetics, and Environmental Change* (Urbana: University of Urbana-Champaign Press, 1989)

Elliott, Brent, 'From people's parks to green deserts', *Landscape Design*, no. 171 (February 1988), 13–15

Environment, Transport and Regional Affairs Committee, *Town and Country Parks.* 20th Report, vol. 1 (London: HMSO, 1999)

Environmental and Recreational Indicators. Report for Audit Commission (London: MORI, 1992)

Eyres, Patrick, '"Naval Warfare": the battle of Peasholm Park', *New Arcadian Journal*, nos 39/40 (1995), 33–48

Field Manual for Phase 1 Survey: A Method for Environmental Audit (London: Joint Nature Conservancy Council, 1993)

Fielden, Bernard M. and Jukka Jokilehto, *Management Guidelines for World Heritage Sites* (Rome: ICCROM, 1993)

Fox, Celena, 'The battle of the railings', *AA Files*, no. 29 (1995), 50–60

Gale, W. K. V., *Iron and Steel* (Telford: Ironbridge Gorge Museum Trust, 1979)

Greenhalgh, Liz and Ken Worpole, *Park Life: Urban Parks and Social Renewal* (London: Comedia in association with Demos, 1995)

Guthrie, J. L., A. Allen and Chris Jones, 'Royal Botanic Gardens, Kew: restoration of Palm House', *Proceedings of the Institution of Civil Engineers*, Part 1, 84 (1988), 1145–91

Hinze, Virginia, 'The re-creation of John Nash's Regency gardens at the Royal Pavilion, Brighton', *Garden History*, 24/1 (1996), 45–53

Holland, Alan and Kate Rawles, 'Values in conservation', *ECOS*, 14/1 (1993), 14–19

Jacques, David, 'The treatment of historic parks

and gardens', *Journal of Architectural Conservation*, 1/2 (1995), 21–35

—, 'What to do about earlier inaccurate restoration?: a case study of Chiswick House grounds', *APT Bulletin: The Journal of Preservation Technology*, 24/3–4 (1992/93), 4–13

Jemison, T., 'Railings', *Landscape Design* (June 1983), 27–30

Jones, Chris, 'Two glass houses, Syon and Bicton', *Architects' Journal* (29 April 1987), 57–62

Krosigk, Klaus von, Gesine Sturm et al., *Garden Art of Berlin: 20 Years of Conservation of Historic Gardens and Parks in the Capital* (Berlin: Schelzky & Jeep, 1999)

Laird, Mark, *Flowering of the Landscape Garden: English Pleasure Grounds 1720–1800* (Philadelphia: University of Pennsylvania Press, 1999)

Lambert, David, Peter Goodchild and Judith Roberts, *Researching a Garden's History: A Guide to Documentary and Published Sources* (Reigate: Landscape Design Trust, and York: University of York Institute of Advanced Architectural Studies, 1995)

Lewis, Peirce 'American landscape tastes', *Modern Landscape Architecture: A Critical Review*, ed. Marc Trieb (Cambridge, MA: MIT Press, 1993), 2–17

London Lakes Project (London: Wandsworth Borough Council, 1997)

Lowenthal, David, 'The American scene', *Geographical Review*, 58 (1968), 61

Marcus, Susan and Rosie Barker, *Using Historic Parks and Gardens: A Teacher's Guide* (London: English Heritage, 1997)

More Grounds for Concern (London: GMB, 1997)

Morton, Brian, 'Iron-framed Conservatories and Greenhouses', in *The Care and Conservation of Historic Garden Landscapes: The Building Conservation Directory*. Special Report no. 2 (London: Cathedral Communications, 1994), 11–12

New Links for the Lottery: Proposals for the New Opportunities Fund (London: HMSO, 1998)

Ornamental Ironwork: Gates and Railings (London: English Heritage, 1993)

Parissien, Steven, *Ironwork*. Guide no. 8 (London: Georgian Group, n.d.)

Park Discovery Project: Teachers' Pack (London: London Historic Parks and Gardens Trust, 1998)

People, Parks and Cities (London: Department of the Environment, 1996)

Phibbs, John L., 'An approach to the methodology of recording historic gardens', *Garden History*, 11/2 (1983), 167–75

Planning Policy Guidance Note (PPG) 15, *Planning and the Historic Environment* (September 1994)

Primack, Mark (ed.), *The Greening of Boston* (Boston: Boston Foundation, 1987)

Railings in Westminster (London: Department of the Environment and Planning, Development Division of the City of Westminster, 1997)

Rice, Graham, 'Pride or prejudice?', *The Garden*, 124/3 (1999), 164–7

Rogers, Elizabeth Barlow, *Rebuilding Central Park: A Management and Restoration Plan* (Cambridge, MA: MIT Press, 1987)

Sanson, Anne and Ros Walmsley, *Ponds and Conservation*, new edn (London: Environment Agency, 1998)

Secretaries of State of the Environment et al., *Biodiversity: The UK Action Plan* (London: HMSO, 1994)

—, *Sustainable Development: the UK Strategy* (London: HMSO, 1994)

Singmaster, D. 'Wrought iron recycled to restore Turner's splendour', *Architects' Journal* (8 February 1996), 36

Social Trends, No. 28 (London: Office of National Statistics, 1996)

167

Sutherland, R. J. M (ed.), *Structural Iron, 1750–1850*. Studies in the History of Civil Engineering, vol. IX (Aldershot: Ashgate, 1997)

The Building Conservation Directory (Tisbury: Cathedral Communications, 1998)

The Quality Exchange Survey of Parks and Open Spaces Managed by the London Boroughs, Metropolitan and District Councils of England and Wales (London: Audit Commission, 1994)

Tunnard, Christopher, *A World With A View: An Inquiry into the Nature of Scenic Values* (New Haven and London: Yale University Press, 1978)

UK Steering Group, *Biodiversity,* vol. I: Meeting the Rio Challenge (London: HMSO, 1995)

Urban Parks Discussion Paper (London: Landscape Institute, 1992)

Wedd, Kitt, *Care for Victorian Houses*, no. 6: Cast Iron (London: Victorian Society, 1994)

Williams-Ellis, Clough, *Cottage Building in Cob, Pisé, Chalk and Clay* (London: Country Life, 1947)

World Commission on Environment and Development (The Brundtland Commission), *Our Common Future* (Oxford: Oxford University Press, 1987)

Index

174